From LeRoi Jones to Amiri Baraka

FOR LA VERNE, ERIC, AND VICKI

From LeRoi Jones to Amiri Baraka:
The literary works

Theodore R. Hudson

DUKE UNIVERSITY PRESS   DURHAM, NORTH CAROLINA   1973

© 1973, Duke University Press

L.C.C. card no. 72-97096

I.S.B.N. 0-8223-0296-9

Printed in the United States of America
By Kingsport Press

Acknowledgments

THE BOBBS-MERRILL COMPANY, INC. For excerpts from *Black Magic Poetry,* by LeRoi Jones (copyright © 1969 by LeRoi Jones), including portions of "Allegro con rocks," "Attention Attention," "Black Art," "Blue Whitie," "The Calling Together," "Citizen Cain," "cops," "Dada Zodji," "An Explanation of the Work," "GATSBY'S THEORY OF AESTHETICS," "Goodbye!" "I Am Speaking of Future Good-ness and Social Philosophy," "I Said it," "Jitterbugs," "Ka 'Ba," "Labor and Management," "THE PEOPLE BURNING," "A Poem for Black Hearts," "A Poem for Religious Fanatics," "A POEM SOME PEOPLE WILL HAVE TO UNDERSTAND," "Red Eye," "The Success," "For Tom Postell, Dead Black Poet," "Three Modes of History and Culture," "THREE MOVEMENTS AND A CODA," "The Visit," "Will They Cry When You're Gone, You Bet," "YOUNG SOUL." Reprinted by permission of the publisher, The Bobbs-Merrill Company, Inc. For excerpts from *In Our Terribleness,* by Imamu Amiri Baraka and Fundi (copyright © 1970 by Imamu Amiri Baraka [LeRoi Jones] and Fundi [Billy Abernathy]). Reprinted by permission of the publisher, The Bobbs-Merrill Company, Inc.

CORINTH BOOKS, INC., PUBLISHERS. For excerpts from *Preface to a Twenty Volume Suicide Note,* by LeRoi Jones (copyright © 1961 by LeRoi Jones), including portions of "Betancourt," "The Clearing," "For Hettie," "For Hettie in Her Fifth Month," "Hymn for Lanie Poo," "In Memory of Radio," "The Insidious Dr. Fu Man Chu," "Look for You Yesterday, Here You Come Today," "The New Sheriff," "Ostriches & Grandmothers," "Preface to a Twenty Volume Suicide Note," "Theory of Art," "To a Publisher...cut-out," "The Turncoat," "Vice." Reprinted by permission of Corinth Books, Inc., Publishers.

GROVE PRESS, INC. For permission to quote letter from Michael Rumaker to Morrie Goldfischer.

HARPER & ROW, PUBLISHERS, INC. For excerpts from "Philistinism and the Negro Writer," by LeRoi Jones, in *Anger, and Beyond,* ed. Herbert Hill (copyright © 1966 by Herbert Hill). Abridged from pp. 51–52, 52–53, 54, 56–57; reprinted by permission of Harper & Row, Publishers, Inc. Note: deletions to be indicated by ellipses.

The System of Dante's Hell (New York: Grove Press, 1965, copyright © 1965 by LeRoi Jones); *Tales* (New York: Grove Press, 1967, copyright © 1967 by LeRoi Jones); and the poems "Black People!" and "leroy," which appeared in *Evergreen Review,* December, 1967.

THIRD WORLD PRESS. For excerpts from *It's Nation Time,* by Imamu Amiri Baraka (LeRoi Jones) (copyright © 1970 by Imamu Amiri Baraka [LeRoi Jones]), including portions of "The Nation Is Like Ourselves" (pp. 7, 8), "Sermon for Our Maturity" (pp. 15–16, 18), "It's Nation Time" (pp. 23–24). Reprinted by permission of Third World Press.

WILLIAM MORROW AND COMPANY, INC. For excerpts from *Home: Social Essays,* by LeRoi Jones (copyright © 1966 by LeRoi Jones), reprinted by permission of William Morrow and Company, Inc.; and from *Blues People: Negro Music in White America,* by LeRoi Jones (copyright © 1963 by LeRoi Jones), reprinted by permission of William Morrow and Company, Inc.

Contents

Introduction

LeRoi Jones is an important American literary artist—one of the most gifted, one of the most individual, one of the most versatile, one of the busiest, and undoubtedly the most influential in the surge, during the late 1960's and early 1970's, of black cultural nationalism.

Unfortunately there exists no comprehensive study of the literary efforts of this man. What writing there is about him and his works consists mainly of isolated articles and reviews of his individual works. The articles purporting to examine or explicate, say, his poetry are, because they are articles, superficial or limited in scope. With the exception of several brief sketches or "profiles," practically nothing biographical about him has appeared in print. In short, writing about Jones and his literary works is fragmentary and incomplete.

I hope with this book to fill the need for a critical survey of the literary work of LeRoi Jones, or Amiri Baraka.

The overall plan is:

Part I: To consider three areas that throw light on his works, these being his life, his characteristic ways of perceiving and thinking, and his characteristic ways of ordering or presenting his material (chapters 1–3). The rationale for presenting the overview of theme and of technique before rather than after the discussion of the various genres is that a prior understanding of his individualistic thinking and unique modes of expression makes for better analysis of the individual works and obviates digressive explanations.

Part II: To analyze and interpret his works and to synthesize elements found in these various works (chapters 4–7). The organization for this part of the study is by genre and then by individual works within the given genre. Treatments of *Home, System, Dutchman,* and *Preface* are relatively extensive. With the exception of *Dutchman,* these works are "firsts" in their respective genres and a number of things said about them need not be repeated in subsequent discussions of other works. *Dutchman* in another sense is a "first"; it was Jones' first major dramatic achievement if not his first dramatic effort and is therefore given relatively more attention. Because *Home* contains so much material that is basic to an understanding of Jones and of all his works, it commands more attention than any other single work. There is relatively little to be gained by surveying Jones' works, regardless of genre, in strict chronological order. For one thing, as we shall see, his artistic and personal development has not followed an orderly, coordinated, or causal progression. In spite of appearing on the surface to be an extremely changeable man, he has always been essentially the same person—changing as any person changes as he experiences and reacts to life. Jones changed in different times, in different ways, in different genres.

Part III: To synthesize and summarize the findings and to arrive at some conclusions and some tentative conclusions (chapter 8).

In most instances I refer to our author as LeRoi Jones. But where emphasis
needed in a given context seems to make appropriate the use of his adopted, or
"traditional," name, I use Amiri Baraka. Occasionally I use simply Imamu, as he
is frequently addressed today.

Because LeRoi Jones is often unconventional in matters of mechanics,
usage, and other components of style, the reader is asked to trust my exactness
in quoting Jones and to accept as accurate what may appear to be unintentional
misspellings and nonstandard capitalization, punctuation, spacing, syntax, and
the like. However, in instances where a clear misreading or unusual doubt might
arise, I have inserted the conventional "[sic]."

I have distinguished between a series of periods in original material that I
am quoting directly and ellipses that I make in original material that I am quoting
directly. Where I have omitted part of the quoted material, I have followed the
MLA Style Sheet by spacing between the periods, as in "Toward the end of his
fellowship years in New York's East Village . . . white America still celebrated
his anger as sacrament." Where three or more periods were already in the material being quoted, I have left no space between the periods, as in "It's the
biggest funeral parlor in the country...got 3 horse drawn hearses...belongs to
that nigger Tom Russ."

When I quote from poems by Jones, I give the title of the poem but not the
page and source. An exception is made for poetry from other than his collected
works; in such cases I indicate the source. In instances where the context makes
clear that Jones is being quoted from a secondary source, the footnote simply
gives the source, omitting the words "Jones as quoted in . . ."

Except in the bibliography at the end of the book, short titles of Jones'
works are used.

I eagerly take this opportunity to express deep gratitude to Dr. Arthur P.
Davis of Howard University. When I was a student there it was he who suggested
this study and who in many indirect and direct ways convinced me that I was
capable of the task. Further, he helped by being the type of literary scholar and
critic I would aspire to emulate. In a more immediate and practical way he as-
sisted me in obtaining a graduate study grant that led to a dissertation that
became the basis for this book. Moreover, he respected my concept of the

dissertation project, made valuable suggestions, and throughout encouraged me to move right along to its completion.

I wish to express appreciation, too, to the other members of my dissertation committee, Dr. Ivan E. Taylor and the late Dr. William D. Washington, both of Howard University, and Dr. Charles E. Larson, of American University, for their suggestions, comments, and other help; and to Dr. Theressa W. Brown, my department chairman at the time at the District of Columbia Teachers College, for being a one-lady cheering squad.

For opening their files for my perusal and for otherwise being most co-operative, I wish to thank the publishers of LeRoi Jones' major works, Grove Press, William Morrow and Company, and Bobbs-Merrill.

I am especially thankful to Mr. and Mrs. Coyt L. Jones for talking with me on several occasions and providing invaluable information about their son and for being hospitable to me in a personal way; to Mrs. Hettie C. Jones for being so gracious about talking with me about Jones' early writing and about the literary and personal milieu in which he functioned at the time; to Mr. Theodore Wilentz for conversation and for leads concerning certain early manuscripts; and to other people who "knew him when" and who "know him now" for their help.

For patience, direction, and more than just professional cordiality, I am grateful to Mr. Ashbel Brice and Mr. W. N. Hicks of the Duke University Press.

And of course I must mention my wife, La Verne, and my children, Eric and Vicki, who supported and endured as only families know how to support and to endure.

Finally, I wish to thank Everett LeRoi Jones—Amiri Baraka, the Imamu—for taking time from an unbelievably busy life to talk with me, correspond with me, and in other ways help make my research and writing about him a personally and I hope academically fruitful endeavor.

Theodore R. Hudson

Washington, D.C.
November, 1972

Part I

Chapter 1. "The struggles away or towards this peace": Chronology

Everett LeRoi Jones was born in Newark, New Jersey, "under Libra" on October 7, 1934. If his family was not middle class in terms of economics, it was middle class in attitude and orientation, with a lineage of preachers and teachers. "I think," Jones says, "black people who had jobs, as my parents did, could be considered middle-class but certainly not middle-class compared to what America is. They had jobs, and they were steady, secure jobs. They were not middle-class in the sense of what middle-class is — they were working class — although I wound up in what I guess is a bourgeoise school, Howard."[1]

His parents, Coyt LeRoy and Anna Lois Jones, will tell one that "LeRoi had the advantage of good grandparents."[2] Maternal grandfather Tom Russ had owned several businesses — store, restaurant, funeral home, barber shop — in Dothan, Alabama. Allegedly resentful whites burned down the store. But Tom was not one to be intimidated easily. As grandson LeRoi was to write years later:

> You built that store back up. You knelt down and scraped the black parts of the wood away and stuck them poles in the ground and got the thing up so fast folks thought you had hypnotized them, and there wasn't really any store at all, only the insane intensity of your vision. So they burned this one too, and said they were going to run you out of town. And just to spite them you knelt back down in those ashes and scraped the black off again, and built again. "It's the biggest funeral parlor in the country...got 3 horse drawn hearses...belongs to that nigger Tom Russ." A vibration can carry a man a long ways. Fancy Tom Russ, funeral parlor so fancy, the niggers killing each other so they can get an excuse to go to it. But the other folks got tired of all that noise, and burned it again. What can a man do? One vibration ain't the world. Your unborn grandson says leave this pisshearted town, Tom. Pack up and move on, Tom. Vibrations are like anything else — there's more wherever you go.[3]

Tom Russ did move, all the way to Beaver Falls, Pennsylvania, where he started a small cooperative business. Businessman Tom Russ was also Deacon Tom Russ. Realizing that he and Southerners like himself were less than welcome in the relatively sophisticated Negro Baptist church there, Deacon Russ and his flock organized and founded their own church, Beaver Falls' Tabernacle Baptist Church. And Thomas and Anna Russ saw to it that their daughter Anna

Lois went to Tuskegee Institute for high school, for there were few Negroes in Beaver Falls and Tom felt that "She's got to know 'bout them vibrations."[4] Then in 1925 Russ moved his family to Newark, New Jersey, where he opened "Russ Produce – Super General Store" and from time to time engaged in other business ventures, seldom working for anyone else and then usually as a temporary expedient.

It was in Newark that Anna Lois Russ, then a student at Fisk University, met Coyt LeRoy Jones. "He is a quiet man, industrious, thin as a string and painfully shy. Tom looks him up and down and asks him is he a good man. This is my father who nods and slides his arm around Tom's daughter. Tom wonders will I look like him, and I nod yes, and he is satisfied and takes out his cigars and chats about the depression."[5]

Later, Grandfather and Grandmother Russ were to try, as grandparents will, to impress upon grandson LeRoi their religious convictions, their self-reliance, and their ethic of decorum and respectability. For example, LeRoi's grandfather pronounced rent parties, if not downright sinful, then certainly as " 'vulgar,' or at least 'wasteful.' "[6] Jones recalls that the "grossest disparagement the 'religious' Negro could make of another was that he or she was 'a heathen.' "[7] Their teachings were not in vain, particularly the "taught" and "caught" attitudes about self-dependence, pride in one's race, and courage in the face of hardships.

Little LeRoi was very close to his grandfather, and Mr. and Mrs. Coyt Jones will tell one that Grandfather Russ had a profound influence on young LeRoi, even though Tom Russ died when LeRoi was only about eleven years of age. They marvel that their son remembers his grandparents with such vivid accuracy.

These grandparents were to be honored by Jones in the published version of *Dutchman and The Slave:* The dedication reads, "For Thomas Everett Russ, American pioneer, and Anna Cherry Brock Russ, his wife." At one time, 1964, Jones was working on a novel, *Instructions for Negroes,* which was to be about his grandfather's life. And in "BLACK DADA NIHILISMUS" he includes his grandfather's name in a catalog of people like Toussaint l'Overture, Denmark Vesey, and Jack Johnson.

On his father's side of the family, LeRoi's grandfather George Jones died before LeRoi could know him. His paternal grandmother, Fannie Jones, is still living in South Carolina. When LeRoi was a boy, going south to see his father's relatives was a ritual. (Coyt Jones recounts that one of LeRoi's earliest experiences with overt discrimination was in Columbia, South Carolina, when the

/

two of them went to a local movie theatre to see Bing Crosby in "Going My Way"
only to be turned away from the box office and told to go to the alley entrance
where "niggers" paid and were admitted to the balcony. As things turned out,
little LeRoi wanted to see the picture so much that he insisted they go anyway,
not realizing the significance of the incident.) Mr. Jones asserts that his grandmother, LeRoi's great-grandmother, was a great story teller who could hold
him and other children spellbound. Many of her tales were about slavery times.
LeRoi's father, like Thomas Russ, had left the South under less than pleasant
circumstances. Coyt LeRoy Jones "left very suddenly" after knocking down a
white usher in a movie house in his native Hartsville, South Carolina. Like any
father of similar mind and status, Coyt was later to teach his son to protect his
person and to defend his manhood, even if in so doing he would have to fight,
physically, a losing battle.

LeRoi's mother "was a social worker, but she started out working in sweat
shops before they started giving black women jobs. Then during the second
World War she got a job as, you know, in the government and after that she sort
of maintained the social worker thing."[8] Mrs. Jones was the type of mother who
would go to school to investigate a teacher's attitude toward her son (as she
does in the biographical fiction "Uncle Tom's Cabin: *Alternate Ending*") and
who would feel a surge of pride in her grown son's activities and accomplishments, today calling him in public Imamu rather than LeRoi.

The remaining member of LeRoi's immediate family was his sister, Sandra
Elaine, now known also by her "traditional name," Kimako. Jones conceives of
her as a once lost, i.e., a white and middle-class oriented girl who succeeded
finally in finding her true self, i.e., her blackness. Miss Jones, identified frequently as an actress and dancer, has had a restaurant-catering service in
Harlem known as Kimako's, and at this time is associated with the House of
Kuumba, a cultural and educational center in Harlem.

It is true that LeRoi Jones' literary works are sometimes autobiographical
(this will be discussed later and mentioned throughout the considerations of
individual works), and therefore it is not surprising to see his parents and sister
and their lives reflected in his writing. Mrs. Jones appears in the poem "leroy" in
which he wistfully states:

I wanted to know my mother when she sat
looking sad across the campus in the late 20's
into the future of the soul, there were black angels
straining above her head, carrying life from our ancestors,

and knowledge, and the strong nigger feeling. She sat
(in that photo in the yearbook I showed Vashti) getting into
new blues, from the old ones, the trips and passions
showered on her by her own. Hypnotizing me, from so far
ago, from that vantage of knowledge passed on to her passed on
to me and all the other black people of our time.

Great Goodness of Life: A Coon Show is "For my father with love and respect,"[9] and the broadly caricatured central figure, Court Royal, is a projection based upon his middle-class attuned and "respectable" father. He looks upon his father as being what a Negro father had to be in his time and place. In "From the Egyptian" Jones says:

I will slaughter
the enemies
of my father
I will slay those
who have blinded
him.

Throughout his writing, as we shall note later, symbol-imagery of postal workers (Mr. Jones) and social workers (Mrs. Jones) persists. Jones' sister is poetically projected in "Hymn for Lanie Poo":

my sister drives a green jaguar
my sister has her hair done twice a month
my sister is a school teacher
my sister took ballet lessons
my sister has a fine figure: never diets
my sister doesn't like to teach in Newark
    because there are too many colored
    in her classes
my sister hates loud shades
my sister's boy friend is a faggot music teacher
    who digs Tschaikovsky
my sister digs Tschaikovsky also

But by the time he wrote *Experimental Death Unit #1,* she had apparently changed to Jones' ideology, and he dedicates this play to "a used to be dead sister," although he will explain that in this instance he really had other people as well as his sister in mind.

LeRoi Jones remembers his boyhood home life as uneventful in a way that the home life of working-class Negro families of the time in a city like Newark was uneventful. His boyhood interests and activities were not unusual. As his writing bears out, he liked football, baseball, and other sports; he avidly read comic strips; he listened to radio programs such as "The Shadow"; he enjoyed motion pictures. He liked to "hang out" with his pals. He got into occasional fights and scuffles with other boys. He disliked certain teachers (he may have understood them too well, it seems). People who influenced him then were people in the community, and people whom he emulated were the athletes and other hero-types for boys.

Yet, there was more going on. "Once, as a child, I would weep for compassion and understanding. And Hell was the inferno of my frustration."[10] In an interview he is quoted as saying, "When I was in high school, I used to drink a lot of wine, throw bottles around, walk down the street dressed in women's clothes just because I couldn't find anything to do to satisfy myself. Neither sex, nor whiskey, nor drugs would do it. People need something to do. If you really have something to do and really want to do it, you use up all that energy and violence in making sure you do it right."[11] LeRoi hung around with the "wrong . . . sort of companions, the 'only middle-class chump running with the Hillside Place bads.'"[12] And fictionally, he writes, "Our house sat lonely and large on a half-Italian street, filled with important Negroes (Though it is rumored they had a son, thin with big eyes, they killed because he was crazy.)"[13]

Actually, LeRoi was not a problem boy. As his parents recall, he never got into trouble, as such. On the contrary, he at one time or another was a Cub Scout, had a newspaper route, earned money by working in a store, and the like. And he was no stranger to the church.

"My own church in Newark, New Jersey, a Baptist church," he once wrote, "has almost no resemblance to the older, more traditional Negro Christian churches. The music, for instance, is usually limited to the less emotional white church music, and the choir usually sings Bach or Handel during Christmas and Easter. In response to some of its older 'country' members, the church, which is headed by a minister who is the most respected Negro in Newark, has to *import* gospel groups, or singers having a more traditional 'Negro church' sound."[14] His first vocational interest was the ministry. After all, he was a descendant of preachers, and at that time in Negro communities a minister was an object of respect, was a leader. "But wow," he says, "there were just too many homosexuals in the church for me."[15] It was in churches, he says, that he "had the funny experience, you know, like those faggies who were sort of magnetized to the church in the choirs and things like that."[16] Such impressions of churches and church people were to find their way into the literary content and symbol-imagery of his later writing. In reacting to interpretation of the boy in *The Baptism* as a Christ figure, he says, "I think that's what I thought that the Christ figure has been — a totally naive person to believe he could go up against these evil persons and not be crucified."[17] Yet when Jones entered Howard University, he considered majoring in religion, explaining, "It was the only reference I had."[18]

When he was very young, Mr. and Mrs. Jones became aware that in LeRoi they had an unusual child, and they did everything they could to develop his gifts. For example, his parents recall that because preschool-aged LeRoi was fond of making political speeches, Mr. Jones would lift him up onto a table, let it serve as a rostrum, and coach his son in speech making. Also, his father saw that the growing LeRoi always had plenty to read, asserting now that "LeRoi has read everything that there is worth reading."[19] That he had talent became more apparent as he grew and matured. For one thing, he had a remarkable memory. His parents tell of the time that LeRoi, about eight years old, to everyone's surprise recited the entire Gettysburg Address. No one had taught it to him or coached him; he simply had heard it or read it and committed it to memory himself. They remember also that as a very small boy he asked if there had ever been any president other than Franklin D. Roosevelt. Mr. Jones got out a book, went over the list with him, and it was not long before LeRoi could recall each president of the United States, in succession. Another unusual thing about this boy was his fertile imagination. He could make up fantastic stories, such as the one which brought several grade-school teachers to the Jones home at lunch time to "see the snakes." LeRoi, tardy that morning, had alternately regaled and terrorized the teachers at school about the snakes that had mysteriously invaded the Jones cellar, bringing about a crisis that had occasioned his late arrival. Too, LeRoi, at about age eight, could frighten his sister with what his imaginary (but real to her) "little men" had said about her and were going to do to her. He was a boy who could amaze white teachers at Central Avenue School and Barringer High School with right answers, a budding Horatio Alger: "'You are a young man & soon will be off to college.' They knew then, and walked around me for it."[20]

In the seventh grade he produced a comic strip, "The Crime Wave." According to Jones, he "Had started trying to be literary in grammar school w/heavy comic strips. Short stories in high school,"[21] mainly science fiction. These early artistic efforts are not extant; he has none of them, and Newark schools were "not in the habit of keeping things that black kids do."[22]

Jones unassumingly makes little of his graduating early from high school, but there is no mistaking the excellence of his academic ability. When he graduated, from several scholarship offers, he chose one in science that Rutgers had offered him.

Discovering the sicknesses: Rutgers, Howard, and the Air Force

But Rutgers was not to his liking: "The effort of trying to prove himself in an 'essentially mediocre situation' and the experience of always being an outsider in any school social activities made him transfer to Howard University."[23] Further, according to Jones, "I had to go to Rutgers before I found people who thought grits were meant to be eaten with milk and sugar, instead of gravy and pork sausage . . . and that's one of the reasons I left."[24]

The important thing about Howard is not the courses that Jones took in its liberal arts college. The important thing is how his experiences at Howard shaped him. As he puts it, "The Howard thing let me understand the Negro sickness. They teach you how to pretend to be white."[25]

Several incidents stand out in his memory of Howard University. Among them is the somewhat apocryphal watermelon episode, an episode that has taken on aspects of a legend. There are several versions. One has Jones expelled from Howard for eating watermelon on Georgia Avenue, a block away from the main campus quadrangle; another has him purposely embarrassing the administration by eating watermelon outdoors on campus; another has him irritating fellow students about their "whiteness" by eating watermelon. And so the versions go. His own version follows:

A student friend (he is now a lawyer in Philadelphia) and I were sitting on the campus studying one day and a watermelon truck passed, and I said, "Let's go buy a watermelon." So we bought this watermelon and went to sit on a bench in front of Douglas Hall. Tom Weaver, the boy I was with, had to go to class, and I was left there alone, sawing on the watermelon. The Dean of Men . . . came up to me and said, "What are you doing?" And I said, "Well, what do you mean? I'm just sitting here." And he said, "Why are you sitting there eating that watermelon?" I said, "Well, I don't know. I didn't know there was a reason for it, I'm just eating it." And he said, "Throw that away, this very instant." And I answered, "Well, sir, I can only throw half of it away, because I only own half.

The other part of it is Mr. Weaver's and he's in class, so I have to wait until he comes out and gets it." The Dean, now quite agitated, replied with great emotion, "Do you realize you're sitting right in front of the highway where white people can see you? Do you realize that this school is the capstone of Negro higher education? Do you realize that you're compromising the Negro?" I was, of course, shocked. [26]

(Even this "official" version leads one to doubt certain details. No highway passes Douglass Hall; it fronts on narrow Sixth Street, by no means a highway but a street used mainly for campus traffic, and its other side faces the campus quadrangle. The nearest "highway" would be arterial Georgia Avenue, its view to Howard's campus blocked by other buildings. And what would a watermelon vendor be doing except by accident on a nonresidential, access street?)

Jones remembers another incident: "James Baldwin's play, *The Amen Corner,* when it appeared at the Howard Players theatre, 'set the speech department back ten years,' an English professor groaned to me. The play depicted the lives of poor Negroes running a storefront church."[27]

A third shaping experience at Howard recalled by Jones is that "the teacher who was in charge of the Music School there told Professor Sterling Brown, and some others who wanted to organize a jazz concert at Howard, that jazz never, never would be played in the Music and Art building. When they finally did let jazz in, it was Stan Kenton."[28]

The result of such incidents, Jones relates, is that:

> Howard University shocked me into realizing how desperately sick the Negro could be, how he could be led into self-destruction and how he would not realize that it was the society that had forced him into a great sickness. . . . These are all examples of how American society convinces the Negro that he is inferior, and then he starts conducting his life that way. So that I find myself, now, reacting very quickly to Negroes who talk about "good hair." There are some who think that being light-skinned is somehow preferable to being dark. It's weird, especially if you are dark, to think like that—to not realize that this is another burden, something they have put on your back to carry around, so that you can't straighten up and confront them as man to man, but rather as man and something else.[29]

In addition to being "beneficial" in the sense that it developed Jones' insights into the "Negro sickness," Howard University was important in other ways. He recalls as important his study of Dante under Nathan Scott, Jr., study which is obvious in *System* and in allusions in other works. He also points out as beneficial the influence of English professor Sterling Brown (considered by most students and scholars to be the patriarch of scholars and critics in the field of Negro literature), not only for what he learned in Professor Brown's class but also for other reasons. "He taught classes in black music. Unofficial classes. A. B. Spellman and I were in the classes, unofficially held in Cook Hall, in the dormitory, at his house sometimes, but mainly in the lounge. They were invaluable. They really turned us on. . . . I think it is important to understand that two of the people who later developed into the well known black jazz critics, A. B. Spellman and I, both developed in his class."[30] Brown, now retired, remembers LeRoi Jones the student but not in any outstanding respect. He remembers Jones' name, his personality to a degree, and that he was one of the students from the university who visited his home from time to time. He also remembers Jones' interest in jazz. Of course, Professor Brown has kept up with his career and knows Jones the writer well.

Howard, unlike Rutgers, did afford Jones a social life. Somewhat reluctant to give details, he hints broadly and with restrained pleasure about the parties, the sallies off the campus, the girls, and other aspects of campus life. Friends and acquaintances at the time, according to Jones, included A. B. Spellman, the Ted Shine who was to go into drama, and (derisively) "a lot of guys who are now professional types—doctors, lawyers—you know, the professionals."[31]

After Howard, Jones entered the Air Force, or, as he terms it, the "error farce."[32] As Howard had taught him the "Negro sickness," the Air Force made him understand the "white sickness": "When I went into the Army it shocked me into realizing the hysterical sickness of the oppressors and the suffering of my own people. When I went into the Army I saw how the oppressors suffered by virtue of their oppressions—by having to oppress, by having to make believe that the weird, hopeless fantasy that they had about the world was actually true. They actually do believe that. And this weight is something that deforms them and, finally, makes them even more hopeless than lost black men."[33]

A sergeant, he was stationed for most of the time in a Strategic Air Command post in Puerto Rico. But he says that he did not travel extensively in Africa, the Middle East, and Europe, as is sometimes reported.[34] Rather, his overseas travel, he says, was limited almost entirely to Germany.

His Puerto Rico stay found him engaged in "heavy reading."[35] As he projects fictionally in "Salute":

. . . this real army life was, like any reality, duller, less flashy than any kind of fancy, and finally a lot grimmer. So the quality of response, and observation. I'd read all day when I could, or walk down near the beaches. I'd read all night if nobody came in to talk with an open jog of rum, and similar sad nostalgias. (These from my few friends, other fledgling thinkers and lost geniuses of feeling.) In those days we were finding out things wholesale, there was so much we didn't know that could be picked up even from the Sunday Times, the air mail copy of which cost seventy-five cents, since it was flown down from the States Saturday night to keep all the colonists happy. I made lists of my reading, with critical comments that grew more pompous with each new volume, even my handwriting changed and developed a kind of fluency and archness that wanted to present itself as sophistication. I made my own frictions. I sent my own brains out into any voids I imagined I could handle.[36]

At the time Jones thought of himself as a painter, but "he was, all the while, writing poetry. 'I had a stack of writing this high . . . And suddenly I said, "Gee, I have all this stuff. Well, I guess that makes me a writer." ' "[37]

From then on, a writer he was.

"Outside the mainstream of American vulgarity": Greenwich Village

Upon his discharge, civilian Everett L. Jones returned to his native Newark. As his mother recalls, "LeRoi and other black young men came back from the service looking for jobs, for opportunities, but they found that the white boys with less to offer were getting the breaks, getting the jobs. We had always tried to work within the system. LeRoi found out that this didn't work out. So he left. He went over to New York, to the Village."[38]

It was in the Village that he met a little, vivacious girl, Hettie Cohen. Hettie had grown up in the New York City area, but had gone to Mary Washington College in Virginia because, as she says, she wanted to be alone with herself, away from relatives and familiar surroundings, away from well-meaning people who wanted to see her married "to some nice Jewish boy."[39] She was back in New York, employed by *The Record Changer* magazine for a dollar an hour when LeRoi came in as a worker, and, as she admits, from then on neither did much work. They just talked. In a way, they were kindred spirits. Hettie had an artistic bent. Literate, articulate, intelligent, she has edited a book of poetry, *Poems Now* (Kulchur Press, 1966), worked in an editorial capacity for *Partisan Review,* edited an anthology of American Indian literature, written poetry, and so forth.

The relationship deepened as it developed. Miss Cohen became Mrs. LeRoi Jones on October 13, 1958, and it was to wife Hettie that husband LeRoi was to dedicate *Preface:* "This Book Is Hettie's."

It is well to note that this period in America, the late 1950's, was a peak era in the drive for racial equality-through-integration. Dr. Martin Luther King's philosophy and program of passive resistance, nonviolence, and "redemptive love," as he termed it, had seized the imagination of American Negroes and many whites. The historic 1954 Supreme Court decision in the Bolling versus Sharpe case in principle outlawed separate schools in the United States. Integration-aimed sit-ins, wade-ins, pray-ins, and the like were in mode. Negroes were being admitted into neighborhoods, occupations, and social situations where they had been barred before. Separatism was in disfavor. A mixed marriage would be looked upon with more blessings, or with less disapprobation, than in any previous time. In the Village especially, biracial couples were common. So the marriage of Negro LeRoi Jones and white Hettie Cohen was no cause for the raising of eyebrows.

The alliance was to cause wonder and outright negative criticism in the years to follow, mainly because of Jones' anti-Jewish sentiment and strong separatist stance. Baraka-who-was-once-Jones is not eager to discuss this marriage. He explains, "I came to the Village looking to be a writer, an artist, and that was one of the first people I met down there."[40] In this connection, it is well to consider — but not to draw conclusions from — certain passages in *Home:*

> Mixed marriages, etc., take place usually among the middle class of one kind or another — usually the "liberated" segment of the middle class, artists, bohemians, entertainers, or the otherwise "famous." (Liberated here meaning that each member has somehow gotten at least superficially free of his history. For the black man this would mean that he had grown, somehow, less black; for the white woman it means, at one point, that she has more liberal opinions, or at least likes to bask in the gorgeousness of being a hip, ok, sophisticated outcast . . .
>
> For the black man, acquisition of a white woman always signified some special power the black man had managed to obtain (illicitly, therefore with a sweeter satisfaction) within white society. It was also a way of participating more directly in white society. One very heavy entrance into White America. (No matter if any of these directions said "Love".) [p. 223]

Hettie and LeRoi had two girls, Lisa and Kellie, both living with their mother now. Villagers remember Jones as a devoted father, even after the separation and divorce. "He was very religious about that," says Theodore Wilentz, Jones' first publisher and a friend of the young family. "Every week-end he would come over to pick up the two kids. In fact, that was one reason why he couldn't be so anti-white, because if any troubles came up they were white, too, you know. He took his fatherhood very seriously."[41]

Today there is still a closeness among daughter-in-law Hettie, the girls, and LeRoi's parents. The Joneses see the girls, and as grandparents will, in their living room they display pictures of these granddaughters, alongside pictures of grandchildren by their son's second marriage.

Hettie and Roi lived at several places in the Village, including the place on Cooper Square where Hettie still lives. Their home was always open to friends. (It was not unusual in those days for Hettie or Roi to lower, by means of a long string, the door key to friends standing on the pavement below in front of the locked main door to the building.) At first there were not a lot of friends. According to Hettie, "When LeRoi and I met there was very little activity at all. There was very little—there was no intellectual elite. There wasn't any such thing as a beat generation, anything. We were about the only people we knew."[42] About a year and a half after they married, Hettie and LeRoi began meeting people and developing friendships. "When we started publishing the magazine [*Yugen*] the house became a sort of place where everybody came on the week-end. And so we had week-end long parties in which there were great exchanges of ideas. LeRoi was really effective in bringing together the more intellectual East Coast people like Frank O'Hara and the other poets and the painters and the jazz musicians."[43] Ted Wilentz, who wonders if Jones' open hospitality may have been a bit of an annoyance to Hettie, recalls, "A very generous guy, Roi. His home was always—you know—people were staying there, people passing through."[44] But Hettie says that she enjoyed the guests, for they liked her, too.

Significant in view of his later anti-Jew statements, a disproportionate number of Jones' friends and associates at the time were Jews. Except for A. B. Spellman, who really came along later, and several others, very few of Jones' Village companions were blacks, and most of these blacks were musicians. The young friends of the couple were the poets, painters, intellectuals who gravitated to the Village—people like Allen Ginsberg, Gregory Corso, Hugh Selby, Gil Sorrentino, Diane DiPrima—and the somewhat older literary and artistic people—people like Ted Wilentz, a sort of combination patron-encourager-editor to the younger writers. "Ted was really very kind to us all the time," says Hettie. "If we needed money we used to borrow it from him. Stuff like that. He was very nice."[45] Important also among these friends and associates were the so-called Black Mountain School group, including artist Franz Kline, writers Charles Olson, Robert Creeley, Edward Dorn. Last but not least were the young, avant-garde jazz musicians such as Ornette Coleman, Don Cherry, and the older but nevertheless avant-garde Thelonius Monk. According to Hettie Jones, a lot more people, especially white artists and intellectuals, became interested in the new jazz as a result of LeRoi's having musicians around and writing about them. With some of these people Jones (and Hettie) developed rather close friendships. It was not unusual, for instance, to find "Cubby" Selby, O'Hara, Oppenheimer, Sorrentino, and Jones having conversation and a drink together at the Cedar Tavern.

Settled with his family and among friends in the Village, Jones continued his intellectual and creative pursuits. (It is often said that Jones earned a master's degree at Columbia University. This is not so, as Jones himself will say.) He was a Whitney Fellow in 1960–61 and a Guggenheim Fellow in 1965–66. He says of these grants that they "had the effect, at the time, of letting me know I had been successful in that particular bag."[46] In 1963 through 1965 he taught courses in post-1945 American poetry and in writing at the New School for Social Research, and during the summer of 1964 he taught a course in modern poetry at the University of Buffalo. Hettie Jones says that he was a very good teacher, well liked by his students. Jones' father recalls people calling him to see if he could use any influence to get them into his son's classes at the New School. Jones says he can remember no student on whom he thinks he had any particular artistic influence. "Wow," he says. "There were so many, you know, in all those classes. I can't remember the names. And I can't point out anyone for sure."[47]

He claims that Hettie had no special influence on his art. However, he and Hettie published *Yugen,* a "little" magazine oriented to the literary vanguard. Published from 1958 into 1963, it has been called "one of the key organs of the [literary] movement [of the time], and had great effect in helping introduce this new poetry."[48] Contributors included writers who became increasingly known and respected in literary circles — writers such as Gregory Corso, Frank O'Hara, Charles Olson, William Burroughs, Edward Dorn. Practically hand made — "I typed out everything on an IBM typewriter. . . . Put it all together with a stapling machine"[49] — it was not widely circulated. Now copies of the magazine are collectors' items. Issue Number Two, for instance, easily brings five dollars for a copy in less than mint condition, and issue Number Four is simply not available.

Another such venture involving Jones was *The Floating Bear,* described as:

One of the most important of all the underground magazines, edited first by LeRoi Jones & Diane di Prima, and now by Miss di Prima alone. A scarce mimeo'd magazine circulated at first solely on a basis of friendship, copies are simultaneously scarce and chock-full of first printings by important poets.[50]

The Floating Bear, like *Yugen,* today is rare and prized by collectors.

Other editorial activities included staff work with Totem Press and Corinth Books. As an editor, Jones selected eleven books to publish, ten of which were published and distributed. His associate in this venture, Wilentz, calls Jones "a brilliant editor."[51] Among those that Jones selected and edited for this Totem series are *The Scripture of the Golden Eternity* by Jack Kerouac and *Empty Mirror* by Allen Ginsberg, both by now considered standards by admirers of these now established authors. Jones' name appears on two publications as the editor; they are *Four Young Lady Poets* and *The Moderns: An Anthology of New Writing in America.* The latter is his major editorial achievement during the time he was in the Village.

Editor Jones' introduction to *The Moderns* states that he wanted to present those writers who for the last decade or so had "something to say in a prose medium that was an adjunct to the artful writing of the marketplace," for "I am most responsive to writing that shows a care for deeper involvement beyond the specific instances of its virtues as 'literature,'" prose that has "some *future* as literary and social phenomenon . . ." (p. ix). Jones had said before in *Poetry* (published later in *Home* as "A Dark Bag," p. 125) that "Anthologies are usually taste-manuals, fashion reinforcers, or, at best, reflections of the editor's personality and total grasp of his material." This statement seems applicable to Jones the anthologist. In commenting later on the book he said that "one of the great values of these writers is that they talk about the Americans who have no vested interests in maintaining some finally invalid image of what America really is."[52] If the writers in this volume were nonconformists in vision they were also, like their editor, nonconformists in regard to literary conventions. Jones saw William Carlos Williams, Pound, the Imagists, and French symbolists as "beginners of a still vital tradition of Western poetry" and not subject to "the Anglo-Eliotic domination of the academies" (pp. x–xi), and one would reasonably suppose that he saw his contributors as further developers of this particular tradition. Appendices in the book reflect Jones' interests and attitudes: "Uses of the Unconscious" by Michael Rumaker; Robert Creeley's dicta on short story form (or nonform), "Preface to Gold Diggers"; "Essentials of Spontaneous Prose" by popular "beat" writer Jack Kerouac; and "Note on Vaudeville Voices" and "The Cut Up Method" by William Burroughs, the latter being instructions for creating literature by literally folding, then cutting, and then patching existing pages of prose so as to form a new, random page. Other writers included in the volume indicate Jones' interest in social and experimental writing: William Eastlake, Edward Dorn, Douglas Woolf, John Rechy, Fielding Dawson, Hubert Selby, Jr., Diane DiPrima, and Russell Edson.

In addition to editorial work, LeRoi Jones was involved in theatrical productions. With others, notably Diane DiPrima, he founded in 1961 the American Theatre for Poets, as the title implies, an experimental group. Too, he continued his study of and promotion of jazz. He sponsored jazz concerts, often in halls and lofts, featuring mainly the rising young musicians who were to become the elite of those later identified with the "New" jazz or, as Jones terms it, the "new Black music." At the time these musicians, artistically controversial people like Ornette Coleman and Archie Shepp, posed problems for established jazz critics who had only lately been able to adjust their critical values to the by then established and relatively popular "bop" and "post-bop" jazz.

Jones the creative playwright-poet-critic-fictionist was not being neglected by Jones the editor-teacher-organizer-promoter. He published in numerous periodicals. Indeed, the list of offbeat, transitory, and limited-circulation organs, some really no more than mimeographed sheets, that Jones published in during his Village days is long. There are, for instance: *Wild Dog, Diplomat, Trobar, Burning Deck, The Naked Ear, Fuck You*, and *Kulchur*, in addition to the already mentioned *Yugen* and *Floating Bear.* Many are most difficult if not impossible to find today. Many of them contain works which found their way into his books. For instance, "Sonny Rollins" (in *Blues People*) and the play *The Toilet* were first printed in *Kulchur*; "The Eighth Ditch" (in *System*) is from *Floating Bear;* the first seven circles of *System* are from *The Trembling Lamb;*[53] and numerous poems in his collected versions are from such publications as *Beat Coast East, Village Voice, Yowl,* and *Matter.* Today Jones continues this practice of publishing in limited-audience media, for example, *Cricket, Soulbook,* and *Black Dialogue.*

This is not to say that Jones found editorial favor only with nonestablishment periodicals and books. He was also writing for *Down Beat, Evergreen Review, Cavalier, Poetry, The Nation, Massachusetts Review,* and other "respectable" or widely circulated publications.

In the late 1950's, Jones began writing drama for semiprofessional stage presentation; he also began writing drama for a reading public. An example of the latter is the just mentioned *The Eighth Ditch*, which eventually found its way into *System* as a combination short story and playlet. In the next five years or so there followed *Dante, The Toilet, The Baptism, The,Slave,* and *Experimental Death Unit #1.*

On March 24, 1964, *Dutchman* opened in the Village at the Cherry Lane Theatre and continued there until February of 1965. It was an immediate success. The reviewers' reactions came as a surprise, for although he had felt that the play was good, Jones had doubted that critics would see its virtues. Later, it won the Obie Award as the best off-Broadway play of the year. (Later, Jones observed that when *Dutchman* was showing downtown, its artistry was respected and admired by white audiences, but when it was presented uptown in Harlem before black audiences, the blacks called it an antiwhite play and, as Jones says, "pulled the money," causing him to discontinue its presentation there.[54]) The two-actor main cast was Jennifer West and Robert Hooks, and one of its three producers was Edward Albee, at that time not so well known. Jones is quick to point out that Albee "was never a friend of mine," but a person who "rose meteorically from within our midst."[55] (According to an interoffice note in the files of the Morrow publishing company, Jones received $500 from Albee when *Dutchman* won the Obie prize, this in addition to the award.) Looking back at Jones' plays of this period, one writer about drama notes, "The LeRoi Jones plays from 1962 to 1964 were more than a beginning of Black Theater. It [sic] was."[56]

His fiction during this Village period was mainly in the form of short pieces for periodicals and occasionally for anthologies, notably *New American Story, The Moderns,* and *Soon, One Morning.* In 1960 he had begun work on *System,* and he published it in 1963, although certain pieces of it had been published separately elsewhere.

Generally, the same may be said about his nonfiction prose. Certain essays in *Home* had been written and published as early as 1960, but the collection was not published until 1966. *Black Music,* 1967, has critical articles dating from 1963. But *Blues People* obviously had been researched for and written as one piece when it was published in 1963, although a comparison of it and *Black Music* shows that he borrowed thoughts from each for the other. Of course, he was writing prose that was never published. For instance, in 1961 when he was getting application papers together for the Whitney fellowship he mentioned as a project a collection of essays called *Attacks on Christendom.*

The thin volume *Preface,* 1961, was his first publication of collected poems, some of which date from 1957. Next came *The Dead Lecturer* in 1964, this too containing in addition to new poems a number previously published individually in various media. The "Sabotage" and "Target Study" poems in *Black Magic* are from this Village period, dating 1961–63 and 1963–65, respectively.

Where was LeRoi Jones artistically and professionally by the end of his Village days? "In 1965, LeRoi Jones was a young, black literary lion," one magazine states.[57] At that time *Playboy* magazine rhapsodized that Jones was "the most discussed—and admired—Negro writer since James Baldwin."[58] Another essayist asserted, "That LeRoi Jones would be heir to the literary baton that had passed from Richard Wright to Ralph Ellison to James Baldwin became apparent a few years after he set foot on the track. Fools alone doubted his speed and ability."[59] His ever growing militancy and blackness seemed not to disturb whites unduly. In fact, "Toward the end of his fellowship years in New York's East Village . . . white America still celebrated his anger as sacrament."[60] Schneck is more descriptive:

He was laved with cocktail party love and lionized with literary laurels and cash monies.

At first, the blase New York culture scene was titillated by his maledictions. He was invited to all the enchanted circle-beautiful people parties, literary events, show business orgies, and hip gatherings. The more he attacked white society, the more white society patronized him. Who'd have suspected that there was so much money to be made from flagellation? Whitey seemed insatiable; the masochistic vein was a source of hitherto untapped appeal, big box office stuff, and LeRoi Jones was one of the very first to exploit it.

Naturally the smart money crowd, the commercial-intellectual establishment, decided he was running a game, that he was into a gimmick, a commercial pose, a successful device. After all, LeRoi had been around the Village for years, had run with the white beatniks in the early '50s, had married a white Jewish girl. So how could he really mean what he was saying? Actually *mean* it . . . ?[61]

What was LeRoi Jones thinking? Poetically, he was saying in "Rhythm & Blues (1" that

I am deaf and blind and lost and will not again sing your quiet
    verse. I have lost
even the act of poetry, and writhe now for cool horizonless dawn.

During the later years of his Village era, he was trying to be less "uselessly 'literary.' . . . trying, as Margaret Walker says, 'to fashion a way,' to clean up and move."[62] He was to explain later:

The writing from the earliest published work is always a concern with the identity of black—my identity of black and what is blackness and just the whole style of being black people. You know, always. Any poetry—early poetry—I've ever written you will see that there. The focus is not always clear. Sometimes it's even self-deprecation, but it's always a deep concern there. It was a matter of developing.[63]

His earliest associates and friends in the Village had been "beats," artistic and philosophical and practicing nonconformists and social outlaws. "The reason I always associate with the people thought of as beats is that they're outside the mainstream of American vulgarity."[64] Even so, by 1964 he found "only one white man in New York I really trust—that's Allen Ginsberg. I trust him and love him completely in that sense [that Ginsberg is empathetic to what Jones thinks and feels]."[65] His distrust of and growing alienation from white America had been, as he would put it, "developing" in the Village.

So, regardless of cocktail parties and writing awards and a promising future, this "irreverent man . . . did not break stride even upon meeting the American Bitch Goddess of Success, and not since Paul Robeson had one fled her boudoir in such utter defiance."[66]

"The guiding spirit of a new event": Harlem

In April of 1965 LeRoi Jones left his wife Hettie, his two daughters Kellie and Lisa, his Village phase, his racially integrated life, and headed north to Harlem where he began an entirely new life. So goes the popular version of the move. However, no such sudden, absolute, and dramatic break occurred. As Jones talks about it, "It wasn't any sudden thing. It was a developing thing. . . . My work kept changing steadily. . . . It wasn't any kind of abrupt, rational decision. It was based on growing, change—like everything else—until one day the whole thing just became unbearable in a physical sense and I just cut out."[67]

It is not possible to say with certainty what were contributing factors in this apparent estrangement of Hettie and LeRoi and how such factors had bearing, if any, on his writing and vice versa. Did his growing black consciousness during this period cause him to turn away from his white wife? "Oh, yeah." Did Hettie cause him to turn away from "whiteness" by some actions, some attitudes, some way in which she related to him? "No. It was a matter of developing, a matter of coming through—a matter of becoming a mature person. A striving to be what I am."[68] Hettie Jones declines to discuss their private affairs, and she declines to react to what others may say about her and LeRoi's private affairs, considering such talk gossip rather than history. Old friends and associates in the Village say they are not sure what happened and are not sure what effect Jones' writing had on his domestic life and what effect his domestic life had on his writing. Jones' father refuses even to speculate, saying flatly that he simply does not know what happened; Jones' mother says she does not know either, but she wonders if pressures from black militants were a factor.

Jones' physical move to Harlem may well not have been a clean break. "It was very difficult, of course, for both of us," says Hettie Jones.[69] A New York *Herald Tribune* feature article of October 31, 1965, stated:

> He says his identity with Harlem is complete, that he has been separated from his white wife, the former Hettie Cohen, for two years, that he has left their Cooper Square apartment to live in Harlem. This comes as a surprise to various people who say they have visited the family in the apartment within the last year.[70]

There was a rumor, a rumor at best yet persistent, to the effect that during his stay in Harlem Jones was subjected to pressure from black associates because of his alleged furtive excursions back to the Village.

Ostensibly, Jones went to Harlem to conduct the Black Arts Repertory Theatre/School (BART/S). It is not true that he went to Harlem for the express purpose of founding this Theatre/School, for it had been in existence in late 1964, while he was still living in the Village. Of this project, Hettie Jones has said, "I don't know a thing about that, really. That was very mysterious doing and we weren't getting along at that particular time. . . . I think he got rooked out of a lot of money at that time. . . . It was very hard."[71] BART/S was short-lived, and in 1965 when it closed Jones had gone back to Newark.

He founded BART/S, Jones says, "to re-educate the nearly half a million Harlem Negroes to find a new pride in their color."[72] It was, a handbill read, "dedicated to the education and cultural awakening of the Black People in America." Drama and other cultural activities were not its only features. About eighty children, ages seven through thirteen, were instructed in remedial reading, mathematics, and in Jones' words, "hard-core nationalism."[73]

Needless to say, such projects must be financially sustained. Jones raised some money by promoting jazz concerts (even back downtown, at the Village Gate night club), by soliciting contributions, and the like. Blacks, alone, it appeared, could not support the project. Then BART/S got approval for $40,000 of federal Office of Economic Opportunity (OEO) antipoverty funds to be used for an eight-week summer session involving 400 students. Later, an Associated Press news release on November 30 read in part:

> Each night in a makeshift Harlem theater a group of young Negroes give vent to their hatred of white people.
>
> They act out dreams of a day when the Negro will stand apart from the white world, and Harlem will be an independent nation.
>
> Their leader is the bitterly antiwhite poet-playwright, LeRoi Jones. . . .
>
> All the productions seethe with rage against "Whitey," an all-inclusive term for whites, who are usually portrayed as homosexuals. . . .
>
> The project's pace stepped up after $40,000 in federal antipoverty funds was made available.

Alexander J. Allen of the Greater New York League defended the grant, seeing as constructive the development of black cultural awareness. And OEO official James Kelleher preferred to see "kids fussing on the stage" rather than in the streets. But as one writer put it, "When *that* got out there was an end to the project. And some of his own people, Harlem sharks, began hustling him. So he left Harlem and moved back to the old home town, Newark, New Jersey."[74]

Just who "his own people, Harlem sharks" were, if any, and why they "began hustling him," if they did, is not at all clear. Harlem habitues and others who generally know what is and has been going on in Harlem claim not to know exactly what happened. But there are those who prefer not to be quoted who will say that Jones was physically attacked by "friends" in Harlem in connection with their efforts to control Jones and BART/S for financial or political reasons. One person believes that Jones fled to Newark because of danger to his person. Another source hints that the basic friction was over whether BART/S would be essentially a cultural operation as Jones insisted it should be or essentially a tool or front for revolutionists. All of this, though, is hearsay, and should be considered as such. It is included here only as an indication of the currents of opinions and rumors concerning the people and ideologies connected with BART/S.

There are, however, other sources of information about Jones and the project, and these sources constitute, though not gospel, something better than hearsay. Jones' father says that BART/S "should be a bad memory for him [LeRoi], but it isn't."[75] Jones' parents claim that their son went to Harlem because he envisioned the realization of an ideal — the involvement of the masses of black people in viable cultural experiences, his job being, basically, to put on a play a week, utilizing the community's human resources and talents. But "parasites and leeches," his parents suspect, sought personal monetary gain. The Joneses insist that their son scrupulously avoided mishandling of funds and that he paid in full all the people who worked under his supervision. But when OEO funds were withdrawn, there simply was no way to continue the flow of what little money there had been. Actors and others connected with the project looked to LeRoi Jones, his parents feel, for continued employment when there were no means of his keeping them on a payroll, with the result that some few of these people became hostile to Jones and BART/S.

Then there is the matter of the "Five Percenters," an alleged group of black terrorists. Members of this group supposedly were employed in the summer of 1965 under the HARYOU-ACT antipoverty program, Project Uplift, and some members of this group were supposedly involved in BART/S, one of Project Uplift's employers of young people. In the eyes of some critics, these youths were being "paid off" to keep down rioting and violence on their part. In defense of employing alleged hoodlums, antipoverty officials rationalized that these were the very type of people their programs were designed to reach and help.

According to a newspaper article the "Five Percenters" were activists in a real sense:

> Its members are blamed for heckling Harlem's Rep. Adam Clayton Powell and Democratic mayoral candidate Abraham D. Beame to the point where the politicos felt compelled to call for police protection and bring a premature halt to a recent campaign tour . . .
>
> By Mr. Jones' own account, two white auditors for HARYOU-ACT fled from their office by a rear exit when he and two other members of the Black Arts appeared at the office a week ago to ask why their funds had been cut off. . . .
>
> Some knowledgeable sources speculate that Mr. Wingate (antipoverty official) may have been talking about the Black Arts rather than the secret hate society called the Five Percenters when he spoke of "an armed group ready to move" if HARYOU-ACT's funds were cut off.[76]

In another article the same writer spoke of reports that this "hate group actually dominated the anti-poverty program" and that "one reason for the refusal of civic leaders to discuss the group appears to be fear of retaliation."[77] In a HARYOU-ACT rally in October of 1965 attended by some youngsters "described by one man as Five Percenters and by others as members of the Black Arts group," Jones is alleged to have talked of employing "killer logic," saying, "If that's what the white man understands, perhaps it's time we take on that mantle; and if they make one shaky move, Watts will look like a picnic.''[78]

Then there is the matter of the "Pakistani Muslims," called by a police official "a secretive organization of extreme Black Nationalists—as militant as you can get.''[79] According to newspaper stories, when police conducted a raid at the BART/S building they found a cache of weapons and bomb materials, dope, a basement firing range, and a wall sign reading "All officers will be obeyed, penalty for disbelievers is death. The law was given by our fathers. It has not been enforced in 1,400 years. It will be enforced now.''[80] By this time, Jones was supposed to have left BART/S and gone back to live in Newark. There was a report, though, that Jones fled the scene and eluded the police. Most people scoff at this. Jones' parents, for instance, say that he had been living with them in Newark for some time before this raid and that he was, in fact, at their home the entire day on which the raid took place.

Detractors were quick to judge the Black Arts Repertory Theatre/School as a failure when it closed, but Jones regards it as a learning experience that was helpful to him thereafter, especially in the organization and operation of Spirit House. It is true that BART/S, though no lasting success, during its life did influence black drama; and it continues to influence black drama. Larry Neal, now a playwright-poet and coeditor with Jones of *Black Fire,* was involved in BART/S activities. Yusef Iman, currently a "name" in the "in-group" world of black drama and poetry, came out of the Theatre/School. Although she was not a member of the repertory group, actress Barbara Ann Teer came from time to time and Jones was her director in one production. Other young poets and actors came through the project, "a lot of people who are still rising,''[81] according to Jones. In addition to its influence on individual blacks, the Theatre/School had and still has impact in black drama. Indirectly and directly it served as a model for the type of community theatre-workshop-school that sprang up in black neighborhoods in other cities in the United States.

During the Harlem stay Jones continued his literary career. Most of his time, naturally, was spent writing, producing, and directing plays at BART/S. But he found time to write essays which were to be a part of *Home,* notably the strong problack ones that end the book, including "STATE/MEANT," his succinct definition of the black artist's role in America. Too, he wrote numerous poems, including many in the "Target Study" and "Black Art" sections of *Black Magic.* And he continued contributing articles and reviews to various journals and periodicals. In tone, content, and technique his writing was indeed becoming "less uselessly 'literary.' ''

Looking back at BART/S and his Harlem experiences, Jones makes this assessment: "We went up town to Harlem and opened a theatre, and blew a billion words into the firmament like black prayers to force change."[82]

Hell or Purgatory?: Newark

Across the river, a short commuter ride from New York City, LeRoi Jones took his ideas and lessons and energy—to force change.

One of his first acts was to organize Spirit House in the heart of Newark's downtown slums. Basically, Spirit House is a self-help operation. In 1967 he said, "The only help we get from them [poverty programs, foundations, and the like] is that they're so stupid they help people see the truth about what I'm saying." Would he accept such money? "Sure I would. But the only way they would give me money now would be to do something they can use against black people. They're not gonna offer me any more money, 'cause even what they think is happening doesn't always have to be happening, you know. They might give you a dollar because they think you're an airplane, and you're really a bird."[83] Spirit House, he explains, is owned by people of the community.

Aside from repertory theatre, "common sense theatre in the sense of being able to teach very literally,"[84] what does Spirit House offer the community? "Anything the community wants—sports, music, parties, meetings, classes; something is going on every night. The plays are only on weekends. We have a permanent ensemble of actors; they're in most of the plays, and of course, we use a lot of kids. We do a lot of children's plays, too."[85]

(Spirit House presentations are generally available free or at nominal cost to the community people, but elsewhere it is a different story. Gerald Weales states that Jones' fee to appear several years ago at the University of Pennsylvania's "Black Week" was $1,500. His Spirit House players cost an extra $1,000, for which they performed two of Jones' plays.[86] Mwanafunzi Katibu, Baraka's secretary, quotes the following fees: lecture by Baraka—$1,500 plus expenses for four people, transportation, and hotel lodging; performance by Spirit House Movers—$750 plus expenses for thirteen people.[87])

The African Free School, named after the first public school in America, is operated by the women of Spirit House. Llorens wrote in 1969, "Community streets in the area of Spirit House are filled with African song at least three days a week as the women of BCD trek through the neighborhood collecting youngsters along the route and singing their way to their little schoolroom where children, often labeled 'unteachable,' demonstrate impressive reading skill and are tiny historians in their own right."[88] Emphasis is upon reading. The school recognizes personality but not individuality in its students, teaching them a value system based upon Kawaida doctrine (discussed later in this book). "It is," says Baraka, "to project our children in our own image. . . . They are taught who they are and what they must grow up to."[89]

Later, a number of Spirit House's activities were moved around the corner to a three-story, former office building on High Street that ostensibly houses the Committee for a Unified Newark. The building contains a tiny office that serves as Jones' base of operations. For some time, he and his family by his second marriage lived on the third floor of Spirit House.

During the summer of 1967, serious civic disorders (or a citizen uprising, a consumer demonstration, a revolt, or riots, as you please) broke out in Newark.[90] Groups and individuals roamed the streets smashing windows, looting, setting fires, destroying property, attacking people. City and state law and military personnel and citizens struggled to contain the violence, using tear gas, firearms, physical force, and appeals. Shots were fired—by the police, the military, and citizens. Scores of people, mainly blacks, were injured; a number were killed, some from gunfire. In an essay which was to appear later in *Raise* as "From: The Book of Life" Jones describes the events as a sort of messianic phenomenon:

> The city is burning! The Devil's city is in flame! And because evil beings have tortured our people by worshiping dumb objects more than human life, our people run through the streets with these objects. Sometimes they are murdered. But also they run with what they need smashing and destroying the temples of the UnGodly. Temples where evil beings sell our people things and keep them chained to illusions of Desire.
>
> *Pop pow pow Boom!!* The flame The Flame. Red shadows moving near the darkness. Devils whirling round and round, frightened that God is near and their deaths are imminent!
>
> Our people dance in the street now! Young men and old men. Arms full. Little girls outfitting their hovels with what they've learned to desire on television. Dancing In The Street!!
>
> On the roofs the marksmen of Shango [Yoruba god of thunder and fertility] and Allah look down and judge the dancers. A devil whirls into the flames, a new eye blind in the center of his skull! Allahu Akbar! . . .
>
> Doom to the devil total death will come soon Doom Doom to the Devil. Young armies of God reformed after 400 years attacking with the most natural

of weapons holding against the scourges of Satan our honor our lives our holy Blackness!

When the devils catch a dancer they murder him at once or else they throw the single human to the earth and stomp and beat him with sticks and try to break his bones and tear out his privates (in terrible envy) and scream "Animals Animals Animals," describing only themselves in their frenzy. [pp. 53–54]

The essay ends with the inscription: "—Essex County Jail/Summer 1967/Year of Rebellion."

During the height of the confusion and violence, LeRoi Jones, accountant Charles McCray, and actor Barry Wynn, riding in Jones' Volkswagon bus, were stopped and arrested by police officers at South Seventh Street and South Orange Avenue in Newark's west side. The charges were unlawfully carrying firearms—two revolvers and a box of ammunition—and resisting arrest. Somehow Jones suffered a head injury that required sutures and a loosened tooth that had to be pulled the next day or so. The police attributed Jones' wounds to his having been hit on the head by a bottle thrown by some unknown person. Jones accused the police of premeditated brutality. As to the guns, Jones claimed he did not know where they had come from but suspected that the police had "planted" them.

What had he been doing out in the streets at such a time? "Actually, we were riding around most of the evening—this was the second night of the riots—picking up people that had gotten hurt and taking them to the hospital. A lot of people were shot and stuff—the police didn't have time to arrest them on the spot, so they would leave them out there in the street."[91] Then what happened, according to Jones? His statement to his lawyer reads in part:

... we were stopped by at least two carloads of white-helmeted police with shotguns and several detectives.

We were told to come out of the car. When I opened the door and stepped down, one detective, whom I recognized as having once attended Barringer High School while I was there, preached to me, screaming that "we were the bastards" who'd been shooting at them. "Yes," he said, "a blue panel truck." (My station wagon is an olive green camper bus.) I said that we had not been shooting at anyone. I told the officer that I thought I remembered him from high school—whereupon he hit me in the face and threw me up against the side of the truck ...

The detective then began to jab me as hard as he could with his pistol in my stomach, asking, "Where are the guns?" I told him that there were no guns.

Suddenly it seemed that five or six officers surrounded me and began to beat me. I was hit perhaps five times on top of my head by night sticks, and when I fell, some of the officers went about methodically trying to break my hands, elbows and shoulders. One officer tried to kick me in the groin—and there were many punches thrown. As they beat me they kept calling me "animal" and asking me, "Where are the guns?" Inside the wagon, the beating continued. They took us from the wagon, and as I was pushed up the stairs at Police Head-quarters, an officer called out, "Wait a minute" and then punched me in the pit of the stomach. I fell to the ground clutching my stomach.

Inside the station, Mr. Spina (the police director) was standing behind the desk. I asked him had he ordered me beaten. He replied, "They got you, didn't they?"—smiling. . . .

We were then taken to City Hospital; I was dragged in and handcuffed in a wheelchair. The "doctors" put in eight or nine stitches, and one doctor shouted at me, "You're a poet, huh? Well, you won't be writing any poems for a long time now."[92]

(In an essay entitled "An article/story about newark policemen using their real names, &c." published later in *Raise,* Jones says of Dominick Spina:

And this ginnie walkin around tellin people he gonna prosecute somebody for turning on a water hydrant in 97 degree weather, and his motherfuckin kids got airconditionin and pools and this fag talkin about how he gonna prose-cute . . . "the maximum." The motherfucker aint wrapped up too tight you askin me. Fuck him anyway. . . .

But I want to describe him, Spina. The chairman (really the director, a pinball machine for his ol haveay handed paisanos. . . . He work for the big ginnies, live out further in the suburbs. It's the same system. The mighty out off some-where hiding from the real shit. They makin shit, fall on our heads. An we wondering, and buckin our eyes, or scarey or shoutin or lying when all the time a creepy european, a drop of blood in em or none at all, the coldest, somewhere fuckin up yr life. [p. 92]

In a footnote, he says that "Spina was indicted in 1968 and 1969 and charges were denied. He was dismissed as Director in 1970 by Kenneth Gibson" (p. 91). Also in *Raise* (p. 63), in the essay "Newark—Before Black Men Conquered" Jones claims "One of the first cops to whip my head during '67 rebellion was an Italian I knew from Barringer, where Italian language was part of the curriculum, Detective Jerry Mellillo.")

At the arraignment, the bail was set at $25,000, an amount Jones described as "ransom, not bail." The bail was made—$2,500 in cash and the rest covered by two homes posted by friends of Jones' parents. The trial came up before Judge Leon W. Kapp sitting in Essex County Court. The jury was all-white. The verdict was guilty.

Between his arrest and the trial, *Evergreen Review* published in its December, 1967, issue the following poem by Jones:

Black People!

What about that bad short you saw last week
on Frelinghuysen, or those stoves and refrigerators, record players, shotguns,
in Sears, Bambergers, Klein's, Hahnes', Chase and the smaller joosh
enterprises? What about that bad jewelry, on Washington Street, and
those couple of shops on Springfield? You know how to get it, you can
get it, no money down, no money never, money dont grow on trees no
way, only whitey's got it, makes it with a machine, to control you
you cant steal nothin from a white man, he's already stole it he owes
you anything you want, even his life. All the stores will open if you
will say the magic words. The magic words are: Up against the wall mother
fucker this is a stick up! Or: Smash the window at night (these are magic
actions) smash the windows daytime, anytime, together, lets smash the
window drag the shit from in there. No money down. No time to pay. Just
take what you want. The magic dance in the street. Run up and down Broad
Street niggers, take the shit you want. Take their lives if need be, but
get what you want what you need. Dance up and down the streets, turn all
the music up, run through the streets with music, beautiful radios on
Market Street, they are brought here especially for you. Our brothers
are moving all over, smashing at jellywhite faces. We must make our own
World, man, our own world, and we can not do this unless the white man
is dead. Let's get together and kill him my man, lets get to gather the fruit
of the sun, let's make a world we want black children to grow and learn in
do not let your children when they grow look in your face and curse you by
pitying your tomish ways.

During the sentencing proceedings, Judge Kapp read this poem aloud in court, omitting what he considered "obscenities" and substituting for them the word "blank." Then followed dialogue between Kapp and Jones:

DEFENDANT JONES: Are you offering that in evidence?

THE COURT: Just a minute.

DEFENDANT JONES: It should be read wholly, if you are.

THE COURT: "The Author: Le Roi Jones, Evergreen Publications, December, 1967."

DEFENDANT JONES: Let me read it.

THE COURT: Just a minute. This diabolical prescription to commit murder and to steal and plunder and other similar evidences—

DEFENDANT JONES: I'm being sentenced for the poem. Is that what you are saying?

THE COURT: —causes one to suspect that you were a participant in formulating a plot to ignite the spark on the night of July 13, 1967 to burn the City of Newark and that—

DEFENDANT JONES: You mean, you don't like the poem, in other words.

. . . .

THE COURT: . . . Another shocking excerpt from a speech which you delivered on September 15, 1967 at Muhlenberg College has been brought to my attention.

DEFENDANT JONES: Did I have the guns then too?

THE COURT: Which reads—

DEFENDANT JONES: Is that what I'm being tried for, Muhlenberg College?

THE COURT: "Unless we black people can come into peaceful power and begin the benevolent rule of the just the next stage of our rebellion will burn Newark to the ground. This time City Hall and the rest of the greco Romans will go down, including the last of these greco Romans themselves."

It is my considered opinion that you are sick and require medical attention.

DEFENDANT JONES: Not as sick as you.

. . . .

THE COURT: It has been suggested by some of your literary friends that you are a gifted writer, which I am willing to concede, except that I abhor the use of obscenities and your foul language. It is most unfortunate that your talents have been misdirected. You have the ability to make a wholesome contribution to ameliorate existing tensions and the resolution of the social and economic problems of our community by the introduction of constructive measures. Instead we find that you are in the vanguard of a group of extreme radicals who advocate the destruction of our democratic way of life by means of criminal anarchy.

DEFENDANT JONES: The destruction of unrighteousness.

THE COURT: . . . If the philosopher can make his own law, so can the fool.

DEFENDANT JONES: We see that.

THE COURT: If the virtuous man can make his own law, so can those who spring from the gutter.

DEFENDANT JONES: Yes, we see that again.

THE COURT: There can be no substitute for freedom but there can be no freedom where anarchy prevails. There can be no substitute for justice but there can exist no justice where law and order have perished. Your behavior, both past and present, constitutes a threat and a menace to our society.

DEFENDANT JONES: And you all are a threat to the world.

THE COURT: The sentence of this Court, on the basis of your conviction for the unlawful possession of two revolvers—

DEFENDANT JONES: And two poems.

THE COURT: —in violation of *New Jersey Statute 2A: 151–41*, a misdemeanor, on Indictment No. 2220–66, is that you be confined to the New Jersey State Prison to serve a term of not less than 2 years and 6 months and not more than 3 years and that you pay a fine of $1000.

DEFENDANT JONES: Sir, black people will judge me, brother Kapp. Don't worry about that.

THE COURT: You are excused. Take him upstairs.[93]

The New York *Times'* headline read, "The Magic Word was 'Prison.'" *Time* magazine of the same week intoned, "Curtains for LeRoi."

The judge's introduction of the poem and of the excerpt from Jones' Muhlenberg College speech and the relatively severe sentence (the average sentence for similar riot-connected convictions was six months, some of this time suspended or on probation) caused some professional and lay disrespect for Judge Kapp. Among those showing concern was the American Civil Liberties Union, which issued a statement which read, in part, "This is clearly a violation of Jones' right to free speech. . . . Actions of this kind tend only to exacerbate an already tense Negro community and do not serve the cause of justice."[94] Another was a "Committee on Poetry" in support of Jones which issued a broadside bearing the names of supporters, including Corso, Creeley, and Ginsberg.

Jones appealed and eventually the conviction was reversed in a retrial.

"Without a shot": The politician

Back in 1965 when he interviewed Jones shortly after Jones had left the Village for Harlem, writer Jack Richardson thought that he discerned "political cunning" in Jones that gave Richardson reason to believe that Jones might have a political future.[95] Mr. Richardson has proved prophetic in that Jones became very much involved in politics — and apparently effectively involved. His political activity contradicts, at least on the surface, Jones' earlier pronouncements in *Home* about the futility of blacks working for change through the existing political structure.

In the spring of 1967 when Jones taught briefly at San Francisco State College, he was impressed by West Coast black leader Maulana Karenga and his program for cultural nationalism, a program called US. Karenga had read Jones and owed much to him, but Karenga knew more about the mechanics of organizing than did Jones. Inspired by Karenga's ideas and methods, after returning to Newark Jones organized in January, 1968, the Black Community Development and Defense Organization, called BCD or "the Organization." Dedicated to a new value system for the black community, its manifestations include new personal names ("traditional" names in place of given or "slave" names), courtesy, propriety, sharing, and certain abstinences such as refusal to eat pork and refraining from the use of tobacco, alcohol, and drugs. Directed by a trio — Balozi Zayd, Mfundishi Maasi, and Jones (by then known as Ameer Baraka) — BCD is one of some thirty-eight organizations, including the political United Brothers of Newark, that make up the Committee for a United Newark (CUN). BCD shares the building at 502 High Street with CUN. Here the sociopolitical is wedded to the cultural-religious-philosophical.

In April, 1968, *Time* reported that Jones was "interested now in achieving black power politically in his native city, where 52% of the 410,000 residents are Negro. As head of the new United Brothers of Newark, Jones said last week, 'We are out to bring back self-government to this city by 1970, and the ballot seems to be the most advantageous way. We are educating the Negro masses that this city can be taken without a shot being fired.'"[96]

Jones was attempting to convert into action a philosophy based upon political realities, a practical philosophy such as he advises other blacks to take:

> You have to control everything of power in your community. You say the Urban League is jive. Sure it is. But you had better control it. If you don't, the white boy will. The poverty program — it's jive. We know that. But we better use it or the white boy will. Make up your mind about who is going to control what's going on in your black community. . . . But you've got to organize. You can't "speechify" things into happening. Organize![97]

Looking at Mayor Addonizio's administration, Jones calculated Italians' power in Newark to be second only to Italians' power in the Vatican. This power, he felt, came from money and "somebody's got to go to jail once they start uncovering the graft that goes on. This town is run by graft, completely. That's why they've been, even on the surface, so unresponsive to so-called social pressures."[98] In 1970, Hugh Addonizio was convicted of extortion and accepting bribes. Then in March of 1972, after going through the appeal process in vain, Addonizio entered prison to begin a ten year sentence.

In 1968 a strange alliance, or perhaps truce would be a precise term, was effected between Jones and Tony Imperiale, leader of the North Ward Citizens' Committee that had formed to protect almost all-white North Ward against "black radical animals" and that was given to riding around in their own patrol cars ("jungle cruisers"). Imperiale and Jones shared a contempt for white liberals from the suburbs and both represented groups who seemed to be political victims rather than the political elite. "LeRoi and I don't love each other but we respect each other," Imperiale said.[99] "I respect him. He doesn't lie like white liberals. He knows exactly what I'm trying to do, and I know right where he's at," Jones said.[100] This understanding "reflects a kind of balance of terror, based on mutually recognized territorial imperatives. . . . The balance is certainly unstable. . . . But at least it exists," wrote Stewart Alsop.[101] And had not Jones said, "Black power cannot exist WITHIN white power. . . . They might exist side by side as separate entities, but never in the same space"?[102]

When incumbent Addonizio, at the time on trial for bribery, opposed challenger Gibson in the mayoral contest in 1970, naturally Gibson was supported by Jones and Addonizio by Imperiale. Gibson was to say later:

> LeRoi is a very dedicated individual, as you probably know. When he decides to do something, that becomes a cause. And he participates to the fullest. There was never a time in the period of the campaign that he could not be called upon for assistance, seven days a week and, you know, any time of night. So you have to respect a man who dedicates himself to his cause.[103]

Jones' plan was to organize what he called the "have-not" Puerto Ricans and blacks and "those white people who don't think it's beneath their dignity to be intelligent . . . to run a kind of unified campaign to see a transfer of power in Newark because black people and Puerto Ricans represent the majority of people in that city."[104] "We know," said Jones, "that the owners will be on the set even after we win; but the morality of the managers will at least be higher than the morality of the owners."[105]

News correspondent Haynes Johnson reported that on election day there was an Addonizio car decorated with flags and a slogan, "It's great to be an American," and warning over a loudspeaker, "Never forget the words of LeRoi Jones. . . . After 8 o'clock tonight he's no longer welcome in our city."[106] One newspaper editorialized: "In circulation was a rumor that Leroi Jones, the militant black playwright, was the man at the wheel of the Gibson campaign; the Addonizio forces pictured a city hall full of black revolutionaries if Gibson should win, and played for a monolithic white vote. That was the intoxicant Wallace served up in Alabama, but Newark, to its credit, wasn't having any."[107]

Gibson won handily. Newark had its first black mayor in history. And Jones was not appointed to his cabinet as rumor had predicted he would be. Yet, months after the election, a major portion of Jones' time was still taken with politics related city activities. During the summer of 1970, Jones admitted doing little creative work at the time, explaining that most of his time was devoted to political work on behalf of black people.[108] In another place he had said, "Oh, I get bored with literary pursuits and the incestuous literary life. A man must be a citizen as well as an artist. I put politics first in my life." [109]

"Self-consciously spiritual": Imamu

What Jones has managed to do since his return to Newark from Harlem is impressive. His art has become even more functional and spiritual during this time. "My work after 1966 is self-consciously spiritual," he says, and this self-conscious spirituality shows. It was not a thing to become surprised at, then, when Mr. LeRoi Jones became Imamu (Spiritual Leader) Ameer Baraka (Blessed Prince), a Kawaida minister. Ameer later became Amiri, with the same meaning. In 1966 he had married his present wife, Sylvia, the mother of two girls by a previous marriage. His new family's "traditional" names became, respectively, Amini, Asia, and Maisha. When Amini bore Amiri two sons they were named Obalaji Malik Ali and Ras Jua Al Aziz.

Jones' early interest in theology has already been pointed out. After he came out of the military service he investigated Christian, Buddhist, and Zen theology. He found "at one level there's a common strain in religions once they leave the priest-craft level — once they get above the desires of individual priests — there is a common strain in true religion."[110] Any religion should be a moral-political-social-cultural phenomenon, he feels, "a way of life, a total thing" that shapes "your entire life."[111] But whites, he claims, have made Christianity "a vehicle for the degenerate — it tends to cover truth rather than reveal it," for they want "a God that they can control . . . an on and off switch for God . . ."[112] As disaffected with Western Christianity as with other facets of Western culture, Leroi Jones sought an alternative. He was first influenced by the late Malcolm X (by the time of his death known also as Hajj Malik) who saw possibilities for social change through the Islamic religion. Jones noticed too that Black Muslim leader Elijah Muhammad taught the morality of Islam as specifically beneficial to the black man. Jones had been further influenced by Yoruba religion. But he did not consider these strains in terms of spiritual philosophy until he had returned to Newark. Finally he was converted to the orthodox Muslim faith by Hesham Jaboa of the Sunni Muslims, but Jones was not to be an orthodox Muslim.

As far back as *System* Jones had said that "Finally, God, is simply a white man, a white 'idea,' in this society, unless we have made some other image which is stronger, and can deliver us from the salvation of our enemies" (p. 153). In 1967 his poem announced that "The Black Man Is Making New Gods." In 1968 in the introduction to *Four Black Revolutionary Plays* he advised:

> say it
> sweet nigger
> i believe in black allah
> governor of creation
> Lord of the Worlds.

Then in 1970 as Imamu Amiri Baraka he set forth in *A Black Value System* the doctrine of Kawaida, meaning "that which is customary, or traditionally ad-herred to, by black people" (p. 4). Actually, Kawaida is a contrived religion. It is based mainly upon a system worked out by Karenga, "a form . . . useful in a total social sense," a value system that "takes into consideration a kind of moral discipline of orthodox Islam and African concepts that are useful to us."[113]

The Nguzo Saba, or seven principles, of Kawaida are Umoja (Unity), Kuji-chagulia (Self-Determination), Ujima (Collective Work and Responsibility), Ujamaa (Cooperative Economics), Nia (Purpose), Kuumba (Creativity), and Imani (Faith). Baraka considers Nguzo Saba the key to the new nationalism.

He does not consider his religion apart from his art. Jihad [holy war] Pro-ductions, operating as an adjunct to his Newark activities, is the agency that today handles his smaller publications as well as those of other black artists, mostly young writers who, according to *Black World* editor Hoyt W. Fuller, might risk "loss of integrity by submitting to the strictures and the judgment of white critics and editors."[114] Jones' father, who spends some time working with Jihad, emphasizes that Jihad always attempts to get royalties into the hands of black writers, preferring that writers not sign over their works to Jihad. Jones, he says, wants black writers to stand independent of any publisher, wants them to hold on to their literary property.

Jihad also produces "Black Communications for the Evolving Black Nation": broadsides, plays, phonograph recordings, motion pictures, posters, monographs, poster-size photographs. Its "constellation of Creators" includes Sun Ra, Don L. Lee, Ben Caldwell, Sonia Sanchez, Gaston Neal, David Henderson, and Katibu. Jones himself may be heard in readings on phonograph recordings "Black and Beautiful" and "Sonny's Time Now!" It is not uncommon for Jihad to be out of stock on certain items; at this writing, for example, it does not have in stock copies of Jones' plays *Slave Ship* and *Arm Yrself or Harm Yrself.*

Jones' writings published by Jihad include the plays mentioned just above and the thin volume of poetry *Black Arts,* which was later incorporated into *Black Magic. A Black Value System* appeared in the summer of 1970. Projected for publication by Jihad are *The Book of Life* which Jones promises will be philosophy, religion, and prophecy. And since Bobbs-Merrill "has the nerve to censor and refuse to publish the play *J-E-L-L-O,* as attacking a public figure's private life . . . Jihad is publishing the play as a side order . . ."[115] This was not to be the case, however; *J-E-L-L-O* was published by Third World Press (a black company) in 1970.

The William Morrow, Grove, Bobbs-Merrill, and Random House companies have been the publishers of Jones' major works during his current stay in Newark. Morrow published *Home, Black Music,* and *Black Fire;* Grove published *Tales, The Baptism* and *The Toilet;* Bobbs-Merrill published *Black Magic, Four Black Revolutionary Plays,* and *In Our Terribleness;* and Random House published *Raise Race Rays Raze.*

The last four works listed show graphically how our author has moved from his earlier Jonesian stances to almost totally utilitarian Barakan blackness. As he has moved through the years, whites have reacted with increasing disaffection, not only to Jones the person but also to his art. Whites no longer celebrate his "anger as sacrament," no longer regard him as a necessary if noisome pricker of their conscience, no longer read him for signs of a breakthrough to a new literary era, no longer abide him as a side effect to be suffered for America's indulgence in racial injustices. A few years ago, he wrote in "I Substitute For The Dead Lecturer" that "They have turned, and say that I am dying." So today Baraka turns from whites and toward his black brothers and sisters. He has been known to do this literally when speaking before mixed audiences.

Today, to most whites he is at best a very talented man who is misapplying his talents and at worst a demented, demagogic, and very dangerous racist plotting their physical deaths. How does he react to being called a racist? In *Evergreen Review* he says, "I'm a racist in the sense that I believe certain qualities that are readily observable on this planet have to do with racial types and archetypes."[116]

If Baraka is a villain in the eyes of whites he is a hero in the eyes of the current generation of black nationalists and their sympathizers. No one so captures the cultural sensibilities of young black cultural revolutionists. He has great drawing power on predominantly black campuses. There is no doubt that among young black readers he is the most consistently read of all the current black writers. As truthful as it is trite is Schneck's evaluation: ". . . he is the poet laureate of this Black Revolution."[117]

If imitation of Jones' artistry is a measure of his cultural leadership, among young blacks he is considered to be without peers. All one needs do is pick up any collection of literature by the current young generation of writers, and there is no mistaking Jones as an important source of inspiration, content, and technique to the likes of Clarence Major, Don Lee, Sonia Sanchez, Nikki Giovanni, Ed Bullins, Ben Caldwell, and Gaston Neal.

He is a culture promoter in other ways. Jihad's productions are an example. But the most important single literary manifestation is *Black Fire: An Anthology of Afro-American Writing* which he edited along with Larry Neal in 1968. The Morrow files reveal a Jones-Neal team insistent from the start upon an anthology of authentic young voices. In fact, they had first considered calling the work *Voices of the Black Nation.* The selections are from such militant-toned and nationalistic publications as *Soulbook, Umbra,* and *Black Dialogue.* Veteran writer Chester Himes characterized *Black Fire* as "unique in the literature of America; it is a young and challenging (I might say daring) book with fresh ideas by young black people, and very, very revealing. . . . After this book, no one can say they don't know what young black Afro-Americans are thinking."[118] Considered for the National Book Award in 1968, it is probably the most comprehensive and accurate representation available of the young black American writers of its immediate time. Most important for black culturists, *Black Fire* gives exposure to writers who would not have access to "standard" anthologies. If anything, the essays, poetry, fiction, and drama in *Black Fire* constitute in general a literary testament of black nationalistic ideology.

"My songs will be softer": The person

In view of his plethora of activities, one wonders when Jones finds the time to get things done. Yet he remains a prolific writer. He is constantly scribbling, writing something. Contributing factors to his productivity are his extraordinary energy, his direct manner, and his constant and intense application to the tasks at hand. He works some eighteen hours a day, each day of the week. During the earlier part of his current Newark residency when he lived in Spirit House, much of his creative work was done early in the morning in the small work room in his living quarters when everyone in the family had gone to sleep and Newark was quiet. Sometimes he will find relative quiet on Sundays in his High Street office. Then too, he writes when he can, for he gives evidence of being able to split his attention without appreciable detriment.

Jones is not a slowly deliberate, painstaking writer; on the contrary, he is a fast writer. He does practically no rewriting and polishing, preferring to work out the mechanics of a piece of literature as he is in the process of writing it. Once he has committed words to paper, for him the artistic process has been completed.

The physical Jones resembles the fictional narrator in "The Death of Horatio Alger," Foots in *The Toilet,* and similar boys and men in his writing. He is slightly built, a bit short, with casually slouching posture. His movements are quick and direct; his fingers move, his eyes dart deftly—with precision. The private Jones seems not to fit the public image at all. One will find him soft-spoken, polite, disarmingly casual (but not "open"), scholarly without being pedantic or overbearing. He says, ". . . the things that I really like to do, you know, are very quiet."[119] Yet his countenance suggests speed and resilient toughness. One black writer speaks of Jones' "gentle acid grin."[120] Jones insists that he is not a violent man, finding art as the most beautiful resolution of potentially violent energies. One woman writer recalls that "when we met, in a room strewn with debris [from a writing conference farewell party], it was the softness of his voice that was startling, his composure and the very slightest tinge of anxiety under the curiosity when he asked, 'You didn't think I was hateful [in *Dutchman* and *The Slave*], did you?'"[121] Perhaps Schneck is correct when he says our man "is obviously not what he seems. He is no martyr, unless we martyr him. Neither is he a black bogey-man, a Mau Mau monster or, as several of his former white friends have described him, a bad-talking clown. He is a poet, a playwright, a conscience, a consciousness."[122]

Still, one cannot overlook that, rightly or wrongly, he has been accused of violent acts against individuals. In 1966 a newspaper reported that Shepard Sherbell, publisher of the *East Side Review,* a little magazine, sought to have Jones arrested. According to Sherbell, he was held against the wall of a Village theatre lobby by two of Jones' companions while Jones punched him and tore a wallet from his pocket. Jones, said Sherbell, contended that Sherbell owed him $100 for printing *Experimental Death Unit #1* in his magazine. Sherbell contended that Jones had let him print the play in order to help the magazine. On another occasion, Jones was accused of resisting arrest and using abusive language, this time in Newark. Then too, there is the already discussed arrest during the riots. As one might expect, there have been reports of threats on Jones' life. The night of the assassination of Dr. Martin Luther King, Jr., Jones' sister told friends that New Jersey government officials and the Mafia intended to "kill" her brother.[123] Today young Simbas from the CUN accompany their spiritual leader from place to place. "Jones is well guarded, and rightly so," says a New Jersey newspaper writer. "There are persons with a pathological hatred of Jones and he knows it."[124]

What is Jones' concept of himself? Early in his writing career, Jones wrote in "Audubon, Drafted":

> I am what I think I am. You are what
> I think you are. The world is the
> one thing, that will not move.

and in "Balboa, The Entertainer":

> Let my poems be a graph
> of me. (And they keep
> to the line, where flesh
> drops off . . .

Where do the graphs point? In "Three Modes of History and Culture" the graph of Jones reads:

> I think about a time when I will be relaxed.
> When flames and non-specific passion wear themselves away
>   And my eyes and hands and mind can turn
> and soften, and my songs will be softer
> and lightly weight the air.

Born Everett LeRoi Jones in a system of hell, our writer committed gradual suicide, became a dead lecturer, and then gave birth to Amiri Baraka, phoenix fashion.

In the same issue of *Evergreen Review* as the poem that got him into trouble with Judge Kapp, there are two others. In one, "leroy," is his legacy:

When I die, the consciousness I carry I will to
black people. May they pick me apart and take the
useful parts, the sweet meat of my feelings. And leave
the bitter bullshit rotten white parts
alone.

Chapter 2. "That's all we are—the body of our thought": Perceptions, conceptions, stances

What, then, is this consciousness that LeRoi Jones wills to black people?

The way any man looks at experience is determined by his perspective, the feelings and experiences that have put him at his individual "window," to use an image favored by LeRoi Jones. Because of Jones' gifted sensitivity to the nuances of life and because of his unusual reliance on intuitive feelings, Jones' coign of vantage is unique. In other words, his "window" is that of an individualistic and sensitive artist. The frame of reference, i.e., "house," for his perspective, i.e., "window," is his life, outlined in the preceding chapter.

An examination of characteristic ideas, reactions, and mental attitudes—what we may call themes—that pervade the corpus of Jones' writing are important for an understanding or explication of individual works or groupings of works. Cutting across genres, these themes cluster about several interrelated general topics: theory of culture and art, the atrophy of Western civilization, theory of literature, the black aesthetic, race relations in America, social politics, black cultural revolution and nationalism.

"As essential as a grocery store": Theory of culture and art

"Culture is simply how one lives and is connected to history by habit," he writes in *Home* (p. 245). If one accepts this statement, one must acknowledge culture as a totality and what people consider art and religion as at once results and causal factors in any given culture. One must acknowledge, further, that how people in any given culture act is the culture, a manifestation of their art or religion. If one does not accept Jones' pronouncement, one may then consider art and religion as adjuncts to, or corollaries of, a given life style. When considering Jones' concept of culture as totality, one may profitably remember Yeats' Byzantium theme and imagery—Yeats longs for the time when and place where art and artisan were indeed inseparable from the functional, utilitarian acts of living. The life style of the people *was* the art, the religion. Said Yeats, "I think that in early Byzantium, maybe never before or since in recorded history, religious, aesthetic and practical life were one . . ."[1] In this connection, one is also reminded of Wittgenstein's idea that ethics and aesthetics are one.

LeRoi Jones, not unlike numerous contemporary theorists of all ethnic and racial identities, sees Western culture as stagnant, debilitated, arid (though others ascribe other causes and prescribe other cures). Because Jones believes so firmly that art should be a fact of day-to-day living, he sees Western art as nonart. "The word 'art,'" he says, "is something the West has never understood. Art is supposed to be a part of a community. Like, scholars are supposed to be a part of a community. . . . Art is to decorate people's houses, their skin, their clothes, to make them expand their minds, and it's supposed to be right in the community, where they can have it when they want it. . . . It's supposed to be as essential as a grocery store. . . . That's the only way art can function naturally."[2] His major point in this respect is that the Western world worships the artifact when it should value the artistic act. This is the central point of "Hunting Is Not Those Heads on the Wall."[3] Overemphasis on the artifact, Jones feels, wrongly negates expression in favor of reflection. "It was, and is," he asserts in *Blues People,* "inconceivable in the African culture to make a separation between music, dancing, song, the artifact, and a man's life or his worship of his gods. *Expression* issued from life, and *was* beauty. But in the West, the 'triumph of the economic mind over the imagination,' as Brooks Adams said, made possible this dreadful split between life and art" (p. 28). So in the absence of a living art, he says in *Home,* Western "white man is in love with the past . . . because it is in the past that he really exists. . . . The white man worships the artifact" (p. 232). And

> . . . their nothing
> grown to sounds
> the deaf take for music.
> ["Style"]

Because art, to whites is

> the spent lover
> smelling his fingers
> ["Theory of Art"]

the creative power has gone amiss, has been perverted and aborted. Western art is dying.

> From Sartre, a white man, it gave
> the last breath. And we beg him die,
> before he is killed
> ["BLACK DADA NIHILISMUS"]

In America:

THE LONE
RANGER

IS DEAD.
THE SHADOW
IS DEAD.
ALL YOUR HEROES ARE DYING. J. EDGAR HOOVER WILL
SOON BE DEAD. YOUR MOTHER WILL DIE. LYNDON JOHNSON,

these are natural
things. No one is
threatening anybody,
that's just the way life
is,
boss.

["THREE MOVEMENTS AND A CODA"]

After all, "what can you say of a society that sends Benny Goodman and Robert Frost to Russia as cultural avants,"[4] he asks.

Yet some life is left in America: "One of the most baffling things about America is that despite its essentially vile profile, so much beauty continues to exist here. Perhaps it's as so many thinkers have said, that it is because of the vileness, or call it adversity, that such beauty could exist. (As balance?)."[5]

What should be the literary man's attitude and role in a crumbling and artistically enervated society? Jones advises:

Make some muscle
in your head, but
use the muscle
in yr heart

["YOUNG SOUL"]

for, after all, "feeling predicts intelligence."[6] Also, he points out that the literary artist can isolate himself from America's artistic mainstream: "Think of the great Irish writers—Wilde, Yeats, Shaw, Synge, O'Casey, Beckett, etc.—and . . . how best they could function inside and outside the imaginary English society . . ."[7] Moreover, the writer should forget abstract art, art for art's sake, and, unfettered by literary conventions, he should concern himself with realistic and conscience-directed art:

High art, first of all, must reflect the experiences of the human being, the emotional predicament of the man, as he exists, in the defined world of his being. It must be produced from the legitimate emotional resources of the soul in the world. It can *never* be produced by evading these resources or pretending that they do not exist. It can never be produced by appropriating the withered emotional responses of some strictly social idea of humanity. High art, and by this I mean any art that would attempt to describe or characterize some portion of the profound meaningfulness of human life with any finality or truth, cannot be based on the superficialities of human existence. It must issue from *real* categories of human activity, *truthful* accounts of human life, and not fancied accounts of the attainment of cultural privilege by some willingly preposterous apologists for one social "order" or another.[8]

The literary artist, Jones warns, should not play

The noxious game of reason, saying, "No, No,
you cannot feel," like my dead lecturer
        ["Political Poem"]

Neither should the artist, as does the narrator in "Heroes Are Gang Leaders," hold a book in front of his eyes "to shield what was going on from slopping over into [his] life";[9] rather, he should engage in a literature of ideas, a literature for social change.

It is not unexpected, therefore, that when Jones considers the black writer he sees him in a peculiarly advantageous position, "completely outside the conscious myopia."[10] In fact, "this is the only way for the Negro artist to provide his version of America—from that no man's-land outside the mainstream."[11] Further, "The Negro writer can only survive by refusing to become a white man . . ."[12]

LeRoi Jones is particularly severe on Afro-American writers who do not write from an orientation of black culture. This attitude is apparent in three key statements: "Philistinism and the Negro Writer," "The Myth of a 'Negro Literature,'" and "The Black Aesthetic," all discussed later in this book. Jones is given to statements about an instinctive, innate divinity available to black writers who will recognize and make use of it. Such statements remind one of the idea prevalent centuries ago, the idea of poets as divine prophets and seers, as priestly artists.

The poem which perhaps most vividly and succinctly presents his conception of the role of black literature is his often quoted "Black Art," which reads in part:

Poems are bullshit unless they are
teeth or trees or lemons piled
on a step . . .
. . . We want poems
like fists beating niggers out of Jocks
or dagger poems in the slimy bellies
of the owner-jews. Black poems to
smear on girdlemamma mulatto bitches
whose brains are red jelly stuck
between 'lizabeth taylor's toes. Stinking
Whores! We want "poems that kill."
Assassin poems, Poems that shoot
guns. Poems that wrestle cops into alleys
and take their weapons leaving them dead
with tongues pulled out and sent to Ireland.
Knockoff poems for dope selling wops or slick
halfwhite politicians . . .
Put it on him, poem. Strip him naked
to the world! Another bad poem cracking
steel knuckles in a jewlady's mouth
Poem scream poison gas on beasts in green berets
Clean out the world for virtue and love,
Let there be no love poems written
until love can exist freely and
cleanly. Let Black People understand that
they are the lovers and the sons of lovers
and warriors and sons of warriors Are poems
& poets & all the loveliness here in the world
. . .

"The new sheriff": Ethnocentrism and race relations

Poems and other literature in the style and with the content of "Black Art" have earned for LeRoi Jones the reputation as racist, revolutionist, terrorist, and the like. In "The New Sheriff" Jones poetically says that

There is something
in me so cruel, so
silent . . .

Perhaps it is the "something" in "For Tom Postell, Dead Black Poet":

> . . . I got something foryou, like you dig,
> I got. I got this thing, goes pulsating through black everything
> universal meaning. I got the extermination blues, jewboys. I got
> the hitler syndrome figured . . .
> So come for the rent, jewboys, or come ask me for a book or
> sit in the courts handing down yr judgments, still I got something
> for you, gonna give it to my brothers, so they'll know what your *whole*
> story is, then one day, jewboys, we all, even my wig wearing mother
> gonna put it on you all at once,

What is Jones' rationale for this apparent hate? "Afro-Americans (Negroes, spades, shades, boots, woogies, *etc.*) in this country can afford, I believe, the luxury of hate. They certainly have enough to hate . . ."[13] And he has said of himself and his work, "People have said about me that I'm hateful and bitter. Sure I'm bitter about a lot of things. I'm trying to work with complications of feelings, love and hate at the same time . . . . What I'm after is a sense of clarity; if it sounds like anger, maybe that's good in a sense."[14]

No matter what is one's definition for hate, one cannot by any stretch of the imagination consider Jones a lover of white Americans. Whites, he feels, have created a convenient concept of the black man, a concept that numbs white consciences and that serves white illusions:

> . . . A point, the
> dimensionless line. The top
> of a head, seen from Christ's
> heaven, stripped of history
> or desire.
>   ["A Poem for Willie Best"]

But:

> . . . We are all beautiful (except white
> people, they are full of, and made of
> shit) . . .
>   ["A School of Prayer"]

Peculiarly, his more pointed contempt for whites is directed toward white political and social liberals rather than toward white political and social conservatives. We have already noted his cooperation with Anthony Imperiale of

Newark. He also has paid grudging respect to Lester Maddox, former governor of Georgia, a man outspokenly and rigidly a racial separatist and who in the opinion of many blacks is a blatant and despicable racist. In both instances Jones has called attention to these conservatives' forthrightness and candor in making known their positions in regard to America's race problems. But the so-called liberals, those who by word or by deed profess a sympathetic sensibility to the situation of the Afro-American, and who by word or deed attempt to change this situation—the Martin Dubermans, the Hubert Humphreys, and the Jules Feiffers of American society—are the objects of heated and derisive abuse from Jones.

LeRoi Jones wants the American way of life radically changed, if not completely destroyed. But, he argues, "even the most liberal white man in America does not want to see the existing system really *changed.* What the liberal white man wants is for the black man somehow to be 'elevated' Martin Luther King style so that he might be able to enter this society with some kind of general prosperity and join the white man in a truly democratic defense of this cancer, which would make the black man equally culpable for the evil done to the rest of the world. The liberal white man wants the black man to learn to love this America as much as he does, so that the black man will want to murder the world's peoples, his own brothers and sisters Moise Tshombe style."[15] Jones claims that even those whites who during the late 1950's and early 1960's went into the South to work in civil rights activities such as voter registration drives were more interested in saving America than in doing anything for Negroes. He doubts that the ends sought by white liberals are really different: "Complete socio-economic subjugation is the goal of both white forces (liberals and non-liberals). What the liberal sees as evil about this program is the way it is being carried out. Liberals want to be leaders rather than rulers."[16] Further, Jones feels that even the so-called empathetic whites really do not understand the black experience. In *Dutchman,* Clay says to Lula, who is roughly representative of socially aware whites:

. . . You don't know anything except what's there for you to see. An act. Lies. Device. Not the pure heart, the pumping black heart. You don't ever know that. And I sit here, in this buttoned-up suit, to keep myself from cutting all your throats. I mean wantonly. You great liberated whore! You fuck some black man, and right away you're an expert on black people. What a lotta shit that is. The only thing you know is that you come if he bangs you hard enough. And that's all.

Others who come in for what seems to be an inordinate and disproportionate amount of negative criticism from Jones are Jews:

Now I know what the desert thing was. Why they fled from us
into their caves. Why they hate me now . . .
having seen them as things, and the resistance to light, and the
heart of goodness sucked off, vampires, flying in our midst, at the
corner, selling us our few horrible minutes of discomfort and frus
tration. Smile, jew. Dance, jew. Tell me you love me, jew.
[''For Tom Postell, Dead Black Poet'']

Jones is as severe with the Negro middle class as he is with any other group, perhaps more severe. In *Blues People* he writes: ''The black middle class, from its inception (possibly ten seconds after the first Africans were herded off the boat) has formed almost exclusively around the proposition that it is better not to be black in a country where being black is a liability. All the main roads into America have always been fashioned by the members of the black middle class (not as products of a separate culture, but as vague, featureless Americans). . . . The black middle class wanted no sub-culture, nothing that could connect them with the poor black man or the slave'' (pp. 123–24, 132).

He now makes a distinction between Negroes and blacks: Negroes (''Knee-Grows'') are those who prefer to be ''Uncle Toms'' or ''imitation white boys,'' as he conceives of them, rather than men. In his earlier works Jones used the term Negro to mean any person of African descent. In the early 1960's he was still calling himself a Negro. By 1961 he had begun using the term Afro-American, ''an historically and ethnically correct term.''[17] Later he was to prefer Black (with a capital ''B'') or Afro-American and he was to use Negro as a derogatory term. Many civil rights leaders and race spokesmen fall within Jones' conno-tation for Negro. He scathingly ridicules them in poems like the ones about NAACP executive Roy Wilkins, ''CIVIL RIGHTS POEM'' and ''Message From The NAACP.'' The same treatment is accorded other prominent Afro-Americans such as actors who would rather play Hamlet than engage in black guerilla theatre, opportunists who assume a posture of blackness when it is personally profitable to do so, writers who aspire to create ''universal'' literature, elected politicians who allow themselves to be manipulated by whites.

Although he may not approve of their actions, Jones will not dismiss such persons as being useless or beyond redemption. A theme in his *J-E-L-L-O, Dutchman,* ''A Poem for Willie Best,'' and other works is the latent blackness in any American of African descent. As Walker, the once integrationist now turned black man, says in *The Slave*, ". . . sometimes the place and twist of what we are will push and sting, and what the crust of our stance has become will ring in our ears and shatter that piece of our eyes that is never closed." And this blackness is a potential power which must be mobilized, by force if necessary:

> Dynamite black girl
> swingin in the halls
> the world cant beat you
> and my slaps are love
>   ["20th-Century Fox"]

by cries for help:

>   SOS
> Calling black people
> Calling all black people, man woman child
> Wherever you are, calling you, urgent, come in
> Black People, come in, wherever you are, urgent, calling
> you, calling all black people
> calling all black people, come in, black people, come
> on in.

or by gentle persuasion:

> I want you to understand the world
> as I have come to understand it
> I'll wait here a few seconds, please come
>   ["Goodbye!"]

When Jones cajoles or threatens Negroes, he is asking them to abandon certain of the ideas, values, plans and aims that they have traditionally nurtured. "The Negro's real problem," he claims, "remains in finding some actual goal to work toward. A complete equality of means is impossible in the present state of American society. And even if it were possible, the society is horrible enough without Negroes swelling its ranks. The only genuine way, it seems to me, for the Negro to achieve a personal autonomy, this equality of means, would be as a truly active moralizing force within or *against* American society as it now stands."[18] In order to know himself, the Negro must separate himself culturally from the white man, Jones feels. Contact with whites tends to bury deeper and to enervate the Negro's latent blackness:

Now they ask me to be a jew or italian, and turn from the moment
of disappearing into the shaking clock of reasonable safety, like reruns
of films, with sacred coon stars. To retreat, and replay; throw my mind out,
sit down and brood about the anachronistic God, they will tell you
is real. Sit down and forget it. Lean on your silence, breathing
the dark. Forget your whole life, pop your fingers in a closed room,
hopped-up witch doctor for the cowards of a recent generation . . .

["THE PEOPLE BURNING"]

Entrance into the mainstream of American life, he insists, destroys the Negro
as a possible agent of dissent. Negroes are fooled, he warns, by tokenism, which
he defines as "the setting up of social stalemates or the extension of meager
privilege to some few 'selected' Negroes in order that a semblance of compromise or 'progress,' or a lessening in racial repression might seem to be achieved,
while actually helping to maintain the status quo just as rigidly . . ."[19]

In view of his thoughts about goals for black people, it is small wonder that
he is not an advocate of nonviolence and passive resistance as preached and
practiced by men like Martin Luther King and Gandhi. He sees such as only
tactics and ploys to maintain the social and political status quo:

In the white West nonviolence means simply doing nothing to change this
pitiful society, just do as you have been doing, e.g., suffer, and by some beautiful future-type miracle the minds of the masses of white men will be changed,
and they will finally come around to understanding that the majority of peoples
in the world deserve to live in that world, no longer plagued by the white man's
disgusting habits. But why, WHY, must anyone wait until these cretins . . .
change...ha ha...their famous minds. . . . Why indeed?[20]

As to bourgeoise Negroes:

Nonviolence can be your "goal" if you are already sitting in a comfortable
house being brought the news of your oppression over television. It can be
the normal conduct of rational men if they believe in the literalness and effec-
tiveness of what they are trying to accomplish by such conduct. But walk, on
any night, from one end of 125th Street (in New York's Harlem) to the other,
and count the hundred policemen and figure out the climate of rational conduct
that is being cultivated by such an environment.[21]

In "Unfinished," he chastises, "You could be in south carolina murdering the
governor, by strangling him with a wide belt, and your knee cocked in the small
of his back."[22]

If LeRoi Jones does not believe in nonviolence and passive resistance as modes for social change, does he therefore believe in literal violence and active resistance? This is hard to determine. He sees little efficiency in approaching white America through speeches, committees, moral suasion, staged demonstrations, and the like. In *print* he is, at least symbolically, uncompromisingly for active physical resistance and violent reaction. Yet he has explained, as we have noted, that art should be used as a substitute for literal violence, that art should be a weapon, that poems should be like "fists," "wrestlers," "daggers," and "guns." In this sense art is a substitute for literal violence. But in another sense such art might be an incentive to literal physical violence. The answer to the question of his advocacy or nonadvocacy of literal violence is further complicated by his seemingly contradictory overt actions: According to *Time,* "On paper few black separatists have sounded more intractable in the past than Playwright LeRoi Jones. . . . Yet when the fires started up this month in Newark, Jones got together with Mayor Hugh Addonizio and city leaders of both races to search for peaceful political solutions."[23] One is impressed too by the fact that this man who claims to be personally nonviolent works in a paramilitary environment at his Newark headquarters and has training in martial arts as an important activity at Spirit House. One is also impressed by the fact that the poet who exhorts his brothers to "smash at jellywhite faces" is also the civic leader who in 1968 proposed that blacks take over Newark in 1970 through politics. Perhaps the question of violence or nonviolence is in Jones' eyes a matter of tactical expediency or rhetoric rather than a matter of philosophy.

Or perhaps it is a matter of aggression as defense. He sees a clear danger of race genocide in America, with blacks as the victims. He expresses this idea repeatedly, in all genres. In nonfiction prose he says that "the only reason the black man is alive in the West today, [is for] continued exploitative use. But one day, and very soon, the white man might just look up, hip again, and see that the black man has outlived his usefulness. Then the murders will break out in earnest."[24] He feels that America, a violent nation, employs exterminators who are " 'licensed to kill.' The American policeman is the foulest social category in the world today, whether domestic, *e.g.,* 'New York's Finest,' or international (Humanitarians dropping out of the clouds, etc.)."[25] He claims that

. . . They have made
this star unsafe, and this age, primitive, though yr mind
is somewhere else, your ass aint.
            ["Jitterbugs"]

and he ends a description of policemen he knew as childhood playmates and associates with the wry

> . . . You wanna stand in front of a bar, with a gun
> pointed at you? You wanna try to remember why you like somebody
> while the bullet comes. Shit.
>   ["cops"]

From this frame of reference, Jones reasons that Negroes should not want "progress" but, instead, freedom — "to be completely free . . . from the domination of the white man. Nothing else."[26] The black man must achieve self-determination, must be free to act in his own best interests if he is to survive.

This insistence that blacks rule themselves is based in part on notions of blacks as racially superior to whites. Some of these notions reach mythic proportions. In the discussion later we shall see that the original virtue of black people became an increasingly favorite theme. In an interview Jones was asked, "Do you believe there's a genetic or generic superiority of the black race over the white?" His answer: "Well, yes. The black man was here on this planet first, and he will be here long after the white man is gone."[27] Blacks, as a "first people, the primitives, not evolving," must "recivilize the world."[28] And blacks can do this, for "our breathing is harnessed to divinity"[29] and "What we do not know, does not exist."[30] In this myth-history, if blacks are racially superior and are possessors of original virtue, then whites are racially inferior and are plagued by original sin:

> . . . In those barren caves, on those inhuman cold scenes the white
> man's hairy ancestors made their first baby gestures to fuck up
> the world. The cold could not sustain human life, witness the
> dogjawed cracker of the west. Who is so cold would wipe his behind
> on the souls of men.
>   ["I said it"]

In a real world politically controlled by "inferior" white men, what practical possibilities does Jones see for "recivilizing" the "Free World"?[31] "Communalism," he says, "cooperative economics is the natural way for men to live, and it will reassert itself."[32] "Capitalism," he asserts, "is just a word — a euphemism for evil. It doesn't exist as any kind of viable economic philosophy. It's just a name given to a form of evil."[33] But he does not see token political power as a means of effecting change in this economic and political structure. What about other political systems as modes? He will have nothing to do with Marxism, for this would be a commitment to European values. He is distressed by blacks who become involved with communistic or Marxist activities, with "all the sinister jive still going down, niggers in french hats, jerked around by some deadwords, many of our fathers know as bullshit, and the corpses of Marx Lenin get raised out of the tomb again."[34] Neither will he have anything to with socialism, seeing it as "just an explanation given by Europeans of how evil [capitalism] should be permuted into good, but that's not gonna happen."[35]

In short, Jones has despaired of reforming or adapting any economic and political structure in existence in the "free world." Regarding in particular the American system, he writes, "What I am saying is that there is *no chance* that the American white man will change. Why should he?"[36] So "There is perhaps a question mark . . . in the minds of many young Negro intellectuals. What is it that they are being asked to save?"[37] Anyhow, "It's much too late. We [Americans] are an *old* people already. Even the vitality of our art is like bright flowers growing up through a rotten carcas,"[38] he wrote in "Cuba Libre" in 1960.

Should the Negro resign himself to hope? Jones says "Hope is a delicate suffering,"[39] and "one *can hope*, but that will not make anything happen."[40]

"The force of evolution": Nationalism

The only alternative, therefore, would be the destruction of the present socio-political structure. In 1963 he wrote, "The only genuine way, it seems to me, for the Negro to achieve a personal autonomy, this equality of means, would be as a truly active moralizing force within or *against* American society as it now stands. In this sense I advocate a violence, a literal murdering of the American socio-political stance, not only as it directly concerns American Negroes, but in terms of its stranglehold on most of the modern world."[41] Of course, his earlier call for the destruction of the American socio-political system must be considered along with his later learning from Malcolm X about "deals," his later political activities in Newark, and his later national political activities.

Whatever the future proves his stance to be, he has been consistent in preaching revolution. Revolution connotes upheaval, violence, drastic, traumatic change. But

> This is the nature of change
> that it must seem jagged and
> convulsed, but remain the smooth speed
> of universal wisdom.
> ["Labor and Management"]

In truth, Jones has not consistently and systematically defined this revolution. At times it seems political, at times social, at times cultural. At times it seems to mean a physical revolution, but more often it seems to mean an ideological revolution. Apparently he appreciates the superior physical power of white America when he advises, "The real work is building, building, building and training and educating and passing on. The white man ain't gonna fall off because a lot of niggers get mad at him . . . . He can take it."[42] "Revolution is Enlightenment,"[43] he declares, and "you must have the cultural revolution, i.e., you must get the mind before you move another futha. There is no violent revolution except as a result of the black mind expanding, trying to take control of its own space."[44]

More than once LeRoi Jones uses the term revolution where others would probably use the term evolution. This being so, it is well to note here that his concept of time is not characterized as past, present, and future. In *A Black Value System* he asserts, "There is no time. Only change" (p. 14). In his introduction to *Black Magic* he says that "we begin to look into the future, which is happening at the same instant, but further away." This concept is also demonstrated in syntactical and grammatical contexts. For example, in *Black Music* he speaks of jazz musician Albert Ayler as a "vessel from which energy is issued, issued" (p. 174).

If there is to be a revolution by blacks, conviction alone will not suffice; there must be unity, among other things:

> But too often, certainly most times in the past, the white man has been able to win out, maintain his stranglehold on us, merely because most of us were so busy looking out for ourselves, which is the "ME ONLY" syndrome, that we were willing to let the worst things in the world happen to our brothers. With black people all over the world dying the most horrible kinds of death imaginable some fools would still be walking around with their behinds in the air saying, "But I'm Cool." Well the word is No You're Not, not as long as one of your brothers and sisters is being messed over by "the man."[45]

Time and again, Jones has called for Afro-Americans to cease dissipating their energies fighting alone or fighting among themselves. However, it appears that in the past he was not different from many other Negro leaders who called for unity when what they were really calling for was devotees to their own particular ideologies and programs. Jones calls for love among Americans of African descent, yet he has excoriated and ridiculed Negro civil rights leaders, the Negro middle class, Negro writers in general, and other subgroups. ("We ain't with youall," he tells the bourgeois Negroes.) He would have all Afro-Americans adopt his value system, become a conscious part of the black nation that he envisions.

It is at times confusing to follow Jones' various statements about black nationalism even when one keeps in mind his concept of time. He talks about a nation that exists: In *Home,* published in 1965, he was saying, "Black people are a race, a culture, a Nation" (p. 248), and "We do not want a Nation, we are a Nation" (p. 239). He talks about a nation yet to come: he writes in "The Black Aesthetic" (1969) that "The purpose of our writing is to create the nation" (p. 5), and he states in *A Black Value System* that "initially our purpose is *Nation* building" (p. 9). Further confusion arises about the kind of nationalism he has in mind. At times, as in *A Black Value System,* he seems to be talking about a cultural nation. At still other times he seems to equate black nationalism with *"independence,* not separation—or assimilation, for that matter,"[46] which implies a sort of self-contradiction. And he talks about political nations: "There might not be America, anyway. It might be a hundred little colonies . . . This can become a little black nation here, a little white nation there . . . It can be like that tomorrow. It *will* be like that."[47] He was to write in "Meanings of Nationalism" in 1969, "If the One World concept as you all have been taught is to work, it must be set up and animated by Black men because we are faster now, and stronger and have the legitimate real life need to build beautiful healthy things. We are not saying wipe out the white people. They will do that to themselves if it is to be done. We are saying we must have a new world. This one is bullshit. And we must do it ourselves."[48]

What seems so contradictory in what Jones sees ahead for white people may be resolved if one considers his pronouncements on the subject to be symbolic or metaphorical. His *The Slave,* for instance, may with justification be interpreted as a projection of the destruction of a way of life, with the Easleys representing the most enlightened state of white conscience. In this sense, not white people but a white life style is being destroyed. The following lines, likewise, can easily be read to mean that white culture will die: ". . . the majority of them are going to die. The ones who are left will be the ones who are submitting to the new doctrine. . . . [They are going to die by] the force of evolution . . . I see it happening in fragments. In some places, violently; in some places through the gradual erosion of white values. . . . Instead of controlling—they will be controlled."[49]

But symbolic readings are more difficult when one considers the *tone* of the poem "Who Will Survive America? / Few Americans / Very Few Negroes / No Crackers at All."[50] which reads in part:

Will you survive America,
with your 20cent habbit,
yo fo' bag jones, will you
survive in the heat and fire
of actual change? I doubt it.
Will you survive woman? Or will your nylon wig
catchafire at midnight, and light up Stirling Street
and you [sic] assprints on the pavement. Grease meltin in this
brother's eyes, his profile shotup by a Simba thinking
who was coming around the corner was really Tony Curtis, and not a
misguided brother, got his mind hanging out with italians . . .

Old people.   No.
Christians.   No.
First Negroes To Be Invisible To Truth.   1944.   Minnesota.
No.
Nothing of that
will be any where.
It will be burned clean.
It might sink and steam up the sea.   America might.   And no Americans
very few Negroes, will get out. No crackers at
all.

If one considers the tone and takes these words as literal, one is inclined also to regard as literal:

(may a lost god dambullah, rest or save us
against the murders we intend
against his lost white children
black dada nihilismus
                ["BLACK DADA NIHILISMUS"]

Chapter 3. "The structure of content": Form, technique, style

Problems of derivation and sources are at best usually inconclusive. Yet there are certain writers and certain milieus that inevitably influence any given writer, for no writer develops in a literary vacuum. LeRoi Jones' literary influences — or perhaps more precisely stated, the people he read and was impressed by — throughout his childhood and young adulthood include the modern writers admired by literary-minded young people of his time and place and include certain other writers he had studied in school or met in his reading. His writing, especially the earlier works, discloses through direct statement, allusion, content, and technique his literary debts and impressions.

Granville Hicks found in *Home* that Jones "refers to Eliot, Pound, Cummings, Apollinaire, Joyce, Keats, Hardy, Kafka, Dylan Thomas, and Baudelaire." He continued, "Somehow, then, in the midst of all this squalor and desperation, the young man managed to get a literary education . . . . that process must have been as important a part of his experience as anything he describes . . . the scheme is a claim to kinship with the makers of Western culture."[1] Still another writer noted, "Indirectly acknowledging the influence of Joyce, Eliot, Pound, and Yeats, among others, he explores their idioms almost at random."[2] The list of other writers Jones mentions or indirectly alludes to, especially in his earlier writing, includes Ford Madox Ford, Masters, Hulme, Herskovits, Melville especially, Dante of course, and Negro writers Chesnutt, Himes, McKay, and two Negroes particularly for their ideas, DuBois and E. Franklin Frazier. One critic discerned that in *Home,* "Joyce, Sartre, Burroughs and Allen Ginsberg come out higher on the scoreboard than Phillis Wheatley, Arna Bontemps, Langston Hughes and James Baldwin."[3]

In various times and places Jones has named specific influences on his development as a writer. They include T. S. Eliot (especially on Jones' earlier, "academic" poetry), Ezra Pound (especially for imagery), William Carlos Williams (especially for a sense of speech in poetry), and Federico Garcia Lorca (for, among other things, helping him break from the Eliot influence). *Current Biography* stated that in the Village, Jones "became a leading, albeit maverick, light on the fringes of the Beat Generation, the insurgent literary movement of that day centered in Greenwich Village. Like Beat poet Allen Ginsberg, Jones recognized a literary debt to William Carlos Williams. Among the major influences in his literary development were Nathanael West ('for blending bitter humor with horror') and Eugene O'Neill. From O'Neill, Jones tried to learn how to be, as a playwright, 'eloquent about America.'"[4] Mark Twain, too, had an impact on Jones: "Jesus, nobody calls Twain's 'Puddn'head Wilson' a novel of racial protest but the comment it makes on what they call race relations is pretty strong. It's a wild book. I've never seen anything so strong. Nobody would say that's social protest, but it's more so than 'The Toilet.'"[5]

It is safe to say that all the writers who gravitated to the Village during the late fifties and early sixties affected each other's work, directly and indirectly, and in varying degrees. Jones was no exception, and there were several who at this time seemed to influence his writing more than others. As does Jones himself, Hettie Jones names Charles Olson as a major influence on young Jones. As Jones poetically states in "To a Publisher...cut-out":

> . . . I ride the 14th St. bus
> every day...reading Hui neng Raymond Chandler/Olson

Others of his early contemporaries named by Jones as having influenced him at that time are Gary Snyder, Frank O'Hara, Robert Creeley, and Allen Ginsberg.

Yet it must be said that regardless of sources and influences, Jones always has been stylistically a distinct writer. It is an understatement to say that the writing of LeRoi Jones is manneristic. There is in it a remarkable absence of mundane, pedestrian expression. Hackneyed language or a cliché is rare in his works, and when it does exist chances are that it originated with Jones and became trite because of his own repetition of it. Indeed, it seems as if he almost perversely determines to create new forms, new ways of structuring content, new phrases for new thoughts. One must agree with the critic who wrote, "Jones triumphs because he is consistently able to inspire language with new life and rhythm."[6] But the very inventiveness of his writing, the "new life and rhythm," makes for difficult reading. Some of his more individualistic and strangely presented works do seem to be either chaos or mere dross. Sometimes one may wonder if Jones is playing games with his readers — or with himself. If one is used to familiar symbols, standard syntax, intelligible metaphors, transparent images, conventional prosody and paragraphing, prosaic diction, then one at first reading usually finds Jones' writing, particularly his fiction and poetry, mystifying.

Three useful keys to his more cryptic writing are his life, his thoughts, and his attitude about and characteristic approaches to style, form, and technique. This is not to say that all of Jones' works can be explicated. But certainly an attempt to discern and understand patterns or schemes of expression is helpful.

First, one must consider his theory of art as it applies to matters of form, technique and style, for Jones simply must be read on his own artistic terms: "Form is simply *how* a thing exists," he says. "Content is why a thing exists."[7] To him, the two are inseparable. What he has said about musical performance is analogous to literary performance: "To my mind, technique is inseparable from what is finally played as content. A *bad* solo, no matter how 'well' it is played is *bad*. . . . No one who can finally be said to be a 'mediocre' musician can be said to possess any technique."[8]

One must keep in mind, too, Jones' tenet that the essence of art is process rather than artifact. One should examine Jones' writing with the attitude that his style is a record of a creative process, possibly a spontaneous creative process. To look only for rational, conscious, and ordered style in Jones' work is to subvert explication and to beg for a misreading or a nonreading. In connection with one's awareness of the spontaneous element in Jones' writing one must also keep in mind his insistence upon initial reliance upon what is felt rather than upon what is thought. In *A Black Mass,* the character Nasafi points out to his fellow divine, Jacoub, that Jacoub's error was "the substitution of thought for feeling." And one must always keep in mind that Jones posits that "feeling predicts intelligence."

"Self-imposed meanings": Language

LeRoi Jones has written that "words themselves become, even informally, laws."[9] The language that Jones employs to make his own laws, or definitions, comes by choice from his personal, sometimes private, and ethnic frames of reference. Shortly after his first published works, he consciously began to avoid "white" language in favor of "black" idioms, grammar, and syntax. Good examples are in *In Our Terribleness,* in which he employs language frequently used by inner-city blacks. This language is characterized by verb-ellipses, reverse meanings, and nonstandard superlatives: "We Still baddest thing on the planet"; by staccato rhythms, dropped syllables and words, street slang, and ethnic conjunctives:

. . . You member
when he beat Chuvalo's ass. Kept stickin his hand in the sucker's
face. Yeh. Man thass a terrible dude. For real.

He was also to increase his use of African and Islamic terms.

When one seeks to explicate Jones' language, one should, then, seek to understand his frame of reference. For example, the derogatory term "faggot" must be understood in Jones' ethnic context. If he uses it to describe an American of African descent, he is usually talking about a male who reacts to challenges (often ethnic-oriented challenges) to his manhood by pretending to ignore, by compromising, by capitulating. In this sense NAACP official Roy Wilkins in Jones' eyes is an "Uncle Tom," a compromiser of his innate blackness, and is therefore a "faggot." On the other hand, if Jones uses "faggot" to describe a white American male, he is talking, literally or symbolically, about a physical homosexual, a degenerated man who has perverted his natural physical urges. The white "faggot" is lower than the black "faggot" on Jones' acceptability scale.

Jones is frequently criticized as being obscene, offensive to good taste and morality. Negro playwright Owen Dodson reasoned, "His use of four letter words . . . seem [sic] to be put in to make life as real as he thinks it is. Playwrights with winning and timeless power have been able to create the same atmosphere that Jones wishes to create with their special language that conjures up our imagination because we have not heard these things before."[10] One magazine, reacting to Jones' statement in *Home* that "This thing, if you read it, will jam your face in my shit. Now say something intelligent!" (p. 15), said, "It will indeed. On almost every page, author Jones, who is now 31 years old, makes reference to evacuations—generally to some form of erotic evacuation. The filth is rationalized as social protest and enshrined in religious allegory . . ."[11] Assuredly, it is easy to assume that Jones is often seeking shock value or is trying to insult his reader for effect.

What are some counter arguments? One is that Jones is presenting reality, that he is being honest. Mr. and Mrs. Coyt Jones point out that nobody in their family cursed, including little LeRoi, although he was an imaginative name caller. "At first," says Mrs. Jones, "I couldn't take it at all." Mr. Jones admits, "I was horrified, too, when I first heard it. . . . When I saw *The Toilet,* I realized that the only words he could have used to make it realistic are the words he did use."[12] The senior Joneses, in other words, look upon their son's use of "profanity" in much the same way many other people do, that is, clinically, considering such language as linguistically valid and therefore acceptable if the writer is to depict life as it is. Another counter argument is that he uses such language for artistic effect, what one writer calls "artistic obscenity."[13] Still another argument is that obscenity is relative, that certain words and images may be obscene in certain segments of society but may not be in others. Jones has said, "Piss is not a dirty word to me. . . . It depends on your linguistic position, your point of reference. Whether or not you are being honest."[14] In the case of our author so much depends upon what he intends.

A passage which perhaps best presents Jones' views of this subject is in "Philistinism and the Negro Writer":

> If . . . you live in a big house and you keep me locked in a room, and you never go in that room, you don't know anything about that room. If I come out of that room to clean many other things in the rest of the house, then I know about the whole house, and if I want to talk, I can talk about the whole house. And if you say, suddenly, that what I am talking about is degrading, is filthy, is obscene, is pornographic, then you must realize that the place that I was forced to live in is that dirty, terrible place I am now describing.
>
> So that a man who tries to tell me that I cannot have a character in a play say "motherfucker" to describe something that my character sees is trying to deny the validity of a certain kind of experience and to deny the expression of that word as honest. He is quite clearly trying to deny a whole world of feeling because he does not know what the word means or how it is used.[15]

Jones' language has what he would call "verb force." To him the verb, or the participle, is equated to the process; the noun is equated to the artifact. He describes the "orchestral language" of musician Cecil Taylor as "a language that still conceives of verb force, i.e., the solo exclamation made fierce by improvisations."[16] In *Blues People* the chapter title "Swing — From Verb to Noun" reflects his sadness about a phase in the evolution of jazz. In *Tales* he speaks of "floating, empty nouns" (p. 11). And in "The dead lady canonized" he projects in poetry the passing of true art in the West:

> (A trail
> of objects. Dead nouns, rotted faces
> propose the night's image.

"Because we have different feelings": Mechanics of style

LeRoi Jones is so stylistically inventive and versatile that it is perhaps foolhardy to attempt to describe categorically and definitely the mechanics of his style. It is wiser to point out certain stylistic predilections or habits (and, later, in the treatment of genres and works, to make individual descriptions).

Especially in nonfiction prose, Jones is discursive, expansive, given to restatement. He tends to write complex and compound-complex sentences, with

frequent appositional, parenthetical, and other subordinate grammatical elements. This is particularly noticeable in his earlier writing. For example, in
"Philistinism and the Negro Writer" there is the passage:

> I once wrote an essay called "The Myth of Negro Literature," which was
> published in a rather weird form in the *Saturday Review,* and the point I tried to
> make there was that, until quite recently, most of what could be called the
> Negro's formal attempt at "high art" was found in his music, and one of the
> reasons I gave was that it was only in music that the Negro did not have to re-
> spect the tradition outside of his own feelings—that is, he could play what he
> felt and not try to make it seem like something alien to his feelings, something
> outside of his experience. In most cases the Negro writers who usually wanted
> to pursue what "they" classify as "high art" were necessarily middle-class
> Negroes, and the art that these middle-class Negroes made tended to be an art
> that was, at best, an imitation of what can only be described as white middle-
> class literature, the popular fiction that was usually about tired white lives. The
> Negro writer who duplicated these tired white lives was only painting them
> black. Therefore he was saying essentially nothing about the Negro except that
> he had been desperately oppressed—so oppressed that he could not even
> remember his own separate experience. [p. 54]

At other times this expansive style is characterized by staccato effects, sentence
fragments, sudden grammatical shifts, exclamatory interpolations, and asides.
For example, in *Black Music* (p. 188) he writes:

> But the significant difference is, again, direction, intent, sense of identifica-
> tion..."kind" of consciousness. And that's what its [sic] about; conscious-
> ness. What are you *with* (the word Con-With/Scio-Know). The "new" musi-
> cians are self-conscious. Just as the boppers were. Extremely conscious of self.
> They are more conscious of total self (or *want* to be) than the R&B people, who,
> for the most part, are all-expression. Emotional expression. Many times self-
> consciousness turns out to be just what it is as a common figure of speech. It
> produces world-weariness, cynicism, corniness. Even in the Name of Art. Or
> what have you...social uplift, "Now we can play good as white folks," or "I
> went to Julliard, and this piece exhibits a Bach-like contrapuntal line," and so
> forth right on out to lunch.

As surely as he can be expansively lucid, Jones can be curtly cryptic. When
he apparently wants to be, he is direct and explicit; when he apparently wants to
be, he is indirect in the sense that his "meaning" is tied up in associational com-

plexes of sound, image, and diction. His more bafflingly dadaistic and surrealistic style is especially apparent in his prose fiction. An illustration is this passage from *System* (p. 104):

> (if we die for the
> two big men. Satyr play shd move next! Change the
> scenery. Get the faggot off, and try to sober him up.
> Chrissakes. Clank (Airthefugginplaceout)
>   ...WAS TP (Hollywood Ted & Co.)
> Everyone alive is a contemporary. As the man who beat
> Louis, or the Georgia heat where Roosevelt's head split.
> We know them together as part of our time.
>   And TP fit
> there. A Friend of The Family, really (as you people are
> now. Knowing so much.) But I envied them, tony, sonny-
> boy, the rest. And it's so easy to cross them now. They've
> failed. Suppliants. Their dancing save them those early
> times. Their coats. But it changed. The sun moved...
> our Gods, I said, had died. We weren't ready for anarchy
> ...but it walked into us like morning.
>   So, look, for the first
> time at Anonymous Negroes and Harry S. Truman.
> (How's that grab you?) yall?) Anarchy, for a time.

Sometimes as in "A Chase (Alighieri's Dream)" the entire piece evokes an impressionistic aura or mood that defies paraphrase into "meaning."

As to punctuation, that in his earlier nonfiction prose is generally standard, or conventional, but in his later nonfiction prose the punctuation is frequently unconventional. His prose fiction and poetry are a different case though, due in part to unconventional syntax but more often due to what must be artistic compulsion. It is not unusual for him to insert a comma between a subject and its verb, even when no elements intervene, as in "White, is abstract."[17] He inserts a comma for separation, for pause, for impact, as in "When Albert might make you think there is no more, space."[18] Jones is fond of parentheses, and, like E. E. Cummings and others, uses the open parenthesis. He frequently will capitalize all letters in a word or group of words, and he frequently uses all lower case letters, even in titles of works. He has a tendency to use the diagonal, or slash, between words or parts of words, usually where meaning is purposely ambivalent, as in "STATE/MEANT." Sometimes he will write a contraction and omit the apostrophe, as "aint," or he will abbreviate a word, as "cd" for "could" and "blk" for "black."

Even though one might point out that Jones insists upon art as expression, insists upon the importance of spontaneous and intuitive artistic creation, a legitimate question arises at this point. Are Jones' eccentric mechanics, syntax, and usage for some intentional artistic effect or accidental or a matter of indifference? When one looks at his letters, his notes, his memoranda, and the like, one notices his constant use of a sort of personal shorthand stylistically very much like certain of his published writing. One wonders if Jones finds the time to be "careful" about technical and stylistic matters. A case in point is "Communications Project,"[19] an outline originally intended for use by the Black Students Union of San Francisco State College. There are abbreviations, a lack of parallelism, needless repetition, apparent misclassifications, apparent interpolations and interjections, and nonstandard mechanics. Actually, the work resembles manuscript pad notes, notes which are to be revised, amplified, polished, and proofread at some later time.

People close to Jones maintain that what he publishes is exactly what he intends; they point out that he is sufficiently skilled in the use of language to use it exactly as he intends. Hettie Jones, who typed many of Jones' early manuscripts, was asked if she ever corrected or edited any of his work, for, after all, she was herself a writer of sorts and had done editorial work. Her reply was that she never changed anything, transcribing accurately what she saw before her on his copy.[20]

Jones is an incurable manipulator of words, almost always in an attempt for straight humor or for satire. He makes puns: His term for Negroes is "Knee-Grows"; he complains that "nobody will . . . sell me a pick axe.' Axe the man who owns one" ("To a Publisher...cut-out"); he tells his Jewish wife who has "been a bohemian / all her life" that she is "RITING BACKWARDS" ("For Hettie"); and of "Crow Jane The Crook" he writes:

Of the night
of the rain, she
reigned, reined her
fat whores and horse.

Another form of his word play is portmanteau words. Only Jones would write, "The undertaker was a stereotype nigger faggunder, taker."[21] Jones also plays with the sounds of words. In *Tales* we find "I sit now, forever, where I am. No further. No farther. Father, who I am . . ." (p. 21). And in the poem "Attention Attention" we find:

Attention Attention

(at tension, we niggers work
supremesmiraclesimpressions, &c.

Still another habit that Jones has with words is to put them into contexts that will twist meanings: he speaks of "Mozart's Ornithology" to connote jazzman Charlie "Bird" Parker's works being bastardized by white musicians. To depict ambivalent feelings he says:

. . . hovering above all the things I
seem to want to be apart of (curious smells, the high noon idea
of life . . .
          ["Vice"]

In the poem "In Memory of Radio" he writes:

. . . Love is an evil word
Turn it backwards/see, see what I mean?
An evol word. & besides
who understands it?

"Fierce, certainly satirical": Humor

A major technique employed by Jones is humor. When he speaks of the "fierce, certainly satirical humor that characterizes a [Thelonious] Monk or a [Sonny] Rollins"[22] he could just as well be describing his own brand of humor. It is incisive satire, satire informed by a certain "hip," or superior, sensibility, by an urbane sensibility developed in street lore, by a contempt born of too much perception. Only a man looking from Jones' ethnic and religious perspective would write, "But they said god was white and you could see him in the chapel of the unity funeral home, waiting for funerals."[23] It is his type of social, economic and political awareness that led him to write of dope addicts as people who "bolster the economy by sticking old needles in their arms."[24] It is a Jonesian type of irreverent, street-corner humor that comes through in this passage from *The Baptism:*

MINISTER: My God! The Lord will strike you dead.
HOMOSEXUAL: That's okay. It never happened before. It might be a gas. I mean
drilled with the holy lightning and all that shit. Wow! (*Sings.*) Drill me baby.
Drill me so I don't need to be drilled no more.

His humor tends to be broad and farcical in his later works, those works intended to be "less uselessly 'literary'"— works intended to be more practical
and more easily grasped by the masses of black people. An example is the poem
"Blue Whitie" in which the speaker asks a white man:

Tell us, sir, why are you so
full of shit? Now, come on, Man, don't be afraid,
speak right up into the microphone.

Another example is his broad caricature of the middle class Negro, the play
Great Goodness of Life: A Coon Show. The same applies to his burlesquing of
male masculinity in *J-E-L-L-O.* And the lines from *The Slave,* when Easley is
dying, must have been intended to convulse certain audiences:

WALKER.   No profound statements, Easley. No horsehit like that. No elegance.
You just die quietly and stupidly. Like niggers do. Like they are now.
   (Quieter)
Like I will. The only thing I'll let you say is, "I only regret that I have but one life
to lose for my country." You can say that.
   (Looks over at GRACE)
Grace! Tell Bradford that he can say, "I only regret that I have but one life to lose
for my country." You can say that, Easley, but that's all.

"Separate, and sometimes abstruse": Symbol and image

Unusual symbolism and imagery, among other things, make difficult the
explication of certain of Jones' works. Of course, as is the case with certain
other kinds of modern writing, explication as getting literal "meaning" is fruit-
less since no "meaning" is intended. Because so much of his symbolism and
imagery is abstruse, it is easy to overlook the fact that Jones does employ conventional symbolism and imagery. Love, eye, cold, and the like are common
denominators of meaning, and he uses them as such. But a reader confronting
as extreme a poem as "Trespass Into Spirit," rather than question his own ability

to appreciate poetry, is likely to question the author's sanity. A reader who must surround himself with reference books in order to check out, sometimes in vain, the likes of Jonas Mekas, steatopygia, The Green Lantern, W. W., floylfloyd, tom russ, buckwheat, and the bronze buckaroo will often wonder whether any such detective work is worth the effort. And often the reference books are useless; either a person happens to know what the symbol-image means or he does not. Jones' persona in "Thieves," a projection of Jones the boy, recalls that "Because the big boys let me sit with them on the steps because I could insult anybody & win dozens constantly. 'Your Mother's a Man.' Separate, and sometimes abstruse. My symbols hung unblinked at. The surface appreciated, and I, sometimes, frustrated because the whole idea didn't get in...only the profanity."[25] Unlike T. S. Eliot, LeRoi Jones does not publish explanatory notes.

Another factor is Jones' intentional strangeness and freshness of expression. He writes in *Blues People,* "In language, the African tradition aims at circumlocution rather than exact definition. The direct statement is considered crude and unimaginative; the veiling of all contents in ever-changing paraphrases is considered the criterion of intelligence and personality" (p. 31). He has at times tried for this type of paraphrase as a way to exercise and expand his intelligence and sensitivity, or so it seems.

Yet, obscure and abstruse as Jones' symbol-images appear to be, some of them do yield meaning.[26] It is symbol-images to which we may direct our attention now.

Once the reader has a superficial grasp of the facts of Jones' life, some of his symbolism becomes apparent and requires no special study. Social workers and postal workers, for example, are obviously his mother and father, projected as decorous, middle-class oriented, and rather alienated from their inherent blackness. It is no accident that Louise McGhee in "Uncle Tom's Cabin: *Alternate Ending*" is employed by the Child Welfare Bureau and is the type of concerned parent (as we noted in the opening chapter) who would take off from work at the office to investigate what might have been a slight that her bright young son had undergone at school. And this same symbolism is at work in *Dutchman* when Lula tells Clay, "Forget your social-working mother for a few seconds and let's knock stomachs." One can see plainly why Jones uses a postal worker symbolically in his description in *Blues People* of the mass exodus of Negroes to the urban North: "You could work for Ford or run an elevator, be a pimp or (soon) a postman, etc. — but the idea was to 'get in,' to 'make it' as best as one could" (p. 106) or in his recalling that "it was [not] really good to wear dark glasses and berets if one wanted to work in the post office or go to medical school" (p. 200).

Symbolism involving radio, movies, sports have meaning when related to LeRoi Jones' childhood interests, as the following illustrate. Favorites of his are the Lone Ranger and Tonto, the former being the white cowboy, a savior-type, the embodiment of idealism, the hero who is always involved in some sort of quest, and the latter being his Indian helper, a lackey-type who is on the surface faithful and primitively strong. With this and the ethnic joke about Tonto's abandoning the Lone Ranger in mind, the irony and message are obvious in this passage from *Home:* ". . . when Charles is up tight all over the world, and will of course ask the black lackeys to help him out, it is high time the black man began to make use of the Tonto-syndrome, i.e., leave the Lone Ranger to his own devices, and his own kind of death" (p. 205). And eroding naiveté and growing cynicism are unerringly depicted by his use of this kind of symbol-imagery in "Look for You Yesterday, Here You Come Today":

> . . . My life
> seems over & done with.
> Each morning I rise
> like a sleep walker
> & rot a little more.
>
> . . . What has happened to box tops??
>
> O, God...I must have a belt that glows green
> in the dark. Where is my Captain Midnight decoder??
> I can't understand what Superman is saying!

> THERE *MUST* BE A LONE RANGER!!!

Titles of various works of his attest to this penchant for using radio and movie characters as symbol-images: *J-E-L-L-O* (the Jack Benny radio and television shows), "Major Bowes' Diary," "The Bronze Buckaroo" (Herb Jeffries, an excellent jazz vocalist who at one time turned to playing cowboy parts in minor motion pictures), "The Insidious Dr. Fu Man Chu," to mention a few. His early and apparently continuing attention to comic strips is seen in his literary works. (It should be remembered that one of his earliest artistic efforts was a comic strip.) Little Orphan Annie and Charlie Brown, for instance, are characters who appear:

. . . Watch out for Peanuts,
he's gonna turn out bad/ A J.D./ A Beatnik/ A
Typical wise-ass N.Y. kid. "X" wanted to bet me
that Charlie Brown spent most of his time
whacking his doodle, or having weird relations
with that dopey hound of his (though that's
a definite improvement over "Arf Arf" & that
filthy little lesbian hes hung up with.)
             ["To a Publisher...cut-out"]

Jones is not given to the use of abstract terms as symbol-images. There are, however, two which bear mentioning, God (sometimes with a lower case "g") and energy. The first, God, is used for normal denotations as well as for symbolic connotations. God, to LeRoi Jones, is a matter of definitions; he sees God meaning different things to different people. One may see a parallel to Montaigne's observation that man makes God in his, man's, image. To Jones the Christian God as conceived by Western whites is a God to suit their purposes. They have used Him,

. . . Biblically, have
fucked him. And left him wanting,
in a continuous history of defeat . . .
             ["Dada Zodji"]

In *Dutchman,* Lula says that her God is "Me," and Clay says that his God is "A corporate Godhead." It is not surprising, therefore, to find Jones later proclaiming that "The Black Man is making new Gods," black gods issuing from black spiritual consciousness. For blacks,

. . . God
is not a nigger with a beard. Nor
is he not . . .
             ["Poem for Religious Fanatics"]

In *Black Music* he says, ". . . God is, indeed, energy" (p. 193), and he thinks of "God as evolution. The flow of is" (p. 198). He advises:

Be somebody Beautiful
Be Black and Open
Reach for God
             ["The Calling Together"]

Energy as Jones uses the term is the divine force for creativity. Energy manifests itself in different ways: Jazz musician Albert Ayler "is a vessel from which energy is issued, issues";[27] Malcolm X talked of politics as a "moving energy";[28] "Breech, bridge, and reach, to where all talk is energy";[29] and the Chuck Berrys and Muddy Waters, folk-oriented black musicians, "first harnessed that energy."[30] Blacks, he feels, are the possessors of natural energies, of divine powers of creativity.

A city boy and man, LeRoi Jones does not use much imagery connected with physical nature. He does, however, use sun, wind, flame, water, and forest. At times he will use sun traditionally, to mean enlightenment, happiness, wisdom, or "energy." He projects a future of

Dead heaps of white ash, vanished, and the sun
allowed to shine. At the front door, baby, at the front
door, or any door, on anything, wail sun, beat on everybody good.
    ["I Am Speaking of Future Good-ness and Social Philosophy"]

At times he will use sun to signify divine blackness, speaking at such times of blacks as "sun people" and warning others, in a reversal of meaning, to

Beware the evil sun . . .
turn you black
            ["Hymn for Lanie Poo"]

Wind as a symbol connotes spiritual essence: "And let us think of soul, as anima: spirit (*spiritus,* breath) as that which carries breath on the living wind."[31] In "The Christians" he recalls that "Somedays wind swept thru my eyes and I'd stare off whistling. This Was An ATTRIBUTE." And in the title poem for *Preface* he writes of

. . . the broad edged silly music the wind
Makes when I run for a bus

Flame, rather conventionally, means the unerring intellect or realistic perception. He assesses himself, in his preface to *Black Magic,* as "the soothsayer, one flayed by evil as a fountainhead of reality finally glimpses of true airflame." Water, river, ocean, wet and their cognates can often be interpreted as fecundity or creative refreshment of an abstract sort. It is that quality necessary for all life, a quality roughly opposite to T. S. Eliot's desert, cactus, and dry. The quality is a catalytic agent: "You are myself's river."[32] Forest, in much the same manner that Dante used it, is a lost or dangerous or uncharted state. In this sense, Jones will occasionally use forest to represent white Western civilization, as in:

> . . . she ran from me into
> that forest.
> > [*"An Agony. As Now."*]

Or he might use it to represent the uncertain future or the unknown present:

> . . . I am
> an animal watching
> his forest . . .
> > ["The Clearing"]

Symbols derived from urban settings include steel, pavement or concrete, hallways, window. Steel, conventionally, is used to project cold, hard materialism that is devoid of feeling. Pavement and concrete conjure concepts of the impersonality, indifference, and hardness of urban life. Hallways are passageways from phase to phase in life. Window is a frequently employed, important Jonesian symbol-image. It stands for a perspective on life, a frame of reference from which one sees and evaluates experience. Conversely, one's concept of another person's perception is signified by looking into that person's window. In *Dutchman,* for example, there are instances of people looking out of and into windows. Lula and Clay's first cognizance of, first assessments of each other, are through windows. People look in at them, they look out at people; occasionally Clay and Lula turn from each other to look out at the darkness rushing past. At one point Clay observes, "Staring through train windows is weird business." Another example is in "The Success" in which the narrator says:

> Among things with souls find me.
> > Picking thru the alphabet
> > or leaning out the window . . .

Jones rarely uses color symbolism, except for green and grey. Green, he supposes in "Vice," is "a color of despair and wretchedness." Predictably, grey symbolizes the white life style and, concurrently, the common connotations of ugliness, spoilage, death. In *Dutchman,* Lula's hair is grey. In *Tales* Jones deprecatingly speaks of the black student leader as "happy to die in a new grey suit" (p. 7).

Sometimes he will use a lady (or "bitch" or "dead lady") to represent Western or white American culture.

Another group of Jonesian symbol-images is based upon the body and its functions. Meat or flesh is sometimes used by him to symbolize intuitive urges, noncerebral and transcendentalistic urges. "The New Sheriff" is

. . . Inside
the soft white meat
of the feelings . . .

In *The Baptism* the homosexual tells the boy that the old woman "takes flesh, just like you did son, but she makes it abstract and useless. So it is holy and harmless." He uses the term in the same manner in "Gluttony": "If my flesh is sweet, my mind is pure. I am awake in your cold world."[33] Fingers are that which draw or evoke feeling. In *Tales* a frustrated narrator is "screaming at my fingers" and later laments that "a vicious sadness cripples my fingers" (p. 8). In a discussion of music, Jones asserts, "Yes, it is music which, under the best fingers, is a consciously Spiritual Music. That is, we mean to speak of Life Force and try to become one of the creative functions of the universe."[34]

A subgroup of body-function symbol-images has to do with sex. Masturbation, as Jones uses it, represents an individualism based upon self-love or it represents love which cannot find external connectives and therefore is turned within. A case in point is the boy in *The Baptism* who has been a masturbator because he had not known where or how to express his love externally, and sought release within himself. He goes to the church and is chastised and ridiculed, but does not find outlets for love there either, although the homosexual would pervert the boy's love. In the instance of Charlie Brown, mentioned above, if one knows that this comic strip character is a "born loser," a constantly frustrated boy, one can understand Jones poetically depicting him as a masturbator who turns within himself in reaction to the world's rebuffs. Homosexuality and heterosexual perversion may be considered as broadly symbolic of misuse of creative energies, as a deliberate turning from what is natural and good, as a degeneracy, as an avoidance of reality.

The two white men in *Experimental Death Unit #1* who seek sexual contact with the black woman are willing to compromise their heterosexual habits when she taunts and then refuses them. They finally beg her for perverted sexual contact. Her willingness to accept contact with the white world on their degenerate and perverted terms is the cause of her death.

(Jones accounts for his artistic interest in homosexuality as follows: "Well,

I think homosexuality was always—I was always very curious about it because there were so many fags in our neighborhood, all the time, it seemed like. . . . In black communities it is a sort of avoidance of reality—a refusal to deal with reality and I don't mean just sexual reality."[35])

Heterosexual intercourse (Jones often uses the term "fuck") indicates the closest possible human interaction. This relationship may be on the physical level, but most of the time it is representative of a spiritual or emotional intimacy in which there is, ideally, a mutually beneficial, intimate giving and getting. In the story "Heretics" the narrator, a Negro somewhat foreign to and a bit afraid of his blackness, is tempted by a woman to immerse himself in a black life style in which he could have meaningful contact with those who truly want and need him, where he could be free from the control of the white world's constrictive influence: "She loved me, she said. . . . We could live together and she would show me how to fuck. How to do it good."[36] Another example is in "Red Eye," which calls for active and close involvement with reality:

The corrupt madness of the individual. You cannot live
alone. You are in the world. World, fuck them. . . .

In *The Baptism* the innate selfishness (unwillingness to have unrequited contact with fellow humans) of the minister is expressed in his line spoken to the homosexual, "I fuck no one who does not claim to love me," and his next words, "You are less selective," imply that the homosexual's contacts with people are open and unregulated by ulterior or selfish motives.

In Jones' works, sterility is often symbolized by urination (he uses the term "pee" and its forms). The opposite symbol would be productive orgasm. Urination implies a useless, wasteful, and unproductive expenditure of creativity. With this in mind, a reading of Jones' *The Toilet* grows richer in symbolism, for he frequently has his characters urinating, flushing urinals, and the like, indicative of the unproductivity and misdirection of their actions in effecting respect and love. In "The Flatterers" Jones talks of "Frozen bums peeing through the windows. For cupcakes. Jelly donuts. Adventure. We laughed about it,"[37] meaning that the perspective (windows) from which whites view experience causes their actions to be spiritually impotent, rewarded only by trivial material gain.

The last symbol-image to be considered here is dance, which he uses to depict the total experiencing of life, for immersion into life. This being so, when Lula entices Clay to dance with her, she is enticing him to engage wholly in her way of life, and on her terms. And the boy in *The Baptism* is still naive, for when the homosexual asks him if he dances, he replies, "Yes sir. I know the popular steps of the day," the implication being that his involvement with life has been only on the superficial or popular level.

As helpful as interpretations of Jones' favorite symbol-images may be, as helpful as knowledge of his life and themes may be, there are Jonesian passages that defy rational paraphrase or explication. When he writes of "24 elephants" stomping out of the subway "with consecrated hardons" he is enigmatic. But perhaps that is what he intends, an enigma.

A spontaneously funny enigma.

Part II

Chapter 4. "The semantic rituals of power": Nonfiction prose

"Going wherever, always": *Home*

Home, a volume of essays covering the period of Jones' nonfiction prose from 1960 through 1965, reveals not so much a carefully delineated, stage-by-stage development of ideas, themes, attitudes, and stances as it reveals the evolution of the same. Certainly there is a dramatic difference between the "American poet" who in "Cuba Libre," the first essay, defensively responds to criticism of America by saying, "I'm a poet...what can I do? I write, that's all, I'm not even interested in politics" (p. 42) and the "Black Artist" who in "STATE/MEANT," the last essay, "must teach . . . White Eyes their deaths, and teach the black man how to bring these deaths about" (p. 252). But the movements are nondramatic, at times subtle. With the exception perhaps of his 1960 visit to Cuba, one looks in vain for traumatic changes, pivotal incidents, or clearly defined and pinpointed emotional or intellectual shifts. Indeed, in retrospect, it seems as if the essential "blackness" of Jones was always there, not quite as clearly articulated as it would be later, but always there.

One notes Jones' perceptive hindsight in his introductory essay for the volume, "HOME":

> I have been a lot of places in my time, and done a lot of things. And there is a sense of the Prodigal about my life that begs to be resolved. But one truth anyone reading these pieces ought to get is the sense of movement—the struggle, in myself, to understand where and who I am, and to move with that understanding. (As for example, the difference in out- and in-look between "The Myth Of A Negro Literature" and "Black Writing"; or a liberal piece like "Tokenism" and the changed thinking that evolved into "The Revolutionary Theatre" or "Black Male.") And these moves, most times unconscious (until, maybe, I'd look over something I'd just written and whistle, "Yow, yeh, I'm way over there, huh?"), seem to me to have been always toward the thing I had coming into the world, with no sweat: my blackness. [pp. 9–10]

His stated purpose of *Home* is "to show just how my mind and my place in America have changed since the 'Cuba Libre' essay. . . . my tendency, body and mind, is to make it. To get there, from anywhere, going wherever, always. By the time this book appears, I will be even blacker" (pp. 9–10).

The reader would hardly suspect that at the time that most of these essays were written their author had a Jewish wife, two children by her, was living a racially integrated, essentially "white" life in cosmopolitan New York City, and was acknowledged as a bright young writer of the predominantly white, establishment, intellectual and artistic American avant-garde. (In fact, Jones had considered entitling the book *The Black Bohemian*.) The year 1961 found him claiming that Negroes can afford "the luxury of hate" for "they certainly have enough to hate" (p. 66). Then in 1962, in "Black Is a Country" he claimed, "we *are* Americans which is our strength as well as our desperation" (p. 85), yet called for a black nationalistic independence which would be neither a separation from nor an assimilation into this same America. As late (or as early) as 1963, while living an integrated life in New York's Greenwich Village he advocated Negroes' isolation from mainstream America as an advantage to black writers. (Of course, as a member of the nonconformist young intellectuals of the time, he was in this sense personally apart from the mainstream.)

Then, by 1964, he had articulated his commitment to what was to transpire in his artistic odyssey: "I write now, full of trepidation because I know the death this society intends for me . . . . But let them understand that this is a fight without quarter, and I am very fast" (pp. 179–80). This manifesto preceded the 1965 physical odyssey from the Village to Harlem. So did his 1964 proposal for a revolutionary theatre which "must teach them [whites] their deaths" (p. 211).

Other pronouncements that he made during his white-black years are not unlike pronouncements of the whites with whom he associated culturally and personally. Many young intellectuals of his time saw a cultural vapidity, an artistic decadence in American culture and art. Jones expressed the same themes. For one thing, white liberal-intellectuals denounced America's racism, as does Jones throughout *Home.* Some saw little hope for America's cultural and political survival; Jones agrees in "The Last Days of the American Empire (Including Some Instructions for Black People)." Some called for new literary forms, as does Jones in "Hunting Is Not Those Heads on the Wall."

Although *Home* shows no traumatic changes in Jones, the reader can discern broadly distinctive periods. As Faith Berry groups them, the 1960–62 essays are "essentially research-reporting"; by 1963 the reportorial style is toned down and "he's behind the scene more than he's on it"; and by 1964 "he's in his own world. . . . He has by this time moved from reporter to commentator to prophet and we are reading a state of mind."[1]

"Cuba Libre" (1960) reveals Jones the journalist on an eye-opening trip to Cuba during which time he articulates his delusions about Cuba and, more important, his awakening disaffection with America. In 1961, in "A Letter to Jules Feiffer," the reader is in the presence of a commentator who, in a statement about the futility of passive resistance, uses the Jews' experiences in Nazi Germany as a point of reference. This commentator is unwilling to be counseled by white people who "think they are peculiarly qualified to tell American Negroes and other oppressed peoples of the world how to wage their struggles" (p. 66), and who prefers the term Afro-American over the term Negro. The next year, 1962, finds Jones acidly pointing out what he considers the hollowness of "tokenism" and the "select coon" ploy, calling instead for black nationalism, seeing promise and hope as futile in the "unnatural adversity" of urban ghetto life. In this same year in "The Myth of a Negro Literature" he asserts that Negro writers must go outside the white culture and into a black frame of reference in order to be creative, and he points toward his yet-to-be-made statements about a black aesthetic.

The year 1963 finds Jones further toward black aestheticism as an absolute, calling in a review entitled "A Dark Bag" for ideological poetry and in another review, "Brief Reflections on Two Hot Shots," condemning James Baldwin and South African writer Peter Abrahams for what Jones perceives as their over insistence upon their individuality and their overindulgence in personal sensitivity. What is needed, Jones feels, is social literary consciousness. In "Black Writing" he advocates realistic presentation of black life styles and the use of ethnic language, and in "Expressive Language" he sees the possibilities of "semantic rituals of power" (p. 169). This same year, 1963, in "What Does Nonviolence Mean?" he inveighs against moral suasion, seeing it as ineffective in achieving social change. In this same essay he derides what he calls the "Liberal/Missionary" syndrome and Negroes' assimilation into American society and culture. Important statements in his ideological journey appear in this essay:

> . . . I advocate a violence, a literal murdering of the American socio-political stance, not only as it directly concerns American Negroes, but in terms of its stranglehold on most of the modern world. . . . The supposed Christian ideal of Nonviolence is aimed at quieting even this most natural of insurrectionary elements. As an actual moral category all rational men are essentially nonviolent, except in defense of their lives. To ask that the black man not even defend himself . . . is to ask that that black man stay quiet in his chains while the most "liberal" elements in this country saw away at those chains with make-believe saws. [p. 151]

Also in 1963, in "The Dempsey-Liston Fight" Jones again takes up an already stated theme, this being the moral, spiritual, and artistic softness of American whites, and he implies another, the physical softness of American whites.

The 1964 essays are essentially manifestoes and position papers. "Hunting Is Not Those Heads on the Wall" is important for its presentation of his theory of art: the act of creating, not the artifact, is of paramount value. "LeRoi Jones Talking" is his formal commitment to "fight without quarter" and warning that "I am very fast" (p. 180). "The Last Days of the American Empire (Including Some Instructions for Black People)" prophesies the death of America. And "The Revolutionary Theatre" presents his credo of black threatre as a social and political force, a theatre of action. The essays of 1965, the year of his physical move from whiteness to blackness, reveal a Jones now theorizing about an innate superiority of black masculinity and about the psychological implications of white-black sex relations, these ideas being expressed in "American Sexual Reference: Black Male." "Blackhope" shows a blanket distrust of whites. "The Legacy of Malcolm X, and the Coming of the Black Nation" presents a politically aware Jones — one who sees the Islamic religion as a political-social-cultural medium, who sees the possibilities of "deals" with whites, who sees politics as a "moving energy" in the movement to black nationhood. The last essay in the book, "STATE/MEANT," defines the black artist's duty. It is short, and because it is a key to an empathetic reading of so much of Jones' work, it is quoted here in its entirety:

The Black Artist's role in America is to aid in the destruction of America as he knows it. His role is to report and reflect so precisely the nature of the society, and of himself in that society, that other men will be moved by the exactness of his rendering and, if they are black men, grow strong through this moving, having seen their own strength, and weakness; and if they are white men, tremble, curse, and go mad, because they will be drenched with the filth of their evil.

The Black Artist must draw out of his soul the correct image of the world. He must use this image to band his brothers and sisters together in common understanding of the nature of the world (and the nature of America) and the nature of the human soul.

The Black Artist must demonstrate sweet life, how it differs from the deathly grip of the White Eyes. The Black Artist must teach the White Eyes their deaths, and teach the black man how to bring these deaths about.

We are unfair, and unfair.
We are black magicians, black art
s we make in black labs of the heart.

The fair are
fair, and death
ly white.

The day will not save them
and we own
the night.
                    [pp. 251–52]

In addition to considering the chronology of ideas in *Home*, the reader profits also by approaching the volume through a consideration of three dominant themes: political-social theory, black cultural nationalism, and black aestheticism. Actually, these three are so interrelated that it is less than wise to attempt in some instances to separate them, but they are sufficiently distinctive to warrant separate considerations.

Several essays are illustrative of the evolution of his political and social ideology, the first being "Cuba Libre." It is important to remember that at the time Jones wrote this essay he conceived of himself as an "American poet," a Negro, and the essay shows a sensitive but politically uncommitted young man, or at least not committed to aggressive action in the field of social politics. And although he feels that "in most cases the so-called American intellectual is not even aware of what is happening any place in the world" (pp. 38–39) because "We reject the blatant, less dangerous lie [slanted accounts of the United States' participation in world politics] in favor of the subtle subliminal lie [that American leaders are "unintelligent but well-meaning clowns"], which is more dangerous because we feel we are taking an intelligent stance, not being had," (p. 39) he sees no alternatives.

During a train ride in Cuba, a Mexican delegate to the Youth Congress questioned Jones at length about American life and politics. Jones reports:

I explained as best I could about the Eisenhowers, the Nixons, the DuPonts, but she made even my condemnations seem mild. "Everyone in the world," she said, with her finger, "has to be communist or anti-communist. And if they're anti-communist, no matter what kind of foul person they are, you accept them as your allies. . . . You people are irrational!"

I tried to defend myself, "Look, why jump on me? I understand what you're saying. I'm in complete agreement with you. I'm a poet...what can I do? I write, that's all, I'm not even interested in politics." [p. 42]

And there is a note of futility near the end of the essay:

> The rebels among us have become merely people like myself who grow beards and will not participate in politics. Drugs, juvenile delinquency, complete isolation from the vapid mores of the country, a few current ways out. But name an alternative here. Something not inextricably bound up in a lie. Something not part of liberal stupidity or the actual filth of vested interest. There is none. It's much too late. We are an *old* people already. Even the vitality of our art is like bright flowers growing up through a rotting carcass. [pp. 61–62]

This ending belies certain germinal ideas, attitudes, and impressions that can be found in the essay. Significantly, it is divided into three parts: "Preface," "(What I Brought to the Revolution)," and "(What I Brought Back Here)." This last part is really the heart of the essay. For one thing, it was during this trip to Cuba that he met and was impressed by Robert Williams, at that time the controversial president of the Monroe, North Carolina branch of the National Association for the Advancement of Colored People (NAACP). Williams had attracted public attention and official NAACP displeasure for advocating that the Southern Negro reject Martin Luther King's method of passive resistance and for proposing in its place violent resistance. Williams by this time, Jones reports, had established "a kind of pocket militia among the Negroes of Monroe, and had managed to so terrorize the white population of the town that he could with some finality *ban* any further meetings of the local Ku Klux Klan. The consensus among the white population was that 'Williams was trying to provoke them and they weren't going to be provoked'" (pp. 18–19). (Williams was later to flee the United States rather than face a charge of kidnapping in Monroe. By 1970 he was back in the United States to begin a legal fight against the accusation.) Further, Jones felt that the trip opened his eyes to the delusions that Americans, and that he too as an American, live under. Before the trip, "it had never entered my mind that I might really like to find out for once what was actually happening someplace in the world" (p. 12).

Jones was impressed by the Castro government's Agrarian Reform Law, particularly its provisions proscribing large land holdings, its provisions for expropriation of large land holdings for redistribution among peasants and agricultural workers who owned no land, and its provisions for land use by individuals rather than by corporations or landlords. "This meant of course," says Jones, "that United Fruit, American Sugar, etc., got burnt immediately. . . . 'That is communism,' one of the ladies next to me said half jokingly. 'Is it wrong?' the tall man wanted to know. The woman agreed that it was not" (p. 31).

The final shaping incident during his trip to Cuba occurred when Jones had returned by train to Havana from the gigantic celebration in commemoration of Fidel Castro's 1953 beginning drive against the Batista government: "I came out of the terminal into the street and stopped at a newsstand to buy a paper. The headlines of one Miami paper read, 'CUBAN CELEBRATION RAINED OUT.' I walked away from the stand as fast as I could" (p. 62).

In "Letter to Jules Feiffer," a rebuttal to a letter Feiffer had published in *The Village Voice,* Jones cites Robert Williams as an example of the efficacy of aggressive resistance to social injustices and oppression, reminding Mr. Feiffer, "(I can think of 5,000,000 people who used to live in Europe, who should've fought back when they were assaulted by racists. Can't you?)" (p. 66). By the time of the writing of this essay, Jones had stopped calling himself a Negro, and he asks Feiffer, "Why so much fuss about Negroes wanting to call themselves Afro-Americans? And if you want to call yourself a Judeo (Judaeo?) American, it's perfectly all right with me. In fact, I think that if perhaps there were more Judeo-Americans and a few less bland, cultureless, middle-headed [sic] AMER-ICANS, this country might still be a great one" (p. 67).

"Tokenism: 300 Years for Five Cents" finds Jones bitingly defining tokenism as "the setting up of social stalemates or the extension of meager privileges to some few 'selected' Negroes in order that a semblance of compromise or 'prog-ress,' or a lessening in racial repression might seem to be achieved, while actu-ally helping to maintain the status quo just as rigidly . . ." (p. 73). Further on he writes:

> Tokenism is that philosophy (of psychological exploitation) which is supposed to assuage my natural inclination toward complete freedom. For the middle-class Negro this assuagement can take the form it takes in the mainstream of American life, *i.e.,* material acquisition, or the elevating of one "select" coon to some position that seems heaped in "prestige," *e.g.,* Special Delegate to the United Nations, Director of Public Housing, Assistant Press Secretary to the President of the United States, Vice President In Charge Of Personnel for Chock Full 'O Nuts, Borough President of Manhattan, etc. The "Speaking Of People" column in *Ebony* magazine is the banal chronicler of such "advances," *e.g.,* the first Negro sheriff of Banwood, Utah; or the first Negro Asst. Film Editor for BRRR films. But the lower class Negro cannot use this kind of tokenism, so he is pretty much left in the lurch. But so effective is this kind of crumb-drop-ping among the *soi-disant* black middle class that these people become the actual tokens themselves, or worse. [p. 80]

A fourth essay concerned mainly with social politics is "City of Harlem" which purports to describe this city within a city "as it exists for its people, as an actual place where actual humans live . . ." (p. 88). He declares that Harlem is "a very different thing" from the stereotyped conception of it as a "pleasure-happy center of the universe, full of loud, hippy mammas in electric colors and their fast, slick-head pappas, all of them twisting and grinning in the streets in a kind of existential joyousness that never permits of sadness or responsibility" (p. 88). Neither is Harlem "the gathering place for every crippling human vice, and the black men there simply victims of their own peculiar kind of sloth and childishness . . . . chances are both of these stereotypes come from the same kinds of minds" (p. 88). Tracing the history of Harlem and the forces which created and determined it, Jones sees it as "a community of nonconformists, since any black American, simply by virtue of his blackness, is weird, a nonconformist in this society . . . . a colony of old-line Americans, who can hold out, even if it is a great deal of the time in misery and ignorance, but still hold out, against the hypocrisy and sterility of big-time America, and still try to make their own lives, simply because of their color, but by now, not so simply, because that color now does serve to identify people in America whose feelings about it are not broadcast every day on television" (p. 93).

In answering the question in the title "What Does Nonviolence Mean?" Jones posits, ". . . it assumes, again, the nature of that mysterious moral commitment Negro leaders say the black man must make to participate as a privileged class among the oppressed" (p. 145). Characterizing nonviolence-committed, middle-class Negroes as "semi-pawns" and characterizing white liberals as those who during slavery "didn't want the slaves beaten" but "not asking that they be freed," he accuses both of turning from realities of police dogs, assassinations, blackjacks, and other terroristic tactics by whites. The poor black, he says, "realizes, at least instinctively, that no matter what deal goes down . . . no help at all is being offered to him" (p. 147) in terms of education, employment, housing. Jones draws an analogy between the nonviolent American Negro and "the European Jews, and more specifically the fate of the German Jews at the hands of Adolph Hitler. The German Jews, at the time of Hitler's rise to power, were the most assimilated Jews in Europe. They believed, and with a great deal of emotional investment, that they were Germans. . . . Even when the anti-Jewish climate began to thicken and take on the heaviness of permanence, many middle-class Jews believed that it was only the poor Jews, who, perhaps rightly so, would suffer in such a climate" (p. 149).

"The Last Days of the American Empire (Including Some Instructions for

Black People)," in energetic, spontaneous, and at times rhapsodic style, calls for unity among American blacks, this unity being necessary if they are to restructure the social politics of America. Declaring that "there is *no chance* that the American white man will change" (p. 198), he says that "the only reason the black man is alive in the West today" is for "continued exploitative use. But one day, and very soon, the white man might just look up, hip again, and see that the black man has outlived his usefulness. Then the murders will break out in earnest" (p. 206). What, then, is America's hope and the Afro-American's alternative? "I say if your hope is for the survival of this society, this filthy order, no good. You lose. The hope is that young blacks will remember all of their lives what they are seeing, what they are witness to just by being alive and black in America, and that eventually they will use this knowledge scientifically, and erupt like Mt. Vesuvius to crush in hot lava these willful maniacs who call themselves white Americans" (pp. 208–9).

"The Legacy of Malcolm X, and the Coming of the Black Nation" speaks of Malcolm X's learning that "Black Conquest will be a *deal*. That is, it will be achieved through deals as well as violence" (p. 239), a tactic that Jones-turned-Baraka appears to have applied later in his political activities in Newark. Jones envisions in the coming black nation the nationalization of all properties and resources so that they can be used to supply the needs of black people. In this connection it is worth noting his earlier (1960) admiration for Cuba's Agrarian Reform Law. In Jones' envisioned autonomous black nation, "No white politicians can be allowed to function within the Nation. Black politicians doing funny servant business for whites, must be eliminated. Black people must have absolute political and economic control. In other words they must have absolute control over their lives and destinies" (p. 249).

So, in these socio-political essays we find Jones positing prominently: social and political change through force, self-determination rather than "freedom," a sense of the futility of working for change within the present socio-political structure, strong anti-middle-class Negro and anti-white-liberal sentiment, a concept of nonviolence as a ploy and therefore inefficacious as a method for social change, and a black nation whose resources will be used to serve the masses. In these essays he does not reveal in what sort of socio-political structure his proposed black self-determination will operate; he fails to detail how the destruction of the present social and political structure will be effected; and he deals in broad or vague generalities about the economic mechanics of his proposed black nation. This thematically related group of essays, then, shows a Jones ranging from a mild, somewhat naive Negro American poet not enamored of but somewhat resigned to what he feels is an immoral and dying socio-political system, to an out-spoken, racially oriented rhetorician-polemicist looking to the day when there will be an autonomous black nation.

Another grouping of essays shares a strong theme of black nationalism — a nationalism that is essentially a unity among blacks, a nationalism more culturally oriented than truly politically oriented. This cultural nationalism is based upon a belief in innate, distinct, and superior ethnic characteristics. The utilization and development of these racial qualities, Jones believes, will help unify blacks to a position of strength. This cultural nationalism is based also upon the premise that integration or assimilation of Negroes into America is neither feasible nor advantageous.

Even in "Cuba Libre" he exhibits a tone of benign moral superiority when he discusses the social, moral, and political faults of the United States. At this point in time it is an assumed superiority of the liberal intellectual that he feels he is rather than an assumed superiority of the black man that he was to feel later. But by 1962 he was to write in "Tokenism: 300 Years for Five Cents" about the moral and spiritual inferiority of the "house nigger," of the middle-class Negro who has taken on the white man's values as his own.

In " 'Black' Is a Country" Jones says, "To a growing list of 'dirty' words that make Americans squirm add the word *Nationalism.* I would say that the word has gained almost as much infamy in some quarters of this country as that all-time anathema and ugliness, *Communism.* In fact, some journalists, commentators, and similar types have begun to use the two words interchangeably. It goes without saying that said commentators, etc., and the great masses of Americans who shudder visibly at the mention of those words cannot know what they mean. And it is certainly not my function, here, to rectify that situation completely" (p. 82). He then goes on to describe nationalism as "acting in one's own best interests" (p. 83) in order to gain independence from an enemy, in this case white America.

No one believes in magic anymore. The Christian church cannot help us. The new nationalists all over the world have learned to be suspicious of "Christianity." Christ and the Dollar Sign have gotten mixed up in their minds, and they *know* that the latter is their enemy. It is time black America got those two confused as well. The idea of the "all black society" within the superstructure of an all white society is useless as well (even if it were possible). [p. 85]

"The Dempsey-Liston Fight" continues the ethnic identity theme. Jones sees the Sonny Liston vs. Floyd Patterson heavy-weight boxing championship fight as symbolic of a black vs. Negro struggle:

Patterson was to represent the fruit of the missionary ethic, in its use as a policy of the democratic liberal imperialist state. Patterson had found God, had reversed his underprivileged (uncontrolled) violence and turned it to work, and for this act become an object of prestige within the existing system. The tardy black Horatio Alger, the glad hand of integration, to welcome those 20,000,000 chimerically, into the lunatic asylum of white America.

In this context, Liston, the unreformed, Liston the violent (who still had to make some gesture toward the Christian ethic, like the quick trip to the Denver priest, to see if somehow the chief whitie could turn him into a regular fella) comes on as the straightup Heavy. I mean "they" painted Liston Black. They painted Patterson White. And that was the simple conflict. Which way would the black man go? [p. 156]

Fortunately for Jones' point, the "blacker" man won:

So a thin-willed lower middle-class American was led to beatings just short of actual slaughter, to prove the fallibility of another artifact of American culture (which, like most of its other artifacts, suffers very seriously from built-in obsolescence). This happened twice. And each time Patterson fell, there was a vision that came to me of the whole colonial West crumbling in some sinister silence, like the across-the-tracks House of Usher.

But, dig it, there is no white man in the world who wants to fight Sonny Liston himself. [p. 157]

Jones warns blacks against making themselves vulnerable to what he considers the debilitating white life style, specifically warning against white-black male-female alliances. The white man's attitude toward sex, Jones claims, is "diseased," but the "black man . . . can enter into the sex act with less guilt . . . is freer" (p. 228). Then (in a sort of illogicality which ignores the fact that at that time in America blackness was at least in part a matter of whites' definitions) Jones makes racial superiority claims which imply the establishment of a black nation by default:

Black creation terrifies the white man, because it is strong, ubiquitous. The white man is like the land, so minute in the world, so in danger from the raging sea, which sweeps the world into any shape it wills. Black creation is as strong as black flesh. If the raped white woman has a child (or the raped black one) it is a black child. The black woman can bring forth nothing out of her womb but blackness, the black man can send out no other kind of seed. And that seed, anywhere, makes black.

The black shows through, and is genetically dominant. The white race will disappear simply enough in genetic time, which cannot be separated from the context of its happening, *i.e.,* social facts which make the genetically weaker whites dangerous in the world, as well as actually diseased. [pp. 232–33]

One may then wonder why Jones would be opposed to integration and inter-racial marriage.

"Blackhope," too, calls for racial unity. Originally a speech delivered in front of the Hotel Theresa in Harlem when Jones was heading BART/S, he ends with "If you want a new world, Brothers and Sisters, if you want a world where you can all be beautiful human beings, we must throw down our differences and come together as black people. And once we have done this, you know for yourself, there is no force on earth that can harm or twist us. No devil left in creation to mess up the world" (p. 237).

Jones' strongest statement about nationalism in *Home* is "The Legacy of Malcolm X, and the Coming of the Black Nation." In essence, the task for black people is to control themselves, defeat the enemy, and usher in the new era. According to Jones, Malcolm X's major contribution was his vision of and work toward the black national consciousness that is necessary for conquest. One can see at this point the ideas which Jones/Baraka was to put to practical use in his political and cultural activities in Newark.

In summary, the black nation which Jones talks about in this cluster of essays is not so much a physical nation of land, boundaries, and political struc-ture as it is a nation of unified black people, a group consciousness, a group pride, a cooperative socio-economic entity and a repository of and progenitor of black culture—all necessary for the survival of the black man in America.

A third major theme of *Home* is black aestheticism. Earlier, in the second chapter, we noted Jones' theory of art as process. This theory leaves little room for imitators of artifacts, but it permits *use,* as different from imitation. This theory also condones nonformalistic (nonpreconceived) art, condones a spon-taneity and intuitiveness in the creative process. As the title implies, the essay "Expressive Language" explores this theme of natural creative process as it applies to the writer's language. Words, Jones insists, should not use artists; artists should use words. Language is social. A pragmatic semanticist, he ad-vises, "Know the words of the users, the semantic rituals of power. This is a way into wherever it is you are not now, but wish, very desperately, to get into" (p. 169). Assuredly, this thinking points toward an art of utility, art as something other than its own end.

In March, 1962, Jones addressed the American Society for African Culture on the subject of Negro literature. This address was later published as an essay in *The Saturday Review* and then in *Home* as "The Myth of a Negro Literature." To make a generalization, Jones sees the corpus known as American Negro literature as really a white literature; ergo, there is no such thing as a Negro literature. He makes the statement, ". . . the literature of the blues is a much more profound contribution to Western culture than any other literary contribution made by American Negroes" (p. 107). So Jones calls for the Negro author to write from the orientation of a Negro, "to go from where he actually is, completely outside of that conscious white myopia" (p. 113). He concludes:

> If there is ever a Negro literature, it must disengage itself from the weak, heinous elements of the culture that spawned it, and use its very existence as evidence of a more profound America. But as long as the Negro writer contents himself with the imitation of the useless inelegance of the stunted middle-class mind, academic or popular, and refuses to look around him and "tell it like it is" — preferring the false prestige of the black bourgeosie or the deceitful "acceptance" of *buy and sell* America, something never included in the legitimate cultural tradition of "his people" — he will be a failure, and what is worse, not even a significant failure. Just another dead American. [p. 115]

Not surprisingly, a number of Negro writers and critics would decline to accept Jones' thesis that a Negro literature does not exist. Cecil Brown, for instance, points out that Jones ignored ethnic and folk elements, particularly the blues, in the works of writers such as James Baldwin, Langston Hughes, James Weldon Johnson. He argues that "It is unnecessary for Jones to ignore the whole of Black literature, simply because the nature of literary form is what it is. It is not necessary to conclude, as he does, that Black literature is mediocre; but then, this is a white critic's judgment, for it implies a comparison between the literature of Black Americans and white Americans, and such a comparison is not possible since we are dealing with completely different things."[2] Possibly the lack of agreement between Brown's commentary and Jones' thinking is simply a matter of degree — Jones calling for greater intensity of blackness as a criterion of quality in Negro literature.

In "A Dark Bag," originally a review of several works for *Poetry* magazine, Jones affirms his belief in a poetry of ideas. These ideas, he says, should be informed by the Negro experience if the author is a Negro. Among his observations are some about specific authors and books: Arna Bontemps' *American Negro Poetry* reflects Bontemps' personality and shows "amazingly noncritical selection" with the result being "another house slaver's manual of verse"

(p. 125). He also criticizes this editor for failing to include work by some of the younger black poets. Langston Hughes' anthology, *Poems from Black Africa* is diagnosed by Jones as having "the same kind of anemia," but still useful simply because so few of its kind exist. *African Songs* by Leon Damas and *24 Poems* by Jean-Joseph Rabearivelo demonstrate "the strength of the French-Negro poets, whether in Africa or in the West Indies" (p. 130). Jacob Drachler's *African Heritage* is "a generally weak willed collection of prose and poetry" (p. 131) but does contain some works of merit. We find in this essay by Jones, as in other of his essays, the equating of poor writing with Western white form and content, or, affirmatively stated, the equating of good writing with black oriented form and content. We find also that Jones does not say, except in a general way and by implication, what, if anything, is distinctly and basically different between "white" and "black" techniques.

Again, this time in "Black Writing," Jones pushes writers with ethnic identifications to write from an ethnocentric position—to write what they know and feel and understand about the world: "'Black writers are stuck because they're always talking about their people.' There is no real answer to that. But who does anyone talk about? Hemingway is always talking about his people, or Joyce. What does anyone think The Dubliners were—abstract literary categories?" (p. 163). America, Jones feels, must be written about in realistic terms. As this applies to black writers, he says:

> I think though that there are now a great many young black writers in America who do realize that their customary isolation from the mainstream is a valuable way into any description they might make of an America. In fact, it is just this alienation that could serve to make a very powerful American literature, since its hypothetical writers function in many senses within the main structure of American society as well. The Negro, as he exists in America now, and has always existed in this place (certainly after formal slavery), is a natural nonconformist. Being black in a society where such a state is an extreme liability is the most extreme form of nonconformity available. The point is, of course, that this nonconformity should be put to use. [p. 164]

The use to which black playwrights in particular (and black writers in general) must put their talent is expressed in "The Revolutionary Theatre":

> The Revolutionary Theatre should force change; it should be change . . . . must EXPOSE! Show up the insides of these humans, look into black skulls . . . should stagger through our universe correcting, insulting, preaching,

spitting craziness — but a craziness taught to us in our most rational moments . . . . must Accuse and Attack anything that can be accused and attacked. It must Accuse and Attack because it is a theatre of Victims. It looks at the sky with the victims' eyes, and moves the victims to look at the strength in their minds and their bodies. . . . The Revolutionary Theatre must take dreams and give them a reality. . . . The Revolutionary Theatre is shaped by the world, and moves to reshape the world, using as its force the natural force and perpetual vibrations of the mind in the world. . . . Our theatre will show victims so that their brothers in the audience will be better able to understand that they are the brothers of victims, and that they themselves are victims if they are blood brothers. . . . This is a theatre of assault. The play that will split the heavens for us will be called THE DESTRUCTION OF AMERICA. [pp. 210–15, passim]

It is well to remember these dicta of his when one assays drama written and produced by Jones, particularly the more ritualistic, communal, participatory drama of the years that followed.

Finally, Jones synthesizes and condenses his thoughts about black aestheticism in the closing piece in *Home,* "STATE/MEANT," quoted earlier in this chapter.

Looking back over the content of *Home,* the reader sees a record of evolution in Jones' thinking — or perhaps more precisely, the repetitious and incremental articulation of Jones' thinking. This collection does, as one review stated, "document his five-year ideological pilgrimage from relatively mild disaffiliation to militant Black Nationalism. This pilgrimage took him from Village Bohemia to Black Harlem — or Home, as he puts it."[3] Major ideas developed in the book are the dishonesty, decadence, and oppressiveness of the social politics of the United States; cultural black nationhood as the major energy for social reform; anti-white, anti-middle-class Negro, and anti-white-liberal attitudes; and black aestheticism as an alternative to white cultural debility. Throughout, Jones is the theorist, the ideologist, for he presents practically no explicit, programmed instructions for the reordering that he envisions.

The form and technique which LeRoi Jones employs in *Home,* particularly in the earlier essays, are conventional in comparison with his poetry and later drama. Paragraphing, sentence structure, syntax, punctuation are for him not unusually innovative. Generally, his sentences tend to be long, and they are sometimes interrupted or followed by long parenthetical material. There is an overall tendency toward a certain expansiveness, a restatement of ideas throughout any given essay ("What Does Nonviolence Mean?" is a good example), as if Jones in a spirit of *copia* wants to make sure that his reader does not miss any key point whatever. He does not write particularly aphoristically, but certain phrases stick out because of their ideological or rhetorical impact. And the poet in him at times triumphs.

The rather conventional mechanics in *Home* does not mean, however, that the essays are not stylistically distinctive. The later essays especially demonstrate Jones' movement to a more individualistic, unconventional, and at times unmistakably spontaneous prose style, as in "The Last Days of the American Empire (Including Some Instructions for Black People)" with its sudden outcries, its dashes and exclamation points, its "I"-"you" point of view, and its crackling imagery. Even the titles of some of the book's essays could have been written only by a LeRoi Jones.

The distinctive Jonesian humor is in evidence. For example, in developing a point against the proponents of love as the prime means of winning the racial struggle, he announces: "FACT: 'People should love each other' sounds like Riis Park at sundown. It has very little meaning to the world at large" (p. 119). And in discussing professional boxing, he notes, "Most of the Dempseys in America now don't have to knock heads for a living (except as honest patrolmen) . . ." (p. 160). Concerning the old idea that slaves were "grinning woogies strumming on the cotton bales," he notes that "men like Caesar, Gabriel, Denmark Vesey, Nat Turner, and so many others were not killed for strumming banjos" (p. 98). And he is not above self-directed humor. For instance, he makes fun of Negroes living a bohemian life "full of beguiling stories about their former existences as underprivileged (i.e., before they, like discovered ART, or THE WHITE THIGH . . ." (pp. 224–25).

In terms of tone as a technique, the chronology of the essays shows Jones growing increasingly positive in attitude, increasingly scathing toward the "enemy," increasingly dogmatic, increasingly prone to generalization without substantive documentation, and increasingly hate-tinged.

Criticism of *Home* in standard reviewing media at the time was mainly negative. This applies to both content and technique. *Atlantic*'s resident reviewer Oscar Handlin concluded: "Formlessness . . . provides cover for the untalented. That accounts for the inflation of LeRoi Jones's reputation. Home . . . reveals how meager are his gifts as a writer."[4] *Time* said, "In his 1964 play, *The Toilet,* Jones gave painful promise of developing his gifts as a writer. In this disjointed collection of essays, the promise is flatly withdrawn. Jones clings raptly to his privileged role as victim, and has settled for a career as blackwash expert."[5] *Newsweek* sadly intoned, "LeRoi Jones is still a young man, but it is now necessary to inter him as a writer, young and kicking. In his collection . . . he writes and harangues himself out of the company of civilized men; and barring some surprising regeneration that is nowhere indicated, he forfeits all claim to serious attention, certainly as a social critic."[6] Robert Bone, of the white critics possibly the most respected by Negroes, concluded that the essays "signal an aesthetic breakdown, a fatal loss of artistic control. The prose disintegrates, the tone becomes hysterical, and all pretense of logical argument is abandoned. The style, shall we say, is severely disturbed."[7]

In addition to style, two things in particular got Jones into trouble with reviewers, his anger and his strong stances on racial matters. Said one review, "Dramatist-essayist Jones styles himself the blackest-angriest writer around."[8] *Newsweek* saw a parallel: "Jones begins with some home truths and fabricates out of them a colossal lie. That lesson he has learned from the true masters of the art. Alter some of the elements and Jones' essays would have gone over big in Berlin and Munich, round about 1933."[9] Where one stands on the question of whether Jones is a racist or an angry realist depends — subjectively and objectively — upon one's orientation and attitude. One who has implicit faith in America's ability and will to recognize and cure her racial ills must view Jones as a supremely paranoid and short-sighted man. One who despairs of America's approaching even near her stated ideals of justice and equality must hopefully regard Jones as a messianic man of truth. All would do well to consider the words of Faith Berry: "He notes . . . 'something...I aspire to is the craziness of all honest men.' In certain passages, before his own beliefs overtake him, he fulfills it, not only with the craziness of his own honesty, but with moments of truth."[10]

"The song and the people is the same": *Blues People*

Blues People is one of the best, possibly the best, book ever written on that peculiarly American phenomenon, jazz. In terms of its scope, stated as "The Negro Experience in White America and the Music that Developed from It," the book is an ambitious undertaking. As a treatise on the social history of jazz, there is no doubt that this book is without peers. Jones calls it a "theoretical endeavor" that "proposes more questions than it will answer" (p. ix).

Blues People is as much sociology as it is jazz analysis. This is the thing which sets this book apart from other histories of jazz — its emphasis upon the sociological (and psychological) causations of jazz. One reviewer went so far as to claim that the book is not about jazz at all, "but a book about the change through history of Negro attitudes and status in the United States, with Negro musicians seen as an index and metaphor of that change."[11] Nat Hentoff, a critic well qualified in the field of jazz and competent in the field of sociology, wrote of the book that it is "The first book of importance which attempts to analyze the history of Negro music in America—particularly jazz—in the context of the psychological, sociological and economic changes in Negro communities as the music evolved. There are debatable interpretations in the book, but as a whole, it has to be considered indispensable for anyone interested in the sources of the Negro American style in music."[12]

The central premise of *Blues People* may be found in its statement that "The most expressive Negro music of any given period will be an exact reflection of what the Negro himself is. It will be a portrait of the Negro in America at that particular time" (p. 137). Jones the social historian sees distinct *"stages in the Negro's transmutation from African to American"* (p. x). A corollary premise of his is that:

> Music, as paradoxical as it might seem, is the result of thought. It is the result of thought perfected at its most empirical, *i.e.,* as *attitude,* or *stance.* Thought is largely conditioned by reference; it is the result of consideration or speculation against reference, which is largely arbitrary. There is no *one* way of thinking, since reference (hence value) is as scattered and dissimilar as men themselves. If Negro music can be seen to be the result of certain attitudes, certain specific ways of thinking about the world (and only ultimately about the *ways* in which music can be made), then the basic hypothesis of this book is understood. The Negro's music changed as he changed, reflecting shifting attitudes or (and this is equally important) *consistent attitudes within changed contexts.* And it is *why* the music changed that seems most important to me. [pp. 152–53]

He goes so far as to say that "It seems possible to me that some kind of graph could be set up using samplings of Negro music proper to whatever moment of the Negro's social history was selected, and that in each grouping of songs a certain frequency of reference could pretty well determine his social, economic, and psychological states at that particular period" (p. 65). He develops, for example, that Afro-American secular music flourished after slavery when masters were no longer around to see that "safe" music was sung and played; that classic or formal blues came into vogue because of rigid segregation of places of entertainment and because Negroes began to assimilate the white appreciation of the artifact; that the eagerness of the rising Negro middle class to take on white culture values increased the contemplative, and decreased the spontaneous and expressive quality in jazz; that social and economic pressures moved swing music from "verb to noun"; that be-bop music reflected the Negro's attempt to drag jazz again outside the bland mainstream of American popular music; that the transition from "cool" jazz to "soul" music was a "form of social regression."

The *why*'s, then, inform this book. And the student of jazz is no student, theoretically, unless he knows these *why*'s. In most instances, Jones reasonably supports his theoretical *why*'s. Goldberg goes so far as to say that "in every instance he has a rational sociological or economic reason for a change in musical style."[13] Another writer, knowledgeable about literature but not generally regarded as knowledgeable about jazz, is not of the same mind: "Jones is hard put throughout the work to isolate the unadulterated African and Negro elements in American blues and jazz, and the elaborate sociological conclusions he draws from his investigations appear somewhat disproportionate to the evidence he offers."[14]

Jones makes no claims about jazz being a strictly Africa-derived art form. To the contrary, he makes the point that jazz is an indigenous art form that could have developed only in America. Regarding the blues, which is basic to all evolved states of jazz, he writes, "It is a native American music, the product of the black man in this country: or to put it more exactly the way I have come to think about it, blues could not exist if the African captives had not become American captives" (p. 17). Jazz, he points out, "is easily the most cosmopolitan of any Negro music, able to utilize almost any foreign influence within its broader spectrum. And blues benefited: it was richer, more universal, and itself became a strong influence on the culture it had depended upon for its growth" (p. 93). Carrying this thesis further, he makes what seems at first to be an un-Jonesian statement:

The point is that Afro-American music did not become a completely American expression until the white man could play it! Bix Beiderbecke, more than any of the early white jazzmen, signified this development because he was the first white jazz musician, the first white musician who brought to jazz he created the *ultimate concern* Negro musicians brought to it as a casual attitude of their culture. This development signified also that jazz would someday have to contend with the idea of its being an art (since that *was* the white man's only way into it). The emergence of the white player meant that Afro-American culture had already become the expression of a particular kind of American experience, and what is most important, that this experience was available intellectually, that it could be learned." [pp. 154–55]

This is not to say, though, that Jones minimizes African influences. Through-out the book he carefully delineates vestiges of African music and other forms of African culture present throughout the continuum of jazz. An early and ob-vious influence was the West African songs which informed the Negro's work songs which in turn were the immediate predecessors of blues. Another is the expressive, as different from the cultivated, human voice. As a jazz instrument, the black voice is not "legitimate" in regard to pitch, timbre, vibrato, and rhythm, preferring the African tradition of indirect expression. Rather than lack of proper training, the jazz singer's hoarse tone, his over- or under-pitch, and his off-the-beat rhythm reflect his degree of artistic individuality or expressive-ness. Jones also points out direct carry-overs and adaptations from African mu-sic. For instance, the upside-down metal wash basin used as a percussion in-strument by early folk musicians was a substitute for the African hollow log drum, and the banjo and xylophone originated in Africa. And he claims that the Negro spiritual "Swing Low, Sweet Chariot" had its thematic and musical origins in a region near the Victoria Falls in Central Africa.

As these few examples show, Jones is keenly aware of African origins and influences on Afro-American music. His job, then, in *Blues People* is to show how these strains were shaped by American social, musical, and other forces into the various phases and types of jazz. As one who is familiar with Jones' thinking might expect, Jones respects those forms of jazz that are closest to "roots" and blackness and are furthest from commercialism and whiteness.

In much of his material Jones is not different from other jazz historians. Like Jones, they point out such things as the transition from call-and-response song patterns to ensemble interplay in jazz orchestras, the closeness of reli-gious and secular Afro-American music, the melding of French and African musical elements in New Orleans, and the difference between the original and the classic blues singers. Like other writers about jazz, for certain source ma-terials on early forms of jazz he relies upon or quotes musical historians and folklorists such as Krehbiel, Odum and Johnson, Lomax, and Ramsey, and upon contemporaries such as Stearns, Ramsey, and Finkelstein — all of these being rather "standard" authorities.

There is no question that Jones was exceptionally well qualified to have at-tempted such a book. No critic denies this. Yet, the expert was subject to human error and human poor judgment. The book has omissions: To note a few, Jones says little about early musicians such as Fate Marable; little about the influence of country and western music on jazz; little about Charlie Mingus as a fore-runner of "the new Black music"; and while negating many aspects of Negro religious music as valid black music he seems to forget that there is a close tie, a reciprocity, between this music and jazz, as manifested by jazz artists like Ray Charles. He makes some historical mistakes: For instance, the truth is Duke Ellington did not attend college; Pee Wee Russell was not a member of the Austin High School gang. Finally, he errs in technical matters: He should know, for instance, that the tone of white, alto-saxophonist Paul Desmond is not "legitimate," for it is as nonclassical as the tone of Charlie Parker, but in a different way; that Billie Holiday was not an "expressive" blues singer, for she relied heavily upon the thirty-two bar popular song form rather than upon the blues form; that John Lewis' music is not a good example of Afro-American elements in that Lewis is noted for European classical elements in his compositions.

Jones is least convincing, least lucid when he must deal with the technical aspects of the music he is writing about. Why this is so is not certain, for Jones does have an understanding of the theory of music. There are two plausible hypotheses for this weakness in the book. One is that Jones simply may not know *enough* about music to grasp fully what is going on in *all* types of jazz, for its forms are varied and it is at times an extremely complex music. The other is that even if he does fully understand the technical aspects of jazz, he may have experienced difficulty in translating his knowledge into terms that the lay reader could understand.

A thing that some object to about *Blues People* is Jones' characteristic positions about anything involving white and black people. Witness the reaction of one critic:

> The undertaking has less . . . to do with information than with public speaking. . . . Yet this fancy-talk of the social sciences is not used to describe or even to analyze, but to condemn and to despise. There are times when the belief in original virtue, a concept Mr. Jones has invented to oppose the original sin of being Black in White America, sounds either histrionic or professional, and in *Blues People,* for all its clever discussion . . . does little more than attempt to create a system or dogma of evil and innocence by sheer classroom oratory. Unfortunately he makes this attempt in the very language of the "deadeningly predictable mind of white America."[15]

As to proportion and balance, in *Blues People* Jones is strong in his discussion of types of jazz in mode around the time that he wrote the book, the jazz that developed during his own time. The London *Times* praised the last section of the book as a "long and complete orientation of the extraordinary, diverse and vital jazz scene today."[16] This is the jazz that he was to write about later in *Black Music.*

As to style, *Blues People* is conventional exposition, conventionally written. It is lucid, interesting. One may find valid reason to disagree with Richard Howard who says that Jones uses "the latest jargon of the social sciences."[17] On the contrary, LeRoi Jones has studiously avoided highly technical jargon in favor of plain diction. If anything, *Blues People* is tinged with common or slang idioms. As we noted earlier, in prose Jones is given to full statement and to repetition, and *Blues People* is no exception. One can find his central theses restated throughout the book, as if he were "padding"; this, however, is a Jonesian way of emphasizing what he considers important. This style annoyed some reviewers, for example one who complained that "Jones has the rare faculty of making a point seem obvious after he has made it. But he has overcomplicated an already complex discussion by his own sense of revelation and his endless italicized modifications. These last are sometimes irritating and unnecessary; too often, we already *know* what he was *talking* about."[18]

All things considered, *Blues People* is the best available book on the sociology of jazz music. It certainly is one of the select, few books that anyone interested in jazz must read. Our author may not be the comprehensive scholar that Sterling Brown is nor the meticulous jazz historian that Marshall Stearns is, but he certainly understands and feels contemporary jazz as well as any jazz authority.

Fortunately, LeRoi Jones' command of language is such that he can write about jazz as well as any authority. And significantly, his writing is invested with a passion and a commitment that give *Blues People* a rare vitality.

"A way into God": *Black Music*

Black Music is an anthology of interviews, reviews, essays, reportage, phonograph album liner-notes, commentary, and criticism written by Jones during the period 1961–66. Most were first published in *Down Beat;* others are from *Negro Digest, Kulchur, Wild Dog,* and other media. Several entries, including the important final chapter, "The Changing Same," which traces the development of jazz to its present state, he wrote expressly for this book. The volume would seem to be a mixed bag, but there is strong thematic unity. (There had been some concern on the part of the publisher about a possible "magazine flavor" that record reviews and interviews might give to the book.) In some way, all works in the book address themselves to The New Jazz—Jones calls it The

New Black Music. In fact, as a composite, *Black Music* is a definitive apology for this phase of jazz. To Jones' credit as a jazz critic, he recognized this coming phase as early as the beginning of the 1960's, at a time when most critics were just beginning to define the waning "cool" and "post-bop" jazz. But it was 1965 before Jones named this phenomenon The New Black Music.

Jones' ideas about the black aesthetic are operative in this book. The music he praises most is that which he feels most closely reflects emotional states and life styles of black people, and the musicians he praises most are those who in words or in music express what Jones considers black cultural nationalism. In his opinion, the more alien the music to what Jones considers the vapid American mainstream of popularized or commercialized jazz, the more valid it is as art. In other words, blackness is the essential ingredient in this new music — the black aesthetic made manifest in music. In one account of a musical performance, Jones graphically describes the plight of a white pianist who, playing with black musicians, finally sprawls on the floor under the piano because he has been "pushed by forces he could not use or properly assimilate" (p. 138).

In keeping with his theory about art as life, Jones insists that this music must emanate from the artist's emotional engagement in black life, from "his own blood tone" (p. 135). In keeping with his theory of the superiority of feeling over contemplation, Jones insists that the music be essentially expressive — that "it should reflect only its maker" (p. 159). Jones exhorts black musicians to exceed the existing limits of form and content:

> The point . . . is to *move* it away from what we already know, toward, into, what we only *sense*. Music is for the senses. Music should make you *feel*. But, finally, unless you strip yourself of outside interference, almost all your reactions will be *social*. (Like a man who digs Mozart because it is "high class," dig it?) But the point of living seems to me to get to your actual feelings, as, say, these musicians want always to get to theirs. If you can find out who you are (you're no thing), then you can find out what you feel. Because we *are* our feelings, or our lack of them.[19]

At this point the musician becomes mystic or prophet or priest: "Yes, it is music which, under the best fingers, is a consciously Spiritual Music" (p. 137). The New Black Music is the "consciousness of social reevaluation and rise, a social spiritualism" (p. 210). It is "a way into God" (p. 193).

LeRoi Jones realizes that the young breed playing this new jazz tends to be trained musicians, that is, they have been formally exposed to western European classical music. Jones claims that "the new musicians have had to break through these whiteners to get at the sound and music they play now'' (p. 202). He warns that "The New Music (any Black Music) is cooled off when it begins to reflect blank, any place 'universal' humbug'' (p. 198). He sees a danger for the young black musicians, "the danger of becoming merely 'stylists,'—hip reflectors of what's going on, rather than explorers, and more than that, finders and changers, which is, believe it or not, finally where it's at'' (pp. 134–35).

Jones is on shaky ground when he tries to apply his dictum of superiority of the expressive over the reflective. Many of the new black musicians, including some whom he praises, approach their music intellectually and meditatively, consciously seeking rational musical composition. It seems that he resolves this contradiction by verbal gymnastics:

> The people who make this music are intellectuals or mystics or both. The black rhythm energy blues feeling (sensibility) is projected into the area of reflection. Intentionally. As expression . . . where each term is equally respondent. . . .
>
> These are categories which make reflection separate from expression; as Pure Expression / and Pure Reflection (if such categories are more than theoretically existent. Expression does not set out to instruct, but it does anyway...if the objects of this mind-energy are so placed that they do receive. Reflection intends to change, is a formal learning situation. . . . I said elsewhere, "Feeling predicts intelligence."[20]

In the new music he finds "the contemplative and the expressive, side by side, feeding each other'' (p. 200).

As to the interpreters and evaluators of jazz, Jones sees the white critic of jazz as disadvantaged, for the white critic appreciates the music, Jones feels, rather than understands the attitude which produces the music. That is to say, the white critic approaches the music without being aware of or suitably sensitive to its emotional and social content. Hence, since most jazz critics "began as hobbyists or boyishly brash members of the American petit bourgeoisie, whose only claim to any understanding about the music was that they knew it was *different;* or else they had once been brave enough to make a trip into a Negro slum to hear their favorite instrumentalist defame Western musical tradition. . . . most jazz criticism tends to enforce white middle-brow standards of excellence as criteria for performance of a music that in its most profound manifestations is completely antithetical to such standards . . .'' (pp. 15–16).

As we noted above, to Jones' credit he was one of the first to identify and interpret the new jazz when it was in its formative stages, before critics, black or white, were sufficiently aware of what was going on. They could not interpret the music for their readers, and they could not do what Jones considers to be the job of a critic, "to tell what is of value and what is not, and hopefully, at the time it first appears" (p. 17). At the time that they first appeared, Jones' critical prescience indicated the future artistic success (or popularity?) of such artists as The Supremes and Dione Warwick. As to instrumental artists, as early as 1961 he identified by name the men considered to be the 1970's avant-garde. Later he was to say, "For the most part [my list] proved accurate, but some of the musicians listed were given more credit, than their later performances, lives, etc. have proved out, usually because at the time they were moving under the influence of some of the real innovators and movers" (p. 79). The "real innovators and movers" who proved Jones' prophetic powers as a critic included Ornette Coleman, Eric Dolphy, Don Cherry, Freddie Hubbard, Wilbur Ware, Charlie Haden, and Cecil Taylor—all became giants in the new jazz. In a 1959 article he "introduced" Wayne Shorter, who was to become a top saxophonist by the late 1960's. In 1962 he predicted that "it will take years before most 'change-ears' even admit Cecil [Taylor] and Ornette [Coleman] are playing jazz" (p. 105).

It must be said, though, that Jones' critical considerations of most of these black musicians are blatantly hagiographic. He is given to writing in superlatives:

. . . John Coltrane is the most impressive voice on the tenor saxophone of our times. [p. 68]

Wilbur Ware backed Earl up with the wildest accompaniment behind a singer I've ever heard. [p. 98]

Sun-Ra's . . . *The Heliocentric World of Sun-Ra* is one of the most beautiful albums I have ever heard. [p. 129]

These two players, Pullen and Graves, are making some of the deepest music anywhere. It wants nothing. [p. 157]

If Jones is given to grammatical superlatives, he is also given to superlatively inventive language in *Black Music*. His diction is fresh, often electrifying in its impact. The Jonesian humor is everywhere in evidence. The well-turned, startling phrase is commonplace. His syntax is erratic, or strange, fitting the intent rather than the rule. The style seems compulsive. Illustrative of these characteristics is the following passage:

> The cool was a whitened degenerative form of bebop. And when mainline America was vaguely hipped, the TV people (wizards of total communication) began to use it to make people buy cigarettes and deodorants...or put life into effeminate dicks (uhh, detectives). Then the white boys slid into all the studio gigs, playing "their" music, for sure.
>
> So-called "pop," which is a citified version of Rock'n'Roll (just as the Detroit-Motown Sound is a slick citified version of older R&B-Gospel influenced forms) also sees to it that those TV jobs, indeed that dollar-popularity, remains white. Not only the Beatles, but any group of Myddle-class [sic] white boys who need a haircut and male hormones can be a pop group. That's what pop means. Which is exactly what "cool" was, and even clearer, exactly what Dixieland was, complete with funny hats and funny names...white boys, in lieu of the initial passion, will always make it about funny hats...which be their constant minstrel need, the derogation of the real, come out again. [pp. 204–5]

Overall, *Black Music* is extremely stylized in comparison with *Blues People.*

This is not to say, however, that Jones is not lucid. He can be as graphic as he is in the following passages which describe in lay terms the complex musical style of John Coltrane:

> The seeming masses of sixteenth notes, the *new* and finally articulated concept of using whole groups of clusters of rapidly fired notes as a chordal insistence rather than a strict melodic progression. That is, the notes that Trane was playing in the solo became more than just one note following another, in whatever placement, to make a melody. They, the notes, came so fast and with so many overtones and undertones, that they had the effect of a piano player striking chords rapidly but somehow articulating separately each note in the chord and its vibrating sub-tones. . . . Coltrane's reaction to the constant pounding chords and flat static, if elegant, rhythm section, was to try to play almost every note of the chord separately, as well as the related or vibrating tones that chord produced. The result, of course, is what someone termed "Sheets of Sound" . . . the long surging chordal line seems at times to shatter into hundreds of different related notes . . .[21]

And he can be as poignant and as lyrical as he is in *The Dark Lady of the Sonnets:*

> Nothing was more perfect than what she was. Nor more willing to fail. (If we call failure something light can realize. Once you had seen it, or felt whatever thing she conjured growing in your flesh.)

At the point where what she did left singing, you were on your own. At the point where what she was was in her voice, you listen and make your own promises.

More than I have felt to say, she says always. More than she has ever felt is what we mean by fantasy. Emotion, is wherever you are. She stayed in the street.

The myth of the blues is dragged from people. Though some others make categories no one understands. A man told me Billie Holiday wasn't singing the blues, and he knew. O.K., but what I ask myself is what had she seen to shape her singing so? What, in her life, proposed such tragedy, such final hopeless agony? Or flip the coin and she is singing, "Miss Brown To You." And none of you cats would dare cross her. One eye closed, and her arms held in such balance, as if all women were so aloof. Or could laugh so.

And even in the laughter, something other than brightness, completed the sound. A voice that grew from a singer's instrument to a woman's. And from that (those last records critics say are weak) to a black landscape of need, and perhaps, suffocated desire.

Sometimes you are afraid to listen to this lady.[22]

In summary, it may safely be said that *Black Music* is a complete survey of this type of jazz as seen by one who understands what is going on in it and who has the verbal powers to interpret and to explicate this music for the public. The very least that can be said about the book is what veteran jazz critic John Wilson declared — that *Black Music* is "the first even adequate explanation of what this new jazz is about."[23]

Kawaida: *A Black Value System*

"Simple faith, like church people say and that's what we want — hardrock emotional faith in what we're doing. The same way your grandmamma used to weep and wring her hands believing in Jeez-us, that deep deep connection with the purest energy, this is what the Nationalist must have" (p. 13). The Kawaida doctrine set forth in this thin publication is to supply just such a need for the "Nationalist." It is based upon seven principles, the Nguzo Saba: Umoja (Unity), Kujichagulia (Self-Determination), Ujima (Collective Work and Responsibility), Ujamaa (Co-operative Economics), Nia (Purpose), Kuumba (Creativity), and Imani (Faith).

Kawaida is really more a practical ethical system than it is a theoretical and structured religion. Or to say the same thing in other words, it is a calculated religion that has as a major goal the ordering of its adherents' lives to the extent that they are "predictable" in their behavior; and this desired behavior is one that Imamu Amiri Baraka feels will unify black people's minds and actions for their mutual well-being. Actually, Kawaida is the doctrine of Maulana Karenga, and it is "the spine and total of the US organization" (p. 2). In *A Black Value System,* Baraka is Kawaida's interpreter, advocate, and priest. He says in the work that at the time the doctrine is in "the head and hands mostly of organization people, and a few key organizers and student leaders around the country. . . . But soon it will be published and available to most of us" (p. 16). In 1972 Baraka published *Kawaida Studies: The New Nationalism,* a collection of six essays which he says in the introduction "are direct interpretations of the doctrine (political philosophy and religion) of Kawaida" (p. 7). (With the exception of "Strategy and Tactics of a PanAfrikan Nationalist Party," the essays in this volume are also in *Raise,* published the same year.)

Once the system of values is known and adopted, *A Black Value System* says, it "will transform black people and by doing this, transform yes, America" (p. 16). The seven principles, he says, are like the Ten Commandments, "yet more profound to us. . . . If there is *Umoja,* for instance, thou cannot kill, steal, bear false witness, commit adultery, or any of the things the western world thrives on" (p. 2). He feels that at any level this black value system is superior to the "practiced morality of Euro-American civilization" and is therefore beneficial to black people.

As one who knows of Jones' insistence upon the totality of religious experience might expect, the value system is applicable in and serves to interrelate all aspects of life—political, religious, social, economic, ethical, creative, historical, institutional. Beyond the pragmatic elements—unity, self-determination, cooperative or communal economics—the adherent is asked to embrace another tenet: he is asked to rely upon faith in blackness first and then upon faith in black leaders, teachers, parents.

Baraka holds that the seven principles are solutions to the political dilemma of black people. One can see easily how adherents to Kawaida, indoctrinated in principles such as unity, collective work, and faith in its leaders, would be in fact a predictable political bloc—at least to the extent that the leaders are predictable. It is when one considers this point that one inevitably recalls history's precedents of political power generated by individuals or leaders who had molded blocs of followers into predictable behavior patterns.

Baraka seems to be advocating individualism and freedom when he calls for black creativity, or Kuumba, as an "antidote to birth or mind control" (p. 12). But at the same time he instructs black creators: "You must ask of each new idea or dissociation that comes to mind, what does this have to do with bringing about unity for black people, what does it contribute to black people's self-determination—does it have anything to do with Ujima, collective work and responsibility, and so on" (pp. 12–13).

Imamu says that Kawaida, calling for no ritual dogma, "is spiritual without being religious" (p. 14). But one is hard put to square this absence of ritual in the value system with the presence of ritualistic drama, greetings, gestures, ceremonies, speech idioms, and the like in his headquarters in Newark. Here there is a formalistic, paramilitary manner in which routine affairs are conducted.

It seems fair criticism to say that in this work Baraka is not specific about just how Kawaida could grow to any more than cult proportions. To say that the system will transform black people is easy enough, but simply saying such a process will take place does not make it happen. For one thing the Nguzo Saba is not really unique; these principles are explicit or inherent in other value systems, ethical systems, and religions. Moreover, simple belief or faith in a principle does not mean that its adherents will live by that principle. Man's principles and man's actions are not often correlated *in toto,* and Baraka's system seems not to have any special features to insure the wedding of the two. Furthermore, this system is still another in a continuum of ethical, spiritual, and other types of panaceas for black people, and it seems not to have any features more attractive than, say, those of the Nation of Islam, the Church of God in Christ, the Catholic Church, or the Black Panthers.

At this point, then, it would be well to look again at the statement by Baraka quoted at the beginning of this discussion of *A Black Value System.* Its adherents are asked to believe, to have "hardrock emotional faith." The Imamu asks his followers to "believe past any bullshit 'rationale' that we may or may not achieve based on 7 million subjective-objective variables" (pp. 13–14).

Those are just too many variables.

"Concrete directions": *Raise Race Rays Raze*

Raise Race Rays Raze, as its subtitle states, is a collection of post-1965 essays. It is a continuation of *Home* in that it presents nothing startlingly or dramatically new in terms of ideology or style. Yet one is aware that the man has moved, that Baraka, not Jones, is the author. He seems to have evolved in inevitable fashion. And one notes that the man has neither retired nor been deterred in this evolutionary process.

The content of the volume varies from essay to essay, but there is a strong thematic unity throughout. Here Baraka is the revealer, the expository writer, as he has always been, but in *Raise* he adds another dimension — he gives more explicit directions. As he, himself, said, the essays in this book "offer concrete direction for the new black man."[24] Baraka is here indeed the Imamu, the spiritual leader who rails against the evil, gives instructions on how to overcome the evil, and provides the shibboleths and the litany for the Jihad.

In "Mwalimu Texts," for instance, he seeks to establish the righteousness of the Jihad:

We mean only good faith and good works and beauty to the world. We are ultimately constructive forces. We are positive spirits. . . . Our ideology is "give power to the bringers of positive change."

We live in a world now, where the real work cannot be spoken of clearly. We believe our children will get to the real work. We will make the real work possible. Before the real work can be done, the disease, the power of evil, must be cleared away. [p. 167]

As he had said as early as 1967 in "The Need for a Cultural Base to Civil Rites & Bpower Mooments," reprinted in *Raise,* "No movement shaped or contained by Western culture will ever benefit Black people. Black power must be the actual force and beauty and wisdom of Blackness...reordering the world" (p. 47). And in "The Fire Must Be Permitted to Burn Full Up: Black 'Aesthetic,'" he teaches:

Revolution, will provide the fire in your loins, them hot rithms, jim. Work is the spirit of rhythm. Carry yr book with you. Hard work. Brutal work. (Sing sing, song in yr back pocket. Build a house, man. Build a city. A Nation. This is the heaviest work. A poem? One page? Ahhhh man, consider 200,000,000 people, feed and clothe them, in the beauty of god. That is where it's at. and yeh, man, do it well. Incredibly Well. [pp. 122–23]

Then in "7 Principles of US Maulana Karenga & The Need for a Black Value System," a very slightly revised (mainly by elisions) *A Black Value System* (discussed earlier in this chapter), he states the Nguzo Saba which must guide the lives of black people as they go about reordering their lives.

The true Imamu, seeing with "the Eye of God," is the exposer and scourger of the hypocritical or mislead brothers and sisters, false prophets, and fallible priests. In *Home* and in other of his earlier writing, Jones often focused condemnation on Negroes, i.e., Americans of African descent who were ideologically more traditional than he. In *Raise* he focuses condemnation less on Negroes and more on those ostensibly more attuned to black nationalism, or those with supposedly high levels of black consciousness. For example, in "Negro Theater Pimps Get Big Off Nationalism" the eye focuses on those he considers the idolators and the misled ("Eldridge Cleaver and his misguided jeworiented revolutionaries"), the exploiters ("Jim Brown, Bobby Hooks all sucking around looking black for white"), the:

> . . . robot kneegrows, lustful winduptoys created by massa in response to the power of Black Nationalism, mack around the pseudo "liberated zones" of America being black, as Weldon Smith says, "for a quick fuck," in for instance literature, theater, graphics, &c. so there are these same pimps, like the dream fulfillment numbers of panting whiteladies who feared their peeholes would dry up under the sudden late SNCC, late Malcolm decamp of young Black people from out the various villages, Haight-Ashburys, &c. existing in the main area of "the movement" itself. [p. 129]

and the Black Panthers, "sincere but purposefully misled brothers, getting shotup because some nigger was emotionally committed to white people, are extreme examples of PimpArt gone mad" (p. 129).

But he will turn away no possible convert, no possible ally or source of ways and means. This idea of using any person or any group or any institution in any way in which that person's or group's or institution's talents and capabilities may help the cause is becoming increasingly an important precept in Baraka's thinking. Imamu does not intend, however, that contact with the less-than-righteous will mean deviation from righteousness. He would use the good and ignore the evil:

> I can learn from anybody and anything. I could learn something from a pile of Nixon under a stoop. But I will not confuse my identity with its. This is the Nationalist's position. We must survive (and this is the only way we *will* survive) as a nation, as a culture. [p. 130]

The 1972 Black Political Convention in Gary, Indiana, in which Amiri Baraka played a key role, had as one of its slogans "Unity without Uniformity," certainly Barakan in thought. One may remember his early political activities in Newark in which he sought an alliance of Blacks, Puerto Ricans, and "those white people who don't think it's beneath their dignity to be intelligent."[25] One may recall, too, Baraka's speeches and public statements since then in which he has made this point.

This precept of using whoever or whatever may be of value in furthering black nationalism is predicated upon the sure knowledge that a few dedicated, spiritual visionaries working alone are not sufficient. In "The Practice of the New Nationalism" Imamu advises:

> In the cities, political power is a national priority. The nationalist aims for an organized community. This is our only survival. *You cannot organize Black people* by shouting *"Kill the Pig."* I know. You can only get the pig to look at you very closely, and try to kill you. . . .
>
> Involve all levels of the community in nationalist programs. Involve nationalism in possibly accomodationist [sic] programs. The *strongest center* will dominate. . . . We must not alienate this mass of Blacks who constitute the majority of us. So that a program for "integrating" administrations of this or that are good programs for nationalists to get behind, because in so doing they can hook up with great segments of the community, usually segments that include professionals as well as the unemployed. [pp. 162–63]

Several other essays in *Raise* bear mentioning, but for different reasons. One is "Poetry and Karma," a key statement of Jones poetic principles, previously printed in the now defunct *Diplomat* magazine. In it he theorizes that "Art is a highvoltage culture-reflect. Poetry the mode of thought trying to spiritualize itself. Sound-rhythm (image) in imitation of the *elementals* of the universe. So it digs deeper, goes to, beyond, the edge of 'meaning' recreates language feeling, to bring us closer to these elementals, beyond where the 'intellect' reaches" (p. 22). Predictably, he asserts that:

> White poetry is like white music (for the most part, and even taking into account those "imitations" I said, which are all as valid as W C Williams writing about Bunk Johnson's band. Hear the axles turn, the rust churned and repositioned. The death more subtly or more openly longed for. Creeley's black box, Olson's revivication of the dead, Ginsberg's screams at his own shadowy races or the creepier elements completely covered up with silver rubied garbage artifacts and paintings and manners and ideas, my god, they got a buncha ideas, and really horrible crap between them and anything meaningful. They probably belch without feeling. [p. 23]

but:

The world we black poets are making is for the new peoples, the growing, the vital, the heroic in the face of, the pure lyric, song above horror, or horror music of the place we are at, or the peace we manage somehow to find, if we know about the godly evolution of life, when it all is refined into spirit.

The people the black poetry speaks of are forerunners and descendants of the inheritors, the spirit people, The First ("primitive") and next "modern" phase. [p. 26]

Second, there are two essays dealing with the concept of nationalism. As we observed in chapter 2, "Meanings of Nationalism" seems to be a Jones continuation toward a crystalization of the concept of black nationalism. A related essay is "The Practice of the New Nationalism" in which he attempts to show how his own New Ark (Newark) is a key to understanding how "consciousness . . . can be given the people as a result of a heightened political involvement" (p. 160).

Third, there are essays and passages, heretofore relatively inaccessible, on Newark. He talks of the before, from the pre-1967 violence through the political turnover (in the sense that a black man, Kenneth Gibson, won the election as mayor over a white man, Addonizio), and the now and the future. The New Ark is envisioned by Imamu as not a provincial and temporal phenomenon but as "a base, an example, upon which one aspect of the entire Black nation can be built" (p. 163).

As can be the case in almost any volume of collected essays, there are gaps. One reviewer, sensing that some important things may have been left unsaid, protested:

Imamu, somewhere in *Raise* . . . we wish you had explained to us the moves that brought you back home to get your head whipped and begin the building of a New Ark. Explain how it felt to lose the grip of time so that the writing you so obviously love no longer could get the attention it needs. . . . Brother, we barely saw you in here. You were moving so fast, trying to describe so much. No pause for reflection. No slow understandings and overnight sittings that let the yeast work on you and cause you to rise in our consciousness as tangible and delicious as fresh baked wheat bread. . . . Explain Imamu 1971 to us. We are listening.[26]

Stylistically, *Raise* is Barakan. The reader who is familiar with this style and who knows of Baraka's creative capacity to use language might unfairly expect Baraka to exceed himself. He does not. And for this reason such a reader might feel a disappointment, perhaps a tinge of tedium. Yet there is enough going on stylistically to make the reading of previously published ideas interesting — interesting in the sense that one reads on, waiting for the Barakan word-magic that inevitably does come. In spots, his prose style is brilliant. It is not hard to agree with Jan Carew, who said in a review of *Raise,* "At his best he can make words ignite and burst into flame."[27] And there are some "bests" in *Raise.*

Chapter 5. "Projections": Fiction

"The flame of social dichotomy": *The System of Dante's Hell*

Much of the fiction of LeRoi Jones is essentially autobiographical. This is particularly true of *The System of Dante's Hell*. However, the reader should not think that the stories in *System* are literal incidents or states in Jones' life adapted to the mechanics and conventions of fiction. Rather, the reader must understand that what Jones has experienced and has seen experienced constitute the starting points for his creative "projections." As he says, "Characters take on different elements that, maybe, I reflected on. Much of it is autobiography—from situations I have been in, but most of it is projections of ideas, much later. . . . They germinate in experience. . . . Most of the time I move from real people that I know, or I move from real experiences."[1] The critical reader, then, should approach Jones' fiction not as history made exciting by narration, but as fiction germinated by history. As a matter of proportion, the creative element far outweighs the historical element.

System does contain bits of ascertainable factual autobiography. A few examples are: The reader learns of Jones' early literary interests and early attitudes about values: "Eliot, Pound, Cummings, Apollinaire were living across from Kresge's. I was erudite and talked to light-skinned women" (p. 31). He was a boy of promise, a prodigy of sorts: "'You are a young man & soon will be off to college.' They knew then, and walked around me for it" (p. 41). He began respecting blackness at an early age: "If I were Raleigh, A negress would walk up my back" (p. 57).

But the important autobiographical element in *System* is not the literal facts; it is the record of his emotional, or one could say spiritual, history. It is these emotional states that comprise the hell that Jones reports. He challenges his reader to expose himself vicariously to this hell: "This thing, if you read it, will jam your face in my shit. Now say something intelligent" (p. 15). The hell that Jones describes in *System* is:

> Hell in the head.
>
> The torture of being the unseen object, and, the constantly observed subject.
>
> The flame of social dichotomy. Split open down the center, which is the early legacy of the black man unfocused on blackness. The dichotomy of what is seen and taught and desired opposed to what is felt. [p. 153]

From the retrospective position of *System,* he can observe that:

> Hell is actual, and people with hell in their heads. But the pastoral moments in a man's life will also mean a great deal as far as his emotional references. One thinks of home, or the other "homes" we have had. And we remember w/love those things bathed in soft black light. The struggles away or towards this peace is Hell's function. . . .
>
> Once, as a child, I would weep for compassion and understanding. And Hell was the inferno of my frustration. But the world is clearer to me now, and many of its features, more easily definable. [p. 154]

The framework of this book is not patterned closely after Dante's *Inferno,* as the title and frontispiece would lead one to believe. For one thing, in terms of proportion and structure Dante's hell is architectonic; Jones' is asymmetrical. Second, Dante is a traveler in hell, a visitor; Jones is a participant, a citizen. Third, Dante is complete and systematic in his description; Jones is disjunctive, casual, impulsive in his. Fourth, Dante's description is essentially objective; Jones' is essentially subjective. A final difference, an important one that we noted earlier in this book, is Jones' placement of the heretics:

> *I put The Heretics in the deepest part of hell, though Dante had them spared, on higher ground.
>
> It is heresy, against one's own sources, running in terror, from one's deepest responses and insights...the denial of feeling...that I see as basest evil. [p. 7]

Jones' sketches of psychological-spiritual states only informally parallel Dante's schema; they fit only by contrivance, tangentially. It is true, as one writer observes, "This scaffolding gives the book an ambitious appearance, but it doesn't seem to me to serve much organic function, except, possibly, providing guidelines to the author's memory and imagination."[2] In *Black Music* Jones defines "use" as meaning "that some idea or system is employed, but in order to reach or understand quite separate and/or dissimilar systems" (p. 73). In this sense Jones has "used" in his *System* Dante's thematic concepts. As one critic phrases it, Jones has borrowed "features of the moral geography of Dante's 'Inferno.'"[3] This being so, the reader does not have to know Dante's work thoroughly in order to interpret Jones' work. Jones is no imitator.[4]

In "SOUND AND IMAGE," a sort of epilogue, he explains that "Hell in this book which moves from sound and image ('association complexes') into fast narratives is what vision I had of it around 1960–61 and that fix on my life, and my interpretation of my earlier life" (p. 153). The aggregate of these association complexes does not depict linear passage of time as in traditionally conceived narratives. With practically no editing, the chapters (or circles) could be shuffled about without appreciable damage to the book as a "novel." Too, almost any in this series of impressions or records of the states of the narrator's soul—for that is what these association complexes really are—could be omitted. Further, there is no real gradation of degrees of sin as one progresses through this hell. (It seems almost as if Jones admits failure to depict *degrees* of state of mind when he provides a note to explain why the heretics are in the deepest part of hell, as if his book does not develop or intrinsically imply why.)

The so-called association complexes convey a feeling of intensity, of compulsion, of the mind's inability to articulate what the senses perceive. Their style is of the impressionistic, but not surrealistic, stream-of-consciousness type. The associations are essentially private, as the following passage illustrates:

> If anyone ever lived in a closet, it was me. There were tracks, streets, a diner, the dark, all got between me and their strings. "You're going crazy...in here with dark green glasses and the light off." It was a yellow bulb tho, and it all sat well on my shoulders. Vague wet air thrashed the stones. It sat well, without those faggots. Or ART, 5 steps up, in a wood house: a true arc.
>
> That, and don't forget the canopied bed. The ugliest green draperies dragged and hooked across the bed. Action as completeness. If I hung out the window, it was warm and people watched.
>
> A guy named powell who is a lawyer. Air pushing. Straight stone streets. A guy named pinckney who is a teacher. (Place again, those fingers, on my strings. Walk in here smiling. Sit yourself down. Rearrange your synods, your corrections, your trees.
>
> Dolores Morgan, who had an illegitimate child*** PROSPEROUS
> Calvin Lewis, who gave it to her****PRIDE
> Think about that: Michael at a beach, in the warm tide. [p. 50]

Passage after passage of this kind of writing prompted writer John A. Williams to say, "Sometimes . . . the novel becomes too personal. It is as if the writer were thinking: I'll be damned if you're going to understand this, reader. The writer's symbols have little relationship to what we know or understand."[5] Another reviewer predicted:

> It won't sell because nobody can understand it and the farout novelists that sell—Selby, Rechy, Burroughs—can be understood. Diffident critics who tend

to find merit in what they can't comprehend can take heart, because Jones' novel offers comprehensive passages that are perfectly terrible.[6]

Still another reviewer, in spite of criticizing what he calls a "violent staccato," concludes that "This kind of writing can grow tiresome, but there is a strong cumulative effect."[7]

This reviewer is right, for as baffling as some of these pieces are, as difficult as they are to dissect and explicate, they do yield impressions—and that apparently is what author Jones intended. Certain titles themselves—"THE INCONTINENT: Lasciviousness," "The Diviners," "Thieves," for instance—indicate what the mind is reacting to and thereby stand as clues, especially if one is familiar with Jones' characteristic ways of thinking and with his attitudes. In others, the impressions or states of mind come through clearly enough. For instance: "Gluttony" is a refusal to participate in the industrialization-commercialism-materialism of urban life. "SEVEN (The Destruction Of America" finds the narrator bemoaning, "I am, as you are, caught" in a place where there is violence against "God, Nature and Art" (pp. 35–36). "The Flatterers" shows a loss of innocence and naiveté, a realization that the narrator, using baseball jargon, is "Good field/No hit!" (p. 45). "THE EIGHTH DITCH (IS DRAMA" is a dramatization of perversion of vision and corruption of the mind brought about by fraudulent counselors, symbolized by a homosexual seduction.

The two "fast narratives" which comprise the last part of the book might more properly be called short stories than might the "association complexes," for they have readily discernible story lines. The first of the two, "The Rape," begins with a group of Negro middle-class and middle-class inclined youths at a party in East Orange. They are under the subtle leadership of the narrator (a Jones "projection" of himself): "THE BEAUTIFUL MIDDLECLASS HAD FORMED AND I WAS TO BE A GREAT FIGURE, A GIANT AMONG THEM. THEY FOLLOWED WITH THEIR EYES, OR LISTENED TO SOFT MOUTHS SPILL MY STORY OUT TO GIVE THEIR WIVES" (p. 107). When a drunken, worn Negro woman happens by, they decide to kidnap and rape her, as a lark, for she is, at best, only an object for their derision. The narrator, as their leader, cannot outwardly show compassion for her. Fortunately for him, they change their minds when she tells them she is diseased, and they toss her from the moving car, while "everybody [is] screaming in the car, some insane allegiance to me" (p. 117). It is easy to apply symbolic meaning to this story, with the narrator representing the promising, college-bred young Negro who is being welcomed into the middle-class, with the young men representing the vacuous and insensitive society in which he is to be a leader, and with the woman representing the distasteful bygone black life that they will look down upon but still use to their advantage.

The other "fast narrative," entitled "The Heretics," tells of two educated, "imitation white boys" from the North who make an excursion into "The Bottom," the rough black community near the military base in the South where they are stationed. The narrator makes a sexual liaison with a local woman who though worldly wise is guileless in her emotions and unspoiled by white values. He is tempted when she asks him to stay and live with her. But being a heretic, he finds himself, to use Jones' words from his introductory note for the book, "running in terror, from one's deepest responses and insights." Then, after being robbed and beaten senseless by thugs, he awakens two days later back in the company of white men, and he is "screaming for God to help me" (p. 152). This story yields a rather obvious symbolic interpretation, especially when considered along with Jones' various other writings on the Negro-versus-black theme.

Both these stories have drawn praise. Typical are the judgments of two critics mentioned elsewhere in this chapter. Hicks calls "The Heretics" the "best in the book."[8] Capouya is even more generous in praise of these two stories, saying that "in these appalling stories the author has ordered his materials as if man were still the master of creation, and the effect on the reader is close to exaltation."[9]

Throughout the book Jonesian themes and attitudes are to be found. In connection with his theories of art and culture there are expressions of the decline of true art, of intuitive feeling as superior to intellectuality and rationality, and of the concept of words as laws. His thinking about racial matters is even more in evidence. For example, "The Heretics," as mentioned above, is an exploration of blacks' attempts to escape from their assumed whiteness to their natural blackness. "The Rape," also as mentioned above, is contemptuous of vacuity in middle-class blacks. And, of course, practically the entire book is a testament of the internal inferno that the narrator finds himself in by the circumstance of being black.

When one considers the style in *System,* one is reminded of theories of writing found in Michael Rumaker's "Uses of the Unconscious," Jack Kerouac's "Essentials of Spontaneous Prose," and the like. One can discern, if he looks for them, traces of or similarities to Joyce, Woolf, Proust, Stein, and others. It would not be inaccurate to characterize Jones' style in this book as being close to the "beat" mainstream, a mainstream that is actually a continuing experimentation that grew out of the Pound-Joyce-Cummings tradition. But regardless of stylistic influences apparent in *System,* the book is essentially Jonesian, for it abounds in Jonesian symbol-imagery, mechanics, syntax, word play, abrupt linguistic units, private allusions, twisted word meanings, "verb force," humor, "artistic obscenity"/obscenity, and dadaistic disregard for conventional form.

Illustrative of his mechanics, syntax, spelling, word play, and spontaneous tone is the following passage:

> William Love: eyes are closed. (Was that Hudson St.? Warren?) He cd, after a fashion appear in Adams' class. He had short stubbed fingers he bit for his nerves. A butt. They called him (not our lovely names...these bastards like Ora, "Big Shot," called him "Bullet Head" or "Zakong.") I had fashioned something easier for his weakness but killers like Murray ground his face in the tar, & William wd chase him. Goof train. Rebound man, wheeld & for a time, as to the properties of his life, dealed. I'm told (and so fell into disrepute. In hell the sky is black, all see what the other sees. Outside the dark is motionless & dead leaves beat the air. [p. 54]

In *System* there is humor, but there is not as much satirical humor as in his other works, possibly because the material, the method, and the purpose do not call for satire. The humor is relatively sudden and spontaneous, the "joning" or "signifying" type that urban youngsters use against each other, for example:

> But that was where the rodeos got in & Slick Andrew from the West. Dead Lillian called him Ungie, & he had a faggot brother who is probably sucking a cock right this moment. On Hillside Place or Waverly Ave. probably. Look him up, the next time you're in that city (or state). [p. 56]

Also, there is the inevitable, perhaps at times unintentional, humor that is a byproduct of any atypical writing style.

Profanity is everywhere. So are depictions of body functions, some artistically stated, some plainly vulgar, some just bad taste. Some profanity is used as symbol-imagery, as in the passage in "The Heretics" in which the narrator describes Peaches' offer to involve him in a new life style that would be compatible with his innermost self, or his true self: "We could live together and she would show me how to fuck. . . . And I felt myself smiling. . . . And felt the world grow together as I hadn't known it. All lies before, I thought. . . . A real world, of flesh, of smells, of soft black harmonies and color" (pp. 146–48). Some pro-fanity is used in an attempt to approximate realistic speech (or thought) as in this line from "THE EIGHTH DITCH (IS DRAMA": "Go fuck yrself, you crooked dick muthafucka. Nobody want nonea your crooked ass peter. Go jerk off" (p. 88). In spite of Jones' "serving up every last putrefied crapulent grind [in a] verbal orgasm," reviewer Despi Tralis found in *System,* "passages of unsur-passed exquisite beauty and personal lyrical expression."[10]

Practically all of the symbol-images discussed in chapter three of this book are in abundance in *System:* water—"We'll travel someplace wide open. Not that slow brown water. A river. Another blue eye washing out land. Water to the east" (p. 28); grey—"The bigboys beat the little boys. The sun itself was grey" (p. 30); wind—"wind shatters lips" (p. 55); meat/flesh—"If my flesh is sweet, my mind is pure" (p. 28); fingers—"The innocence of myself. Of you, under me. Of each finger dying. Egyptians, Praxiteles, Lester Young. Sources, implements under the ugly sea" (p. 25); pee—"He died in a bathroom of old age & segre-gation. His nose was stopped up and he could pee all over anybody's floor" (p. 28); pavement/concrete—"Frank was little for a long time but suddenly grew up big. Up thru the silent pavements" (p. 73); and so on.

If *System* has any claim for recognition in twentieth-century American let-ters, it will be for Jones' inventive use of language. "I don't think there is a single cliche in the book," poet-critic Dudley Randall says.[11] As to the book's con-tent, although it reveals a sort of representative hell that some blacks in America experience, the states of mind that comprise this hell are not sufficiently de-veloped and delineated to be of more than passing interest. As to themes, he expresses them better in other works.

With regard to form, the book is not really an autobiography; neither is it a novel. At least it is neither of these in the commonly accepted meanings of these terms. When one considers the form of this book, it seems to be really a themati-cally and stylistically controlled anthology. This suspicion is reinforced when one learns the following bibliographical facts: The first seven circles had been published in *Trembling Lamb;* "The Eighth Ditch" had been published as a play in *Floating Bear;* as editor of *The Moderns,* Jones had included "Hypo-crite(s)" and "Thieves" as his own contributions to this book; "The Christians" and "The Rape" had been published in Herbert Hill's anthology, *Soon One Morning;* and "The Heretics" had attracted some critical praise when it was published in *New American Story.*

Perhaps *System* could be called a novel somewhat in the sense that Virginia Woolf's stream-of-consciousness *To the Lighthouse* or James Joyce's expressionistic *Finnegan's Wake* are called novels. Or perhaps it could be a novel in the way Rumaker thinks the novel has to become: "Open, without the past clumsinesses of easy connections of plot and characterization. Done the way life does assault body and spirit: immediate, without dress, without apology or explanation—yet, all revealed." To Rumaker, *System* is "a tortured nightmare, excruciatingly honest and alive, painful and beautiful."[12]

The simple truth is that *System* defies categorization. It is simply LeRoi Jones' *System,* and its success or failure must be assessed on his terms.

Generally, critical reactions to the book have been uncomplimentary. A good cross section are those which appeared in *Newsweek, Atlantic Monthly, Bibliographic Survey,* and *The New York Review of Books. Newsweek* breezily dismissed it: "The entire book, not really qualifiable as a novel, is a diary of bad dreams, a remembrance of things aghast."[13] Phoebe Adams stated that the book is "a cryptographic narrative . . . the work of any conscientiously over-sensitive young egoist."[14] *Bibliographic Survey,* which aims for objectivity in its abstracts, called it "a collection of sixteen rambling, disconnected tales, somewhat autobiographical in nature."[15] Bergonzi guardedly phrased his judgment of the book: ". . . it doesn't seem to me a success, not, at least, by any of the standards I am used to employing."[16] The complimentary criticism that the book has generated is mainly directed, as pointed out earlier, to the "fast narratives." It could be that these particular stories are closer to traditional narratives and for this reason are received more favorably than are the "sound and image" selections.

To borrow a phrase from Jones' own definition, it is just possible that *The System of Dante's Hell* itself is "unseen object, and, the constantly observed subject."

The system of Ray's Purgatory: *Tales*

Fortunately, Jones imposed no overall schema on his *Tales,* so that he had no need to force his materials, as he may have had to do for his artificially structured *System.* Yet *Tales* is more visibly a novel than is *System.* True, this book makes no pretensions to being a novel, but as a collection, an anthology, of stories there is a thematic unity, an overall sense of chronology, and a development—from the anxiety-driven youngster in the first story who escapes an unnamed and unknown pursuer, to the self-confident narrator in the last story who elatedly realizes that "Love was heavy in the atmosphere."

One writer, complaining about the book's "erratically uneven quality," characterizes it as "an ad hoc product put together and packaged synchro-nously with its author's current notoriety."[17] But regardless of possible com-mercial purposes and the artistic merits of the individual stories, *Tales* is a unified collection. It is, as *Choice* says, "a mixture of wit and terror, projected like a missile against the white establishment."[18]

Some of the selections in *Tales* would have fitted well in the first part of *System,* for they are "sound and image" pieces that convey tortured states of mind and spirit. These include "A Chase (Alighieri's Dream)," "The Largest Ocean in the World," "New-Sense," "New Spirit," and "No Body   No Place." "A Chase (Alighieri's Dream)" is particularly Dantean. Instead of a dark wood with three beasts endangering him, the narrator here is fleeing through the wilderness that is Newark, and his dangers are undefined and unknown to him and are therefore even more terrifying. One piece, "Words," could qualify as an essay of the sort found in *Home.* The rest of the entries are similar in technique to the "fast narratives" in *System.*

As in *System,* there is autobiographical material in *Tales.* There are literal autobiographical elements, to be sure. For instance, street names in the stories are those of real streets in Newark, "THE SHORT SKINNY BOY WITH THE BUBBLE EYES" (p. 43) is by all accounts descriptive of LeRoi Jones the boy, the school that this boy attends is Jones' alma mater, Central Avenue School, and the allusions to sports accurately reflect Jones' boyhood interest in and participation in sports. In addition, the tales contain allusions to, and include as characters, actual persons such as Lynn Hope, Charlie Parker, and Sun-Ra. Most of the material is not literal autobiography but, again, Jones' fictional "projections." Author Jones, as the narrator-participant, uses incidents and perceptions from his life as starting points for the creation of fiction, as is his custom. "Salute," for example, has as its narrator a young Negro artist and writer-to-be in the military service in Puerto Rico. Jones' father, for example, is the real-life person upon whom Jones builds the fictional father named Michael in "The Death of Horatio Alger." The lines, "A window at each end. One facing the reservoir, the other, the fine-arts building where Professor Gorsun sits angry at jazz, 'Goddamnit none of that nigger music in my new building. Culture. Goddamnit, ladies and gentlemen, line up and be baptized. This pose will take the hurt away. We are white and featureless under this roof,'" (p. 23) for example, constitute a fictional reference to a former dean at Howard University.

Important in *Tales* are the autobiographical themes and stances that the stories reveal. The early tug of black versus white and black versus Negro are central in such stories as "The Alternative." The emptiness of American culture is a theme in stories like "The Largest Ocean in the World," with its lines "The dead fill the streets. And their dead thoughts. I do not know this place" (p. 33). There are expressions of an insistence upon an interrelatedness of concrete and abstract aspects of existence, such as the flat statement in "Uncle Tom's Cabin: *Alternate Ending":* "The psychological and the social. The spiritual and the practical. Keep them together and you profit, maybe, someday, come out on top. Separate them, and you go along the road to the commonest of Hells. The one we westerners love to try and make art out of" (p. 37). Art as expression is enunciated in such passages as "Having understood the most noble attempts of white men to make admirable sense of the world, now, reject them, along with any of them. And the mozarts are as childish as the hitlers. Because reflect never did shit for any of us. Express would. Express. NOW NOW NOW NOW NOW NOW" (pp. 96–97). Negroes and the Negro middle-class are attacked in lines like "These are cool Knee Grows who have a few pesos in their pockets (earned by letting whitey pass gas in their noses)" (p. 101). There are others of Jones' themes—ethnic artists as priests, creation as revelation, original virtue of blacks, black unity—practically the entire corpus of Jones' themes is in *Tales* in some form.

In addition to being read for their composite and cumulative impact, the stories may profitably be read as individual entities.

"A Chase (Alighieri's Dream)" succeeds in conveying a mood of undifferentiated fear that propels the narrator. He tells himself, "You should be ashamed. Your fingers are trembling. You lied in the garage. You lied yesterday. Get out of the dance, down the back stairs, the street, and across in the car. Run past it, around the high building. Court Street, past the Y. . . . Up one block, crooked old jews die softly under the moon. Past them. Past them" (pp. 1–2). He executes "A hip, change speeds, head fake, stop, cut back, a hip, head fake" until he can get to the place where he can "Change clothes on the street to a black suit. Black wool" (pp. 3–4). It is then, on a hill, that he can finally see "4 corners, the entire world visible from there. Even to the lower regions" (p. 4)—the hell that is Newark. Jones makes the pace of this story montage so breathless, so frantic that the reader is drawn into the story and races alongside, relaxing only after the escape has been made.

The physical setting and the premise for "The Alternative" are based upon dormitory life at Howard University. Late at night, the narrator, "The Leader," among noisy, slangy, empty-headed fellow students, ponders "Where I am, will go, have never left" (p. 7). The narrator declines to take part in their harassment of a student who is entertaining a local homosexual in his, the student's, room. The narrator tries to dissuade his classmates and for his troubles is knocked to the floor where he hears "Their voices, all these other selves screaming for blood. For blood, or whatever it is fills their noble lives" (p. 29). The problem that the narrator faces is which alternative to choose: to continue (and if so, how) his leadership of classmates who are preparing to live middle-class lives and to strive, himself, for "whatever it is fills their noble lives" or else to reject them and follow his intellectual and emotional impulses. The story is indicative of the dilemma of the individual who must decide whether to obey the impulses triggered by his sensibilities or to accept a pre-patterned and perhaps more blindly comfortable life.

In "The Screamers" Jones attemps verbal translation of the sort of ritualistic, almost mystical communal experience motivated by honking and stomping musicians who as "Ethnic historians, actors, priests of the [black] unconscious" (p. 76) finally so excite five or six hundred "hopped-up woogies" that they all pour out of the dance hall into the streets, "Ecstatic, completed, involved in a secret communal expression . . . . laughing at the dazed white men who sat behind the wheels" (p. 79). For sheer rendition of mood and atmosphere this story is artistically superb.

"Words" is a quiet and poignant vignette of an almost wasted writer who has just broken from a white way of life and who finds in Harlem little empathy:

> When I walk in the streets, the streets don't yet claim me, and people look at me, knowing the strangeness of my manner, and the objective stance from which I attempt to "love" them. . . . You will think of old facts, and sudden seeings which made you more than you had bargained for, yet a coward on the earth, unless you claim it, unless you step upon it with your heavy feet, and feel actual hardness. [p. 89]

He asks:

> Why does everyone live in a closet, and hope no one will understand how badly they need to grow? How many errors they canonize or justify, or kill behind? I need to be an old monk and not feel sorry or happy for people. [p. 90]

He realizes:

> The purpose of myself, has not yet been fulfilled. Perhaps it will never be. Just these stammerings and poses. Just this need to reach into myself, and feel something wince and love to be touched. [pp. 90–91]

Finally, he concludes:

> We turn white when we are afraid.
> We are going to try to be happy.
> We do not need to be fucked with.
> We can be quiet and think and love the silence.
> We need to look at trees more closely.
> We need to listen. [p. 91]

Some of the other stories do not succeed as well as the above examples. "Going Down Slow" is a story of a man, himself unfaithful, who discovers that his wife has been unfaithful. He attacks her lover, leaving him possibly dead. The ending is painfully amateurish: the husband goes to get high on dope, apparently for the first time. "Answers in Progress" hardly qualifies as science fiction. In it, blue-colored creatures from space make an invasion, and there is "Bamberger's burning down, dead blancos all over and a cat from Sigma Veda, and his brothers, hopping up and down asking us what was happening" (p. 128). The spacemen will not be satisfied until they have some Art Blakey phono- graph records, for "The spacemen could dig everything" (p. 128). The point of this story seems to be that black people have an affinity with all that is superior in the cosmos, but the story flounders badly. The best that Jones can contrive to end the story is to say, "That's the way the fifth day ended" (p. 132).

Jones' occasional ineptness fades when one considers his overall tech- niques, for in *Tales* he is an effective writer. For one thing, he is character- istically funny. For example, he speaks of Howard University as a place that nurtures one for "a new world of lies and stocking caps" (p. 16), asks "How can you read *Pierre* if you think your wife's doing something weird [being unfaithful]" (p. 54), and describes himself as:

> The leader, at his bed, stuck with 130 lbs. black meat sewed to failing bone. A head with big red eyes turning senselessly. Five toes on each foot. Each foot needing washing. And hands that dangle to the floor, tho the boy himself is thin small washed out, he needs huge bleak hands that drag the floor. And a head full of walls and flowers. Blinking lights. He is speaking.
> "Yeh?" [pp. 5–6]

Moreover, the reader looking for Jonesian symbols and imagery is not disap- pointed. The ones he used in *System* are here also, freshly used and still ar- tistically operative; and there are new ones. Further, there is a force and a sheer lyricism that characterize most of the stories. Even in mediocre stories there are passages of redeeming majesty. Almost always Jones the poet manages to eschew the straight declarative statement in favor of poetic metaphor and indirection. Indeed, it is the language that lifts *Tales* above the level of mediocrity. Resnik is correct when he says that Jones' "sense of poetry carries him far beyond the mere telling of his own story."[19]

One may read *Tales* just to see what it is possible to do with language.

Chapter 6. "Thought trying to spiritualize itself": Poetry

> . . . (I mean I think
> I know now
> what a poem is) A
> turning away...
> from what
> it was
> had moved
> us...
>   A
> madness.
>   ["Betancourt"]

LeRoi Jones wrote these lines early in his poetic career, while he was in Cuba in 1960. Later he was to write:

> They characterize
> their lives, and I
> fill up
> with mine. Fill up
> with what I have, with what
> I see (or
> need. I make
> no distinction. As blind men
> cannot love too quiet beauty.
>   ["Joseph To His Brothers"]

His poetry was to be more than exercises in aesthetics: "I do believe, desperately, in a 'poetry of ideas.' Poems have got, literally, to be about something."[1] Further, his ideas were to be more than exercises in philosophy:

> Art is a high-voltage culture-reflect. Poetry the mode of thought trying to spiritualize itself. Sound-rhythm (image) in imitation of the *elementals* of the universe. So it digs deeper, goes to, beyond, (the edge of "meaning" re-creates language feeling) to bring us closer to these elementals, beyond where the "intellect" reaches.[2]

So we see a poet subjugating the aesthetic, the intellectual, and the mundane to the spiritual.

One of the functions of Jones' poetry is to reveal himself to himself:

A morning poem
is to dig any new
change, inside
the skull's hairy
dynamism.
        ["Allegro con rocks"]

Poetry also functions as emotional catharsis. "I have to write poetry," he has said. "I'd last about maybe a day if I didn't. I'd go crazy. Any artist has a lot of energy that won't respond to anything else."[3] Beyond these private functions, he considers his poetry to have revelation for the society in which he finds himself:

I write poetry only to enlist the poetic consistently as apt description of my life. I write poetry only in order to feel, and that, finally, sensually, all the terms of my life. I write poetry to investigate my self, and my meaning and meanings.
    But also to invest the world with a clearer understanding of it self, but only by virtue of my having brought some clearer understanding of my self into it.
            ["GATSBY'S THEORY OF AESTHETICS"]

It is therefore not surprising to see expressed in his more recent pronouncements the idea of the black poet as the messiah, the priest, the magician whose duty it is to discover and verbalize intuitions and feelings and perceptions and to relate them as a collective spiritual consciousness, this consciousness to be used by black people as a basis for a life style.

"Nobody sings anymore": *Preface to a Twenty Volume Suicide Note*

Once he had discovered that he was a writer, Jones thought of himself as a poet primarily. This early poet, as all young poets tend to do, tested, experimented with matters of form and technique, groped and probed his own feelings and ideas. He was not quite sure of himself.

His first findings are recorded in his first volume, *Preface to a Twenty Volume Suicide Note.* Here we see, by turns, the romantic believer and idealist:

Saturday morning we listened to *Red Lantern* & his undersea folk.
At 11, *Let's Pretend/* & we did/ & I, the poet, still do, Thank God!
            ["In Memory of Radio"]

the confused young man:

It's so diffuse
being alive . . .
> ["Look for You Yesterday,
> Here You Come Today"]

the disillusioned idealist:

People laugh when I tell them about Dickie Dare!
What is one to do in an alien planet
where the people breath [sic] New Ports?
Where is my space helmet, I sent for it
3 lives ago...when there were box tops.

What has happened to box tops??
> ["Look for You Yesterday,
> Here You Come Today"]

and the despairing young man so poignantly poetized in the title poem:

Lately, I've become accustomed to the way
The ground opens up and envelopes me
Each time I go out to walk the dog.
Or the broad edged silly music the wind
Makes when I run for a bus...

Things have come to that.

But the troubled, complex, and changeable poet in this volume is also the
fantasizing incipient maverick:

I dream long bays & towers...& soft steps on moist sand.
I become them, sometimes. Pure flight. Pure fantasy. Lean.
> ["The Turncoat"]

a young man with urges and promptings too strong to be repressed:

Sometimes I feel I have to express myself
and then, whatever it is I have to express
falls out of my mouth like flakes of ash
from a match book . . .
This is *not* rage. (I am not that beautiful! Only immobile coughs
& gestures towards somethings I don't understand . . .
Mosaic of disorder I own but cannot recognize. Mist in me.
> ["Vice"]

an artist-poet who sees the failings in potentially creative artists because they:

> . . . are fools
> who hang close
> to their original
> thought.
>> ["Betancourt"]

a young man considering alternatives:

> . . . I am
> an animal watching
> his forest.
>> ["The Clearing"]

a man with a growing sense of self-sufficiency but who must still reassure himself:

>> If
> I think myself ugly
> I go to the mirror, smiling,
> at the inaccuracy . . .
>> ["The Insidious Dr. Fu Man Chu"]

and, finally, a man and artist in an alien and dangerous place who warns:

> . . . Inside
> your flat white stomach
> I move my tongue
>> ["The New Sheriff"]

The developing awareness and disaffection that we see in *Preface,* we rightly suspect, will grow into the contempt and the rage that are important energizing forces for the later poetry by this sensitive and morally self-righteous poet.

The collected poems that comprise *Preface* are lyrics in the sense that they explore deeply personal feelings and emotions. They are also lyrical in the sense that they are soft, reflective, meditative. Even the ominous "The New Sheriff" is quiet in manner. There is an absence, in this volume, of emotion-charged diction, of profanity, of phillipic, of inflammatory rhetoric. The overall mood is one of gentle insistence and calm exposition rather than devastating polemic. For pure lyricism, the title poem and the fourth stanza of "Hymn for Lanie Poo" seem unrivaled in this volume.

Of these delicate poems, several of the best are those about his wife at the time, Hettie Jones. "For Hettie" is a wistful and gentle poem which includes descriptive lines:

My wife is left-handed.
which implies a fierce de-
termination. A complete other
worldliness. ITS WEIRD, BABY. . . .

But then, she's been a bohemian
all her life...black stockings
refusing to take orders. I sit
patiently, trying to tell her
whats right. TAKE THAT DAMN
PENCIL OUTTA THAT HAND. YOU'RE
RITING BACKWARDS. & such. . . .
& now her belly droops over the seat.
They say it's a child. But
I ain't quite so sure.

"For Hettie in Her Fifth Month" expresses a husband's awe at his pregnant wife's eccentricities and ends in intellectually "hip" good humor:

A slit in the flesh,
& one of Kafka's hipsters
parked there
with a wheelbarrow.

The father-to-be is also in "Look for You Yesterday, Here You Come Today":

. . . Suddenly one is aware
that nobody really gives a damn.
My wife is pregnant with *her* child.
"It means nothing to me", sez Strindberg.

There is a poem for his sister, "Hymn for Lanie Poo." (Lanie Poo has been Mrs. Coyt Jones' nickname for daughter Sandra.) There are references to, if not poems about, Jones' friends, associates, and literary models of the time, people like Jack Kerouac, Gary Snyder, Franz Kline.

In terms of technique and form, here Jones is not unlike the other young poets of his time and literary milieu in that he continues the free verse tradition. As we noted earlier, his artistic and physical environment at the time was the world of young, maverick intellectuals and artists, all alienated in various degrees and in various ways, seeking intellectual and artistic fulfillment. Jones' forms are really nonforms, in the manner of such people as Charles Olson, who conceived of form as simply an extension of content. Jones' forms are fluid, seeking to adjust to the poems' contents. In other respects he is also derivative of modern experimentation. His lines are of irregular length and meter; there is no rhyme; poetic syntax and punctuation are, by traditional standards, unconventional; spatial techniques come from E. E. Cummings and his artistic descendants; the imagery is of the Pound-Williams school; diction is conspicuously free of cliches.

Yet there are characteristic Jonesian techniques. One is his use of comic strips, motion pictures, and radio shows as allusive to American culture. Another, of course, is the use of his own symbol-images. Most important is the creative uses to which Jones puts language. The language in some passages is effective, even exquisite, poetry. For example, this imagery in "Ostriches & Grandmothers" is unfailing:

Here, it is color, motion;
the feeling of dazzling beauty
Flight.

As
the trapeeze rider
leans
with arms spread

wondering at the bar's
delay

There is in *Preface* an unusual sense of rightness of the lines (even the more abstruse lines) that suggests that Jones was at this time a young craftsman taking time to shape, chisel, and polish, as he was not to do in his later poetry. In other words, his poems here seem to be self-conscious and composed in contrast to his later poems which seem to be spontaneous and impulsive.

All things considered, *Preface* was an auspicious beginning for LeRoi Jones the poet.

"The crucial seeing": "Sabotage" and *The Dead Lecturer*

Two works comprise the graph of Jones during the several years following his first volume; they are *The Dead Lecturer,* published in 1964, and "Sabotage," written in 1961 through 1963 but not published in collected form until 1969 when it appeared as the first section of *Black Magic.* In both, the tentative and introspective young speaker is being replaced. The new speaker focuses more on his external world, resolves some of his earlier indecisiveness, better and more positively articulates for others as well as for himself what must be done. At the beginning of this phase of his poetic career, Jones:

> . . . practices
> loneliness,
> as a virtue.
> > ["As a possible lover"]

wistfully thinks:

> . . . about at time when I will be relaxed
> When flames and non-specific passion wear themselves
> away.
> > ["Three Modes of History and Culture"]

but finally he is forced to exercise the alternative:

> We have awaited the coming of a natural
> phenomenon. Mystics and romantics, knowledgeable
> workers
> of the land
>
> But none has come.
> (*Repeat*)
> > but none has come.
>
> Will the machinegunners please step forward?
> > ["A POEM SOME PEOPLE WILL HAVE TO UNDERSTAND"]

Committed as he tells himself he is, the narrator still harbors vestiges of his earlier ambivalence. But he pushes aside these soft feelings, these fond looks backward, afraid that they will vitiate his Jihad:

> The Lord has saved me
> to do this. The Lord

has made me strong. I
am as I must have
myself. Against all
thought, all music, all
my soft loves.

                    ["I Substitute For The Dead Lecturer"]

There are strong xenophobic statements. One type is anti-America, such as
he expresses in *"An Agony. As Now."*:

I am inside someone
who hates me. I look
out from his eyes. Smell
what fouled tunes come in
to his breath. Love his
wretched women . . .

But it has no feeling. As the metal, is hot, it is not,
given to love.

It burns the thing
inside it. And that thing
screams.

Another is anti-"Negro," as exemplified in this passage:

. . . What man unremoved from his meat's source, can
    continue
to believe totally in himself? Or on the littered sidewalks of his
    personal
history, can continue to believe in his own dignity or intelligence.
Except the totally ignorant
who are our leaders.
                    Except the completely devious
                    who are our lovers.
                    ["Green Lantern's Solo"]

And another is anti-Western culture, symbolized in the brief "Crow Jane" series
of poems. He knows that:

She is looking
for alternatives. Openings
where she can lay all
this greasy talk
on somebody. Me, once. Now
I am her teller.
             ["Crow Jane In High Society"]

Having identified the issues along racial as well as along aesthetic lines,
Jones proselytizes:

We must convince the living
that the dead
cannot sing.
             ["A Guerilla Handbook"]

Paradoxically, although he is not moved to compassion:

. . . For the deadly idiot of compromise
who shrieks compassion, and bids me love my neighbor. . . .
             ["Rhythm & Blues (1"]

he says:

I want to be sung. . . .
As what I am
given love, or time, or space . . .
And let you, whoever
sits now breathing on my words
create a self of your own. One
that will love me.
             ["The dance"]

Finally, our lecturer, through death, has found his true self:

             Where ever I go to claim
my, flesh, there are entrances
of spirit.
             ["The Liar"]

and

I fondle what
I find
of myself. Of you
what I understand.
                    ["Dichtung"]

In *The Dead Lecturer,* LeRoi Jones continues the technical experimentation evidenced in *Preface.* His diction, however, has become ever so slightly more declarative, hinting at poetry-of-statement. In doing so, he sacrifices some of his poetic compression and becomes a bit blunt, less sharp. There are intermittent flashes of brilliant poetizing in this book, but not with the same degree of frequency as in *Preface.* As to form, he is approaching no norm, even for himself, except for a tendency toward tighter spatial arrangements of the words.

More than subject-matter, technique generated unfavorable critical comments about *The Dead Lecturer.* Typical is the judgment of Richard Howard who claimed that "technical devices . . . merely blur . . . uncertain margin of intent: single parentheses, slash marks, phonetic spellings, Poundian contractions, aberrant punctuation, broken lines, the absence of any 'formality' beyond the decorum of arrangement on the page and, perhaps, a pattern of breathing." More than any other aspect of technique, form got Jones into trouble with the critics. In Howard's opinion, "Certainly not one of these poems is wholly *made,* or even whole. Nowhere do I recognize in these shattered phrases, in these abrupt releases of attention, the impulse to shape, to seek the containing form."[4] The *Times'* reviewer was more succinct: ". . . the jazzing goes nowhere."[5] Clarence Major, then a practically unknown young black writer who was to go on to become a poet, an anthologist, and a critic of some promise, concluded that "Sometimes . . . his preoccupation with various forms . . . is mere exercise, and at the very worse, derivative."[6]

In "An Explanation of the Work" in *Black Magic* there is a passage which seems apropos of what Jones was doing in *The Dead Lecturer.* In it Jones calls his early poetic works "a cloud of abstractions and disjointedness, that was just whiteness. European influence, etc., just as the concept of hopelessness and despair, from the dead minds and dying morality of Europe." But, he continues, "There is a spirituality always trying to get through, to triumph, to walk across these dead bodies like stuntin [sic] for disciples, walking the water of dead bodies europeans call their minds." The clouds of white abstraction and disjointedness, then, would have to give way to black realities and unity, both in form and in content.

In terms of technique and thought, "Sabotage" moved further from *Preface* than did *The Dead Lecturer.* One may reasonably suspect that Jones held back the "Sabotage" poems until he was sure that they were what he really wanted to say, until he was sure that he really wanted to burn the bridges behind him. By 1969 when he published these poems in *Black Magic* he had committed himself to their content. Particularly in diction is the change in technique apparent—the relatively reasonable and subjective and passive poetic statement gives way to the aggressive assertion; the carefully turned phrase gives way to the impulsive exclamation; the euphemism gives way to the hurled invective. The poem that was once the position paper has become the bullet. As Jones explains in the introduction, "*Sabotage* meant I had come to see the superstructure of filth Americans call their way of life, and wanted to see it fall. To sabotage it, I thought maybe by talking bad and getting high, layin out on they [sic] whole chorus."

Rather than remain in the land of the dead, our narrator tells us, he has committed suicide to the part of his self that had lived there. Once he had committed that act, he found that:

What I never wanted, came back
for me to love. (Above the sirens
and bogus magic of the laughably damned) Came back,
in a new way, into new heart . . . old things considered
there light struck me, social songs, racial songs,
and love, like a versified cliche, came down on me
hard, in its casual way.
                    ["The Visit"]

The reclaimed part of self made possible Jones the social poet, the functional poet, and he tells himself:

Roi, finish this poem, someone's about to need you. Roi,
dial the mystic number, ask for holy beads, directions,
plans for the destruction of New York. Work out your problems
like your friends on some nice guy's couch. Get up and hit
someone, like you useta. Don't sit here trembling under the
hammer. . . .
. . . Your time is up
in this particular feeling. In this particular throb of meaning.
                    ["Citizen Cain"]

Jones rationalizes his conscious turning from Western aesthetics on the premise that the expressive is superior to the reflective (as if the expressive were not also a part of Western tradition). Suspecting that whites "belch without feeling," he accuses them of creating a poetry that is physical "in its attempt to make FORMS which endure past their meanings as organic creations . . . a poetry of ratiocination or post-volitional ratiocination."[7]

"Gonna put it on you all at once": *Black Arts* and *Black Magic*

His post-1964 poetry manifests his theories about poetry. It becomes increasingly nonverbal, impulsive, aural, ritualistic, and antirational. At the same time, in terms of purpose, his poetry becomes more overtly propagandistic, moralistic (according to his value system), inflammatory, and utilitarian. In other words, he is making poetry a "black art" available or relevant to the virtuous, i.e., the black masses whom he would influence and shape into a cultural and spiritual nation. Significantly, the poetry becomes less lyrical, less private, and more dramatic and incantatory, moving toward poetry expressly for public performance.

Jones' third collection, before *Black Magic,* is the thin volume entitled *Black Arts* (not to be confused with "Black Art"—without the final *s*—which is the third section of *Black Magic*). The fifteen poems that comprise this collection, most to become a part of the yet to be published *Black Magic,* exemplify this shift in content and technique. He talks directly to black people, tells them what to do:

. . . O black people full of illusions
and weird power. O my loves and my heart
pumping black blood screaming through
my thickened veins.

Do not obey their laws
which are against God
believe brother, do not
ever think any of that
could shit they say is
true. . . .
                    ["A School of Prayer"]

Here the poet-priest delivers the call:

                              S O S

Calling black people
calling all black people, man woman child
Wherever you are, calling you, urgent, come in
Black People, come in, wherever you are, urgent, calling
you, calling all black people
calling all black people, come in, black people, come
on in.[8]

He talks directly to them, teaching the doctrine, leading the incantations, invoking the magic. He evangelizes, using the language of the congregation:

    . . . Say-Pop. Say Yeh
Pop pop. Say. Hey. Pop & Pop Pop
you got a terrible thing going brother
You got a really terrible thing going
(devil dropped a book on my head)
dont stand up please & sit back
down, keep on standin
& standin
& keep a really Black Thing
grogrroov beebeep

        Ah bee-bee
        Ah bee-bee
        Ah bee-bee

Keep a real good strong healthy
fast intelligent groo-groovy black
thing goin
                ["Live Niggers—Stop Bullshitting"]

He declares the Jihad against the "devils":

May this bitch and her sisters, all of them,
receive my words
in all their orifices like lye mixed with
cococola and alaga syrup

feel this shit, feel it, now laugh your
hysterectic laughs

> while your flesh burns
> and your eyes peel to red mud
> ["Babylon Revisited"]

And he delivers the benediction:

> . . . Huge Beast Of The Night, awake to be the whole
> of creation, the thing breathing, a breast silhouette, under supercool
> new moons of turning into
> ["Part of the Doctrine"]

This little volume shows, too, changes in technique. The Poundian allusions, the William Carlos Williams imagery, the "arty" diction, the erudite indirection are gone. In their places are the prose-poetry declarative statement, the breezy and slangy street idiom, the nonsense line, and the aural (or nonverbal) line. At this point he was more polemicist at times than he was poet.

But let us turn our attention again to *Black Magic.* The "Target Study" section of *Black Magic,* as Jones explains in the forenote, "is trying to really study, like bomber crews do the soon to be destroyed cities. Less passive now, less uselessly 'literary.' Trying to see, trying to understand . . . trying, as Margaret Walker says, 'to fashion a way,' to clean up and move." As Kessler put it, "How to destroy the devil without destroying himself is the burden of Target Study."[9]

Jones identifies himself and his purpose; he identifies the enemy. Then he assays the price of opposition:

> . . . even bitter water
> which we get used to, is better than
> white drifting fairies, muses, singing
> to us, in calm tones, about how it is better to die
> etcetera, than go off from them . . .
> ["Will They Cry When You're Gone, You Bet"]

Opposition will lead to no greater danger than now exists, for:

> . . . They have made
> this star unsafe, and this age, primitive, though yr mind
> is somewhere else, your ass aint.
> ["Jitterbugs"]

Moreover, there is no alternative to the holy war. He goes to battle, invoking the spirit of Malcolm X and declaring:

. . . let us never breathe a pure breath if
we fail, and white men call us faggots till the end of
the earth.
[''A Poem for Black Hearts'']

About "Black Art," the last section of *Black Magic,* Jones says in his introduction, *"Black Art* was the crucial seeing, the decision, the move. The strength-
ening to destroy, and the developing of willpower to build, even in the face of
destruction and despair, even with, or WITHOUT, the confrontation of blank-
ness, whiteness, etc." The central thrust of this section is the same as the
previously mentioned *Black Arts.* Increasingly, he emphasizes the divinity of
black people, trying to make them see their cause as spiritual and their actions
as religious duty. Tied in with this theme is myth-history of the black man as the
possessor of original virtue. He would have black people believe:

We have been captured,
brothers. And we labor
to make our getaway, into
the ancient image, into a new

correspondence with ourselves
and our black family.
[''Ka 'Ba'']

Certain poems in *Black Magic* have attracted public and/or critical attention.
Several are to an extent autobiographical: ''GATSBY'S THEORY OF AES-
THETICS'' is really not a poem but rather a short poetic essay delineating
Jones' key principles of poetry. ''Numbers, Letters'' also is revelatory of his
theory of poetry. ''I don't love you'' renounces white America and her values.
''For Tom Postell, Dead Black Poet'' contrasts the early, ''imitation white'' Jones
and the later anti-Semitic Baraka. Then there is the lyrical ''leroy'' in which he
makes his aesthetic will. Others are those frequently anthologized: ''A Poem for
Black Hearts'' in praise of Malcolm X, which is ''made breathless,'' say Emanuel
and Gross, ''through punctuation and mounting emotion and lengthening line,
a poem as darkly sincere as its brooding author'';[10] ''Black Art,'' which finds its
way into other publications on the strength of its imagery, its poetic sincerity,
and its shocking way of saying that art should not exist if it has no social value.
Others are known for still other reasons: ''Jitterbugs'' and ''cops'' are considered by black aestheticians to be good poetic statements about the danger

that blacks are in. "Black Bourgeoisie" and "CIVIL RIGHTS POEM" are effectively satirical of the "Negro" middle-class and of "Negro" leaders. Two of the better known poems expressing the idea of the divinity of the black man and his cause are "THREE MOVEMENTS AND A CODA" and "The Black Man Is Making New Gods." One more poem needs to be mentioned, but not because of any intrinsic philosophical content or technical expertise. It is "Black People," catapulted into prominence by Judge Kapp at the 1967 trial of LeRoi Jones.

Homilies, paeans, and photographs: *It's Nation Time, In Our Terribleness,* and Other Later Poetry

The later poetry continued mainly in the style and ideology of his "Black Art" poems. Much of it is poetry-for-performance, such as "Jim Brown on the Screen."[11] in which he even includes stage directions: "(hand slap)," "(hand/slap, stomp, wheel)." Another, "Black Power Chant,"[12] is comprised of more stage directions than verse, making it hard to categorize this work as ritual, poem, or drama. Other poems, though they have no explicit stage directions, lend themselves to dramatic readings, for example, the popular "Who Will Survive . . ." One which Baraka delivers especially well is "It's Nation Time." It does appear that Baraka is more and more writing poetry for his own voice, that he seems to be taking into account his personal rhythms, intonations, and sound values. His *Spirit Reach* is a thin collection of poetry which seems to have been composed especially for oral presentation by Imamu himself.

Jones is a skillful reader of his own poems, a crowd pleaser. Weales, in an account of a lecture by Jones at the University of Pennsylvania, reported that Jones read "tricky typographical poems . . . beautifully, making admirable oral sense of what often looks like chaos on the page."[13] He reads with dramatic skill indicative of his experience in the world of the theatre. At times he speaks with incredible rapidity—distinctly; at times he speaks with deliberation; he changes pitch and intonation, creating the effect of different speakers in different moods; and he makes his body a complement or extension of his voice.

In 1970 Jones, as Baraka, published *It's Nation Time* and with Fundi (Billy Abernathy), *In Our Terribleness.* The first is openly evangelistic, obviously written for his own voice. An unpretentious little volume of twenty-four pages, it contains three poems that Jones is given to speaking and dramatizing in whole or in part at his public lectures and readings: "The Nation Is Like Ourselves," "Sermon for Our Maturity," and the title poem.

The first poem begins by defining the nation:

The nation is like our selves, together
seen in our various scenes, sets where ever we are
what ever we are doing, is what the nation
is
doing
or
not doing
is what the nation
is being
or
not being

In this poem he cries out:

Doctor nigger, please do some somethin on we
lawyer nigger, please pass some laws about us
liberated nigger with the stringy haired mind, please lib
      lib lib
you spliv er ate
US . . .
please mister liberated nigger love chil nigger
nigger in a bellbottom bell some psychodelic wayoutness
on YO people, even while you freeing THE People, please
just first free YO people . . .

On and on he goes, cataloging and pleading with all "the sweet lost" blacks
who are "our nation" that "we need you bbbaby man, we need all the blood."
    "Sermon for Our Maturity" exhorts Negroes (the term is used advisedly here)
to fulfill their potentials as blacks:

Stretch out negro
            Grow "Gro
            Gwan "Gro Grow
Stretch out Expand
Bigger than a white boys shack
You the star nee-gro, you touch all points
w / yr circular self . . .

Aint no Italian suit can contain you
    Yr body is all space
    Yr feet is valley makers
Aint no Italian shoes can contain them
You a black foot Buddha face . . .
You can dance Nigger I know it
Dance on to freedom
You can sing Nigger sing
Sing about your pure movement
in space
Grow . . .

Those addressed are promised:

Not gon' call you Negro if you keep
    gettin up
You grown Blood

"It's Nation Time," like the previously mentioned "SOS," calls for all blacks
to emerge and unite:

niggers come out, brothers are we
    with you and your sons your daughters are ours
    and we are the same, all the blackness from one black allah
        when the world is clear you'll be with us
            come out niggers come out
            come out niggers come out
It's nation time eye ime
            it's nation ti eye ime
                    chant with bells and drum
                    its nation time

These poems, like those in the later *Spirit Reach,* are uneconomically written.
Moreover, individual lines and passages are too cumbersome for good aural
effect, except, perhaps, for delivery by Jones himself. Mnemonic devices, fluid
lines, rhythm, and other features that make for effective oral rendition are
missing. Too, there are some abstract lines that are so trite that they surprise
one who is used to Jonesian linguistic gymnastics.

In Our Terribleness: Some Elements and Meaning in Black Style is Jones'
most physically pretentious book. Following the preliminary pages there is a

leaf of heavy aluminum paper; in the center of this aluminum sheet are the words "IN OUR TERRIBLENESS." The sheet is to serve as a mirror by which the reader, presumably black, may see his "terrible" self and identify with:

Some terrible
folks
these inside here.

The book is encased in a handsome black jacket bordered on the front with red and on the back with green — the three colors of the black liberation flag. A photograph entitled "Flight (The Glory of Hip)" adorns the front of the jacket. Priced at $7.95 clothbound, the book has thick, glossy paper of good quality. Each page is bordered in black; there is a generous amount of white space on each page, several pages having only a line or two of print. The pages, art-gallery style, are not numbered. Overall, the book is rather precious, as if Baraka succumbed to the notion of creating, of all things, an artifact.

(Baraka asked the publisher, Bobbs-Merrill, to finance a $1,000 publicity party to introduce the book to the public, the party to be held at his sister's catering service, Kimako's, in Harlem. The company demurred, for, according to one of their spokesmen, they had not allotted that much money for the book's coming-out party.)

In Our Terribleness is a combination of photographs of black people by Fundi and complementary text by Baraka. Undoubtedly, Fundi is a sensitive and highly skilled photographer who can do with a camera what a good poet can do with language. His pictures are specific, honest, and refreshingly candid. There is something graphically dignified, even majestic, about his subjects, whether they be a group of small children around the door of a tenement ("Across the Street from Spirit House in LeRoi J's New Ark New J"), three street "dudes" ("cats who are PEACOCKS strut"), an aged black man and a young boy ("Old Man & Simba hence ETERNAL LOVE"), or the portrait of an eloquently plain young "sister" ("Uncrowned Queen").

Unfortunately, too many of the photographs and text of *In Our Terribleness* are not clearly coordinated, almost as if Baraka wrote the text and then fitted the pictures to it rather than the other way around. The pictures are not captioned. One must look in a sort of index ("IMAGES") in the back of the book to find the titles of the individual photographs. Even so, since there are no page numbers, the pictures are identified only by "Order of Appearance."

There are instances in which word and photograph are well, even artistically, coordinated. One such is a picture of a girl ("Love") for which Baraka writes:

Hey, man, look at this woman.
She is fine. Fine.
I cant say nothing else.

We need to give her something. . . .

This is why we ourselves speed to grace.

Another is a photograph of a confidently smiling construction worker ("Tooth-pick In dus try Smiles"). For this picture Baraka's poetic perception dictated the lines:

. . . What's pictured here is
our nation
Like this blood with the tooth pick . . .
. . . The touch of light.
Transformed wood. A wand. Transmutation. A dumb wood now
vibrating at a higher rate. With the blood. His mouth wand.
The toothpick of the blood is his casual swagger stick.

A final example is a picture of an elderly lady, too proud to be tired, standing erect, composed, and dignified, waiting for, perhaps, a bus. For this photograph are the lines:

When the old sisters get to standing
there waitin for us. Been waitin for so long, like that
endless patience (Man,
you better play both them numbers) all our souls can be seen.

Amiri Baraka defines his terms early in the book. Proceeding from the ethnic meaning of "bad" as superior or exceptionally fine, he claims:

. . . Our beauty is BAD cause we bad. Bad things.
Some bad bad bad ass niggers

and then explains:

To be bad is one level
But to be terrible, is to be
badder dan nat.

This is his theme, then, for this book: the total and absolute beauty of black people.

The beauty, he writes, is inescapably divine:

the word will be given by niggers
we are in our most holy selves niggers
god is a nigger really
ask who god is and he will answer if you ask right

As divine creatures, black people should consider the routine of their lives as:

always
continuing exercise
          of astonishing grace.

But, he reasons, they must rid themselves of poor self-images; they must refute those who:

. . . Always talk so bad about the blood.
"The blood aint ready. A nigger aint shit. Negroes aint got no
values. Man, these spooks'll make you tired, with they shit." And
on and on. Trapping ourselves in screens of negative criticism.
We know we bad. Shit, we here. We here and gonna survive.

Throughout the volume Baraka probes for worth in black people — from the "doo-rag" (stocking cap) wearing urban hipster to the just-released-from-jail Herman to the leather, suede, and alligator hide accoutred street "dude" insouciantly seated on a doorstep, open switchblade in hand. One is reminded of the Burnses and Whitmans of poetry who found worth and beauty in those whom society had rejected.

The Kawaida doctrine is espoused in this book as the doctrine that will save black people. There is a cycle, Imamu preaches. The white man's phase of this cycle is dying; blacks must ready themselves for the power to come. This means:

           Simply that one way of life will
pass. Like any man's life. From babyhood to middleage to death.
(Change.) And the west will pass, and we who are the slaves will
take control. Let it be the beauty in us that takes control. Let
it be even longer than 5000 years that we rule this time.
The scientists must show us the way to survive the endless cycle
of back and forth. The pendulum of rise and fall. The Religious
Scientists.

It seems that the thing which does not get through in this book is its theme's elemental simplicity. "Black is beautiful" is an essence, an uncomplex essence. This premise is lost, however, in Baraka's verbiage. He has overwritten his point — both in terms of sheer words and in terms of the too mystical diction and imagery. This is not to say that he eschews plain language — the examples above are fair samplings of the street idioms, ethnic expressions, and crude or coarse language in the book. It is simply that the masses of blacks, or the literary elite, for that matter, will find too much esoteric and abstract talk in the book. The more one looks through *In Our Terribleness,* the more one is reminded of the Chinese adage: "One picture is worth a thousand words."

Looking back over the corpus of Jones' poetry, we notice a gradual change from a subjective, tentative lyricist to an activist priest-poet. As to subject matter, the Jonesian and Barakan themes are there: the negative themes — anti-middle-class Negro, anti-Jew, anti-white liberal, anti-Christianity, anti-Western culture, and the positive themes — blacks as the saviors-survivors in the coming world, the need for new gods, black aestheticism, theories of art and culture, revolution as necessary and justifiable on spiritual grounds, the physical and spiritual beauty of black people.

As to technique, we notice a gradual change from avant garde "beat" style to a "black art" style. By Western standards, Jones deteriorated; by black aestheticians' standards, Baraka grew. Throughout, we find our poet characteristically satirical, inventive in imagery, expressive, consummately in command of language, occasionally lyrical, playful with words, partial to only a few symbol-images (his own), "profane," and disdainful of conventions of form and mechanics. We find our poet in his later works depending more than before upon ritualistic and dramatic devices and partial to the language of the masses of black people.

"Establishment" and academic critics are often appalled by his ideas, regretful about his failure to master and control accepted poetic techniques. Young black critics and writers and others of Baraka's ideological persuasion are generally sympathetic to his ideas, rejoice that he is seeking to establish by example some black literary criteria. Typical of the former is Margolies, who writes:

One suspects . . . that from the beginning Jones has mistrusted poetry, possibly hated it (as an expression of white civilization), and that he has devoted his career of purging himself of his poetic sensibilities. . . . What was once a source of strength, an energizing force in Jones's poetry — his rage, his contempt — has lately become a monomaniacal obsession, and his recent poems are fragments of fantasy, feeling, and ideas tossed together in a whirlpool of hysteria.[14]

Typical of the latter is one who calls Baraka "the greatest poet ever to live in twentieth-century-america."[15] Between the two are voices like that of Darwin Turner, who says:

> Since 1964, Jones has concentrated on the use of literature—poetry and drama especially—as the force of revolution. To this end, he has revised his poetic style to make it more meaningful for community residents who have found little relevance in the traditional, formal language of American poetry. His success is evidenced in the extreme popularity of his frequent public readings in community assemblies. Thus, Jones has revitalized poetry for many people.[16]

It is just possible that the truth lies squarely in the middle.

Chapter 7. "Not the weak Hamlets": Drama

As early as 1958, *Yugen* advertised *A Good Girl Is Hard to Find,* a play by LeRoi Jones, to be presented at Sterington House in Bloomfield, New Jersey. By 1959 LeRoi Jones had written *Revolt of the Moonflowers,* the play often said to have been his first. The manuscript for *Revolt of the Moonflowers* is not extant, but Jones feels no great sense of loss, saying, "It was a bad play, anyhow." In 1961 his *Dante,* a "sort of dramatization of the False Comforters theme" in *System,* was performed at the Off-Bowery Theatre in lower New York City. Another early drama was published first as a play in *Floating Bear* and later was incorporated in the fictional *System;* this was *The Eighth Ditch.* None of these semiprofessional works attracted public attention.

Then came 1964, in two ways the biggest single year in the career of Jones the dramatist. First, it was a prolific year, for he wrote, published, or had produced *The Baptism, The Toilet, Dutchman, The Slave, Experimental Death Unit #1,* and *J-E-L-L-O.* Second, 1964 saw Jones catapulted into public attention when *Dutchman* won the Obie Award. For the first time, LeRoi Jones was the subject of serious critical consideration by the American theatre establishment. By 1966, he had committed himself to what he calls "common experience theatre,"[1] this year bringing forth *Madheart* and *Great Goodness of Life,* both obviously written primarily for black audiences. In the ensuing years there was more drama of similar intent and technique. *Home on the Range* and *Police* were published in 1968. Thereafter came *A Recent Killing, Arm Yrself or Harm Yrself, The Death of Malcolm X, Insurrection, Junkies Are Full of (SHHH...), Bloodrites, Columbia the Gem of the Ocean,* and others, including the occasional little dramatic, pageant-like presentations at Spirit House.

In all his plays, there are manifestations of his theories of theatre. "The Revolutionary Theatre" essay in *Home* articulates what he was in fact doing all along in drama, that is, using the theatre as a device for edification and motivation. As in other genres, his practice of his own theory became more evident as time passed, so that now, in retrospect, it is easy to see, say, *Home on the Range* as incitement when it is compared with *The Baptism,* which is more along the lines of exposition. Although Jones has a reputation as a changeable person, the sort of pronouncements about theatre that he is making now he has been making all along. A recent essay along these lines is "Negro Theatre Pimps Get Big Off Nationalism."[2] Although the thrust of this article is derogatory of Negro actors who in his opinion prostitute their blackness, there are passages reminiscent of some earlier statements about the role of black theatre:

> Everything we do must commit us collectively to revolution ie; NATIONAL LIBERATION. Theater that does not do this is bullshit, any art that does not do this, no matter on what level it speaks, lyric, scream, funky shake, is no where. Black Theater has gotta raise the dead, and move the living. Otherwise it is a teacup in a cracker mansion. [p. 8]

In another place he says, "But a play—it seems to me—a work of art—should talk to you . . . at least carry as much information as somebody on the sidewalk, saying, 'Get off the sidewalk.' "[3] In other words, a play should make one "Move. Or get up. Or shoot."[4]

From the beginning playwright LeRoi Jones moved toward plays that would have this as their purpose.

Adam and Eve, alternate ending: *Dutchman*

Of the plays that LeRoi Jones has written, the best known is *Dutchman*. Starting as part of a twin-bill offering, along with *The Zoo Story* by Edward Albee, it has proved durable as theatre fare. (There is even a motion picture version. Produced in 1967 and directed by Anthony Harvey, it has never attracted much attention, playing mainly at small, "arty" motion picture houses.)

On the literal level, *Dutchman* is concerned with two people, a Negro male, Clay, and a white female, Lula, who strike up a chance acquaintance on a subway train. They size up each other: To Clay, Lula is a white liberal, a bohemian type, a bit flirty; to Lula, Clay is a typical middle-class, intellectual young Negro anxious to achieve success in white America, the type who should feel honored or pleased that she offers him her company.

The two engage in flirtatious small talk during which Clay agrees to take Lula along to a party that he plans to attend that night. Continuing their bantering, they exchange good-natured, playful jibes. Then Lula teases Clay about compromising himself in order to get along in white society. Clay becomes resentful. Lula persists. "You're a murderer, Clay, and you know it," she says, referring to his avoiding his identity as a black man. She upbraids him, calling him a "liver-lipped white man . . . just a dirty white man." Clay is not the type to succumb to her wiles if this entails being insulted. Pushed to the point where he loses his composure, he angrily rebuffs Lula, declaring that it is his right to be whatever he is or wants to be regardless of whether she approves or disapproves. Indeed, his manner of living is a way of controlling his violence: "I sit here in this buttoned-up suit to keep myself from cutting all your throats. If I'm a middle-class fake white man — let me be. The only thing that would cure my neurosis would be your murder." He continues until Lula, enraged, rather reflexively stabs Clay to death while other subway riders look on passively. She orders them to throw Clay's body off the train, and they do, silently. Then when a similar young Negro boards the subway train at the next stop, Lula begins what apparently is going to be a similar temptation routine.

Jones has stated that something along these lines actually happened to him and that he knows the tough bohemian type that his character Lula is. He says:

> . . . I showed one white girl and one Negro boy in that play, and the play is about one white girl and one Negro boy, just them, singularly, in what I hope was a revelation of private and shared anguish, which because I dealt with it specifically would somehow convey an emotional force from where I got it — the discovery of America — on over to any viewer. . . .
>
> But I will say this, if the girl (or the boy) in that play has to "represent" anything, I mean if she must be symbolic in the way demented academicians use the term, she does not exist at all. She is not meant to be a symbol — nor is Clay — but a real person, a real thing, in a real world. She does not represent any thing — she is one. And perhaps that thing is America, or at least its spirit. You remember America, don't you, where they have unsolved murders happening before your eyes on television. How crazy, extreme, neurotic, does that sound? Lula, for all her alleged insanity, just barely reflects the insanity of this hideous place. And Clay is a young boy trying desperately to become a man. *Dutchman* is about the difficulty of becoming a man in America.[5]

Popular symbolic interpretations of *Dutchman* have Lula representing a white America that abides Negro America as long as Negro America respectfully accepts whiteness as the norm — even while white America derides Negro America for being imitative. Popular symbolic interpretations have Clay representing a Negro America that wears a mask of respectability and nonviolence, a schizoid Negro America that tries on one hand to accept America on white terms and on the other hand to accept its own identity. As one review aptly stated, it is this symbolism, this "mythic dimension, as well as its complex poetic structure [that] raises *Dutchman* so far above sociology."[6]

The symbolism in *Dutchman* is maintained in the action, in the dialogue, and in certain motifs. Jones seems to tell us that Lula, like America, does not know the Negro except as a type:

> CLAY: Hey, you still haven't told me how you know so much about me.
> LULA: I told you I didn't know anything about *you*...you're a well-known type.
> CLAY: Really?
> LULA: Or at least I know the type very well.

Lula, like white liberal America, knows that whatever the black man is, he hides, even from himself, behind a facade of imitation whiteness:

> LULA: . . . What've you got that jacket and tie on in all this heat for? And why're you wearing a jacket and tie like that? Did your people ever burn witches or start revolutions over the price of tea? Boy, those narrow-shoulder clothes come from a tradition you ought to feel oppressed by. A three-button suit. What right do you have to be wearing a three-button suit and striped tie? Your grandfather was a slave, he didn't go to Harvard. . . . Who do you think you are now?
> CLAY: . . . Well, in college I thought I was Baudelaire. But I've slowed down since.
> LULA: I bet you never once thought you were a black nigger. . . . A black Baudelaire.
> CLAY: That's right.

When the Negro enters into the white mainstream, his innate creativity is aborted:

> LULA: . . . Real fun in the dark house. Hah! Real fun in the dark house, high up above the street and the ignorant cowboys. I lead you in, holding your wet hand gently in my hand . . .
> CLAY: Which is not wet?
> LULA: Which is dry as ashes.

Once the Negro, in hopes of being accepted, professes that he loves America, he will continue to lie to her:

> LULA: . . . You'll say to me very close to my face, many, many times, you'll say, even whisper, that you love me.
> CLAY: Maybe I will.
> LULA: And you'll be lying.
> CLAY: I wouldn't lie about something like that.

LULA: Hah. It's the only kind of thing you will lie about. Especially if you think it'll keep me alive.

Once white America knows that Negro America has succumbed to her temptations, she will wrest whatever pleasure she wants from Negro America, regardless of what embarrassment it may cause him:

LULA: . . . Come on, Clay. Let's rub bellies on the train. The nasty. The nasty. Do the gritty grind, like your ol' rag-head mammy. Grind till you lose your mind. Shake it, shake it, shake it, shake it! OOOOweeee! Come on, Clay. Let's do the choo-choo train shuffle, the navel scratcher.

When Negro America refuses to "dance," white society's latent feelings of master-to-be-obeyed surface.

At this point the latent manhood in the Negro is aroused. Negro America can either lash out at the tormenter or simply ignore the tormenter. Clay chooses the former, and for this white America summarily murders him. Unpliable clay (Clay) is rendered to dust (death). His murder is ignored by the rest of America (the other subway riders), for under the circumstances it is perfectly normal, almost ritualistic to murder. After all, Negro America has declined to "dance" with white America.

Two key supportive motifs are at work in *Dutchman*. From the beginning, Lula is the aggressor, even down to the blatant symbolism of the apples which she from time to time eats and which she offers Clay ("Eating apples is always the first step."). Even though somewhere in his past Clay has been taught, perhaps intuitively, not to partake of the "fruits" of America's white life, he consents to take her to a party with him and then go home with her. She muses:

LULA: And with my apple-eating hand I push open the door and lead you, my tender big-eyed prey, into my...God, what can I call it...into my hovel.
CLAY: Then what happens?
LULA: After the dancing and games, after the long drinks and long walks, the real fun begins.

A second motif is the subway train. It is significant to connect the train with the title of the play. One reasonable interpretation of this motif is that black and white America, Clay and Lula, are rushing headlong through darkness, literally and symbolically seeing nothing on the way to vague destinations. They do not "see" where they are going, for the train is traveling so fast that they catch only glimpses of "light." Both are captives aboard a slave ship, for neither is free to love or reject the other honestly and openly. In this interpretation the title *Dutchman* is an allusion to the Dutch East India Company, the best known slave ship company of the seventeenth century and whose flagship for the voyages between West Africa and America, tradition says, was named *Flying Dutchman.* Another possible referent for the title *Dutchman* is the literary legend of the Flying Dutchman in which the central character is ever in pursuit of prey that can never be caught.[7] In either case, Lula as white America and Clay as black America fit as symbols.

Besides for its rich symbolism and allegory, *Dutchman* has been acclaimed for its characterization and for its dialogue. Jones created Lula as an intellectual white liberal who "knows" everything in the way Western civilization "knows" (is the source and repository of) everything that needs to be known in order to be in control. It is with this type of person that Jones builds his paradox: Lula "knows" only what she has been taught to know—lies—and consequently is blind to the real Clay, blind to his "pumping black heart." But rather than deal with her own self-deception, a form of insanity, she turns from the truth ("I've heard enough.") and kills the bearer of that truth. Clay, as a character, shows a dramatist in control of his materials. By his dress, demeanor, and conversation, Clay is established as a cleanly scrubbed and decorous young black intellectual, the type of young man Jones himself affected in his tweed-wearing, intellectually and artistically oriented early Village days. Clay is not the aggressor in their relations, for he knows better and is wary; but when he realizes that the vivacious and beautiful Lula is serious about offering herself to him for the evening, he feels surer of himself, warms and loosens in anticipation. He compromises himself, Lula catches him doing it, and when she tells him the truth about himself, Clay finds the truth too much for his vanity, his integrity, and his composure. Clay is a plausible character.

The dialogue is precise, poetic, with a pace and tone that fit the narrative movement and the characterization at any given point. There is an easy alternation of the two characters' lines, a natural and unforced alternation. When one considers the type of characters Jones has created to speak the lines, the dialogue seems inevitable. The high point in the dialogue is Clay's soliloquy about whites' ignorance of blacks. In a crescendo and diminuendo of rage, he tells Lula:

> . . . You don't know anything except what's there for you to see. An act. Lies. Device. Not the pure heart, the pumping black heart. You don't ever know that. . . . You great liberated whore! You fuck some black man, and right away you're

an expert on black people. What a lotta shit that is. The only thing you know is that you come if he bangs you hard enough. And that's all. The belly rub? You wanted to do the belly rub? Shit, you don't even know how. You don't know how. That ol' dipty-dip shit you do, rolling your ass like an elephant. That's not my kind of belly rub. Belly rub is not Queens. Belly rub is dark places, with big hats and overcoats held up with one arm. Belly rub hates you. Old bald-headed four-eyed ofays popping their fingers...and don't know yet what they're doing. They say, "I love Bessie Smith." And don't even understand that Bessie Smith is saying, "Kiss my ass, my black unruly ass." Before love, suffering, desire, anything you can explain, she's saying, and very plainly, "Kiss my black ass." And if you don't know that, it's you that's doing the kissing. . . . If Bessie Smith had killed some white people she wouldn't have needed that music. She could have talked very straight and plain about the world. No metaphors. No grunts. No wiggles in the dark of her soul. Just straight two and two are four. Money. Power. Luxury. Like that. All of them. Crazy niggers turning their backs on sanity. When all it needs is that simple act. Murder. Just murder! Would make us all sane. . . . Ahhh. Shit. But who needs it? I'd rather be a fool. Insane. Safe with my words, and no deaths, and clean, hard thoughts, urging me to new conquests. My people's madness. Hah! That's a laugh. My people. They don't need me to claim them. They got legs and arms of their own. Personal insanities. They don't need all those words. They don't need any defense. But listen, though, one more thing. And you tell this to your father, who's probably the kind of man who needs to know at once. So he can plan ahead. Tell him not to preach so much rationalism and cold logic to these niggers. Let them alone. Let them sing curses at you in code and see your filth as simple lack of style. . . .

It was dialogue like this and other elements in *Dutchman* that prompted Littlejohn to call the play "race-war literature,"[8] that prompted California's superintendent of instruction to ban its use in that state's black studies programs, and that not long before the Watts riots prompted the banning of advertisements of Jones' plays from the Los Angeles press.

But Jones insists that "I'm not a violent man — that's what I'm trying to say in 'Dutchman.' "[9]

No exit: *The Slave*

Riding on the critical excitement caused by *Dutchman,* Jones soon followed with a presentation of *The Slave.* There had been theatre-world talk to the effect that James Earl Jones would play the lead, but the play opened with

Al Freeman, Jr., in that role. Nan Martin and Jerome Raphel played the other two parts. Planned for an opening on October 7, 1964, to coincide with the playwright's thirtieth birthday, it actually opened in December of that year at St. Mark's Playhouse in New York City.

If in *Dutchman* Jones created two valid protagonists (or two antagonists), he created in *The Slave* an antagonist within the protagonist, Walker Vessels, and the two ostensible antagonists, Grace and Bradford Easley, are merely a chorus, a convenient audience, an efficiency gauge for Walker's cathartic mouthings. (As Bradford Easley says, "Oh, don't get so worried, Grace . . . you know he just likes to hear himself talk...more than anything...he just wants to hear himself talk, so he can find out what he's supposed to have on his mind.") This is to say that there is no dramatic tension between Walker and the Easleys. Walker has committed himself to an action that he may be incapable of stopping, and he is articulating his rationale for his action, depending—he and the audience know to be in vain—on the Easleys to convince him of his error, if he has erred, and to make him change his course of action.

The Prologue, delivered by Walker, establishes his uncertainty about himself. It also seeks to establish an attitude necessary for speculation, necessary for an open mind on the part of the viewer if the viewer is to be objective in his perceptions of the play:

> . . . Whatever I am or seem . . . to you, then let that rest. But figure, still, that you might not be right. Figure, still, that you might be lying...to save yourself. Or myself's image, which might set you crawling like a thirsty dog, for the meanest of drying streams. The meanest of ideas . . . Yeah. Ideas. Let that settle! Ideas. Where they form. Or whose they finally seem to be. Yours? The other's? Mine? . . . just because they're *right*...doesn't mean anything. The very rightness stinks a lotta times. The very rightness. . . . Brown is not brown except when used as an intimate description of personal phenomenological fields. As your brown is not my brown, et cetera, that is, we need, ahem, a meta-language. We need something not included here.

After all, he seems to say, both positions—that of the white liberal and that of the black revolutionary—are tenable.

With this audience conditioning attempted, the story unfolds. Walker is a black leader who has come to the Easley's home during the height of a physical revolution in which his side is obviously succeeding. Grace and Easley, white liberals, cannot understand why Walker has come to torment them, for Grace is his former wife and Easley is his former professor, and neither has harmed him nor carried ill-will toward him insofar as they can see. There are upstairs asleep two girls, daughters of Grace and Walker, and it is supposed that he has come either to take them, to see them, or to make some demands upon the Easleys in connection with them.

Walker knows that he cannot make the Easleys understand why he has taken the course in life that he has taken. What the "liberal" Easleys can understand is that the Walker they knew as an intellectual and poet is now as dangerous as any other Negro and should be repressed, contained, put in his place:

EASLEY: Look...LOOK! You arrogant maniac, if you get drunk or fall out here, so help me, I'll call the soldiers or somebody...and turn you over to them. I swear I'll do that. . . . No! I mean this, friend! Really! If I get the slightest advantage, some cracker soldier will be bayoneting you before the night is finished.

and

GRACE: . . . Ohh! Get away from him, Walker! Get away from him . . . you nigger murderer!

WALKER: . . . Oh! Ha, ha, ha...you mean...Wow! . . . No kidding? Grace, Gracie! Wow! I wonder how long you had that stored up.

There follows more talk by Walker which Grace characterizes as "the mad scene from Native Son" delivered by a "second-rate Bigger Thomas." The dialogue becomes increasingly wordy and philosophically speculative — albeit superficial — each examining and contesting the other's ideology, with Walker finally telling why he had had to leave Grace:

Oh, goddamn it, Grace, are you so stupid? You were my wife...I loved you. You mean because I loved you and was married to you...had had children by you, I wasn't supposed to say the things I felt. I was crying out against three hundred years of oppression; not against individuals.

Continually drinking, Walker becomes intoxicated and reveals that he had been there earlier while they were out, had already seen his daughters, and now wanted to take them. Grace sees no reason why the girls should suffer because of Walker's "self-pity, and some weird ambition." Easley and Walker fight, during which Walker shoots, killing Easley. Shortly thereafter, an explosion shakes the house and Grace is pinned under beams and debris. Dying, she cries for Walker to save the children, but he shouts that they are already dead.

As the curtain falls, "There are more explosions. Another one very close to the house. A sudden aggravating silence, and then there is a child heard crying and screaming as loud as it can."

If *The Slave* is tragic, its tragedy is in Walker's being forced into an attitude of hate that enslaves him, even if his side is the winner in the insurrection. The irony is that, although he is the victor, he is at once the enslaved. He no longer has a capacity for love and compassion; he had gone from disaffection to specific rage against a social order to undifferentiated hate for all white people.

In *The Slave* playwright Jones is teacher Jones. His subtitle for the play is *A Fable*, indicating that the play should not be considered as literal and that it should be considered as instruction. This being so, one must see how well it succeeds as fable.

It hardly hits the mark as moral instruction. One fault is that the ideas expressed by the characters remain on the surface level. The talk about why liberals are ineffective, why some blacks dislike all whites, what a liberal feels when he must act on the basis of his rhetoric, and the like are explored to no greater depths than they have been in letters-to-the-editor columns of daily newspapers. By the time that Jones wrote this play, everyone should have heard the pro's and con's that he explores—that there is latent racism in white liberals, that whites who think they know everything about Negroes are fooling themselves, that in an Othello-Desdemona racial relationship there is likely to be an Iago about, that few liberals expect to be rejected by Negroes, that revolutionary blacks may exhibit a love-hate syndrome, and so on. And how LeRoi Jones says these things in this play is not exciting as drama. Littlejohn, in explaining why he thinks the play "is a blatant, unmodulated scream of racial abuse" for "authorial self-gratification," notes that "The stopper to one argument, a dramatic moment typical of the play's subtlety, is: 'Go and fuck yourself.' It is so devoid of conflict, of dramatic content . . .'"[10] In *The Slave* there is little that ignites or provokes thought, little that is quotable. But perhaps this is the point the Prologue intends—that the parade of mental cliches is all that blacks and whites have given themselves as a means of coming to grips with matters of race.

One commentator, George Dennison, reporting his observations of audience reactions to a presentation of the play, recalled that there were three high points in audience excitement: "The first occurred when the Negro revolutionary beat up the liberal-intellectual (judo); the second when the revolutionary enacted a brief rape of his former wife; and the third when the

.

revolutionary finally shot the intellectual." He claims that the responses of the young Negroes in the audience "were not triggered by the actions, but by the well-turned and very plentiful put-down-Whitey phrases that accompanied them. . . . When Jones's young supporters parrot his phrase about a canon of Negro values, they are saying, alas, that they will cling to the self-aggrandizing conceits which make them feel good precisely in the absence of values."[11]

It does seem that in *The Slave* Jones is not as interested in art, in the usual sense of the word, as he is interested in presenting a "feel good" session for blacks. What apparently happened is a failure between Jones' idea and his artifact, a failure of execution. Of this play Jones himself says, ". . . I wasn't ready for it yet. It's o.k. I respect it. But the complexity has to be worked on." Unfortunately, he never got around to working on this complexity.

No Obie winner, *The Slave* nevertheless did win the drama prize at the First World Festival of Negro Arts held in Dakar, Senegal, in the spring of 1966.

Naturally, speculation may arise about the autobiographical content of this play. Again the reader is reminded of Jones' habit of making projections from actual situations. This play is no more "real" than, say, *Great Goodness of Life* is "real." Simplistically, Walker as LeRoi, Grace as Hettie, and the two girls as Kellie and Lisa may fit. But beyond this likeness no other likeness exists. Hettie has not remarried, no white professor taught both Hettie and LeRoi, and, of course, no such revolution has occurred. Further, the play is, after all, a fantasy. When Hettie Jones saw the play on opening night she was noticeably moved. But this was not because she saw it as a depiction of herself and LeRoi and not because she saw it as a prophecy (she and LeRoi were getting along very well together at the time). Rather, she was overwhelmed by the intensity of horror generated by the fantasy and by the sheer power of the overall dramatization. She had known about the play before:

We used to call it *Roi's Bad Dream* [Laughter.] . . . I was just so horrified when he wrote it—and then, you know, of course—we just called it *Roi's Bad Dream* for a year. And then finally somebody was going to put it on, and I never even thought about—to go to the rehearsals so to diminish the shock, because the kids had the chicken pox, I remember.[12]

But a play on paper and a play on stage are different things. Not attempting to view the play clinically, as a work of art, abstractly, Hettie simply reacted to a powerful play in the same manner that anybody else might react to a powerful play.

"Just like I was a radio": *The Toilet*

The Toilet was presented in December of 1964 at St. Mark's Playhouse in a double bill with *The Slave.* The lead roles were played by James Spruill as Ora, Jaime Sanchez as Karolis, and Hampton Clanton as Foots. By this time, Robert Hooks, who had played the part of Clay in the successful *Dutchman,* was conducting in his 28th Street apartment a drama workshop for young blacks who could not afford conventional training in drama. Five of the boys who played in *The Toilet,* selected from 250 who tried out, came from Hooks' workshop and none of these had had previous stage experience.

Jones admits that of his plays written by that time, "I like it best . . . it came so much out of my memory, so exact. Just like I was a radio or something and zoom! I didn't have to do any rewriting . . ."[13] Supposedly written in six inspired hours one night, *The Toilet* projects in drama the same autobiographical Ray projected in fictional pieces — replete with pop-eyes, small and wiry stature, nominal leadership, and capacity for human compassion.

The scene is a boys' toilet in an urban high school. Several young Negro toughs, including Ora, really the antagonist in the play, are waiting for their comrades to round up and bring to the toilet Karolis, who has insulted their leader, Foots (Ray), by sending Foots a love note. They are planning to force Karolis into a showdown fight with Foots, for Foots must maintain his tough-guy image and his leadership. While the boys wait, they engage in idle chatter, profanity-for-profanity's-sake, boasting, and horse-play, some leading to a brief bit of action in which Ora threatens and then knocks a boy named Farrell to the floor. Ora is plainly at the top of the group's pecking order and thereby is both a foil for and a threat to Foots. When Karolis is dragged into the toilet Ora is the main one to bully him. Foots enters soon after and it becomes apparent, even though he has a veneer of toughness and bravado, that he would just as well let Karolis go; after all, Ora and one or two others had a short time before already roughed up Karolis when they caught him in the hall and tried to get him down to the toilet.

Foots is "the weakest physically and smallest of the bunch, but he is undoubtedly their leader," Jones tells us in a stage direction. Foots tries to avoid the fight without losing face. Karolis, though, insists that he wants to fight Foots. They fight. Karolis gets a grip on Foots' throat and begins choking him. Incited, the others, led by Ora, jump in and thoroughly beat Karolis. They then help Foots to his feet, and Ora throws water from the commode on Foots' face. The gang leaves. Left alone with a badly beaten Karolis, Foots begins to regain his senses, sees the condition of Karolis. The play closes as Foots, now Ray as Karolis preferred to call him, "runs and kneels before the body, weeping and cradling the head in his arms."

Baraka now finds the ending of this play, as he now finds some of his other early works, embarrassing:

> When I first wrote the play, it ended with everybody leaving. I tacked the other ending on; the kind of social milieu that I was in, dictated that kind of rap-prochement. It actually did not evolve from the pure spirit of the play. I've never changed it, of course, because I feel that now that would only be cute. I think you should admit where you were even if it's painful, but you should also understand your development and growth. . . . But that was ground that I walked on and covered, I can't deny it now.[14]

Love is the subject of *The Toilet.* Jones poses the question: Can only the calloused survive in a society so inhuman that one cannot openly express love? In the vicious society that he finds himself, Foots/Ray could be honest with neither his gang nor Karolis nor himself. As Jones conceives it, the play is about "how they love and hate and desire and suffer in the limited world they know."[15] The fact that the love in this play is homosexual is to an extent irrelevant, except for the dramatic staging. The fact that the love in this play is biracial is also irrelevant. One need only imagine the racial identities reversed, with Karolis a black and the others Caucasians, to understand that race does not control the narrative line and the play's inherent drama. As much as some Jones admirers might want to object to its being said, *The Toilet* is universal.

Negative reactions to the play are not so much directed at what the play says as they are directed at how Jones says it. Controversial, or objectionable, language abounds. Measured in terms of intensity and frequency of controversial idioms, *The Toilet* is Jones' most "obscene" play. And Jones' characters are not using this language exclusively for any symbolic content. Jones here is striving for linguistic fidelity, for realism. The question, then, is how much realism is art? The answer to this depends upon one's orientation and one's concept of the purposes and the nature of literature. Clearly, Jones has attempted to portray the brutal aspects of modern life and its resultant constriction of human expressions of love. The language which men use to control others' lives is in a sense "profane," no matter how "acceptable" this language is to society. (One must remember Jones' dicta on language and laws.) In this sense, "decent" language used to pervert man's attempts to love is "indecent."

The same principle applies to the physical setting and physical action of the play. A toilet is symbolic of the world that Jones is trying to describe through drama. It is a world of "peeing" people who go about their business of dehumanizing other people in the least pleasant "rooms"[16] of the world. A dirty toilet is most compatible to their purposes, and they are so intent on their evil purposes that they are oblivious to the room's filth and stench. The actions of the boys in the microcosmic toilet are reflections of the vacant, ego-boosting, cruel, and finally useless actions that pass for human relations in a vicious society, a society where humans find personal fulfillment in predatory acts upon other humans.

Whether Jones' use of language, setting, and action in *The Toilet* is or is not art is, finally, a consideration of degree. One is reminded of the question, how long should a piece of string be? In a poem written several years before *The Toilet,* Jones recalls the situation upon which the play is based:

> Was James Karolis a great sage??
> Why did I let Ora Matthews beat him up
> in the bathroom? Haven't I learned my lesson.
> ["Look for You Yesterday, Here You Come Today"]

Jones, it appears, had decided in the intervening years to have too much rather than too little string.

Comic blasphemy: *The Baptism*

In *The Baptism,* LeRoi Jones concerns himself with two hypocrisies, religion and, to a lesser extent, love as a tenet of religion. Neither, he dramatizes, exists freely and honestly. The person who naively and instinctively seeks either will not be understood. Neither will he be appreciated. Love (sex) and spirituality (religion) are perverted by the priestcraft and their followers.

The tone and the action of this play smack of allegorical burlesque, as if Jones never had thought of a morality play but instead decided to use his theme in a bawdy farce, with three Jonesian symbol-images standing out: dance, homosexuality, and heterosexuality.

The play opens in a church with a minister and a homosexual thinking aloud about love. A boy comes in, sobs, and asks the minister to pray for him, a sinner. The minister is ineffectual as an agent for the absolution of the boy's sin, and the homosexual awaits an opportunity to try to seduce the boy. Meanwhile an old woman enters and accuses the boy of masturbating (by the homosexual's calculations, 1,095 times) while saying his prayers. She would not have the minister intercede on the boy's behalf:

BLASPHEMER.   You spilled your seed while pretending to talk to God. I saw you. That quick short stroke. And it was so soft before, and you made it grow in your hand. I watched it stiffen, and your lips move and those short hard moves with it straining in your fingers for flesh. Not God. You spilled the seed in God's name? And then that fluid, what all life needs, spilled there in your fingers, and your lips still moving begging God to forgive you.

The homosexual points out the old woman's hypocrisy, saying:

Bah. She takes flesh, just like you did son, but she makes it abstract and use-less. So it is holy and harmless. I pee on her Jesus if he but dare to tell me who and when I can get laid. . . . If God is omnipotent, it is his doing, as well. And who killed all those Egyptians with all that water? Satan? Bullshit. That ignorant woman's lord in his wretched community of sterile eavesdroppers.

Also, the homosexual sees the minister as a hypocritical politician for religion and a fascist one at that. As to himself, he admits:

I be Giotto of the queers. I be Willie Mays of the queers. I not be lim-lim limited to tiny nigger songs. Dance with me, boy. . . . I make all my beds, and baby, I lie in them.

When a chorus of women—the "virgins of Christ's love" and the minister's "usherettes"—enters, the boy observes them and exclaims, "Father, I must be baptized! I feel the sin returning. That hardness in my flesh." The women then think they recognize the boy as Jesus, "Beautiful screw of the universe!" The boy denies any claim to divinity, and the homosexual admiringly muses that the boy "has put these art majors in a trick." The women and the minister turn to the boy, prepare to punish (crucify) him, but he announces, "There will be no second crucifixion!"

At this point, a messenger on a motorcycle arrives to take the boy away, saying:

The man sent me. . . . Yeh. The man. Your father. . . . Yeh. I'm closing up this whole deal. The man don't like none of the action. It's all finished.

Then the following dialogue ensues:

BOY: But he sent me here to save them. This earth.

MESSENGER: Yeh, I know. But you been fuckin' up royally. You agree?
BOY: Agree? No. I don't agree. I have brought love to many people.
MESSENGER: Well, it's not my doing. The man says you just blew your gig.
BOY: That's not true.
MESSENGER: I don't have time to argue, Percy, orders is orders. The man's destroying the whole works tonight. With a grenade.

Over the boy's protests, the messenger follows his orders and forcefully whisks the boy away. As the lights dim, only the homosexual arises from the pile of bodies on the floor; he looks around and blithely leaves in order to get to the bars before they close.

The rather obvious allegorical and symbolic interpretations of this play are the boy as a latter-day Christ, the minister as organized religion, the women as Christian society, and the homosexual as the devil (he calls himself "the son of man"). Asked if he regards the boy as a Christ-figure, Jones says that the boy is, in a sense, "A kind of modern adaptation of it—really, a kind of naive—I think that's what I thought that the Christ-figure has been, a totally naive person to believe he could go up against these evil persons and not be crucified. That's Percy,"[17] In this context, then, Jones shows in the play that God does not consider the modern world worth His passion, and He forcibly rescues His Son, the agent of love, from a meaningless crucifixion. The devil, homosexual that he is, is at least honest about his religion (or irreligion) and remains to cruise about looking for human prey. In other words, Christianity has failed not so much because the devil (the homosexual) ensnares people, for no one in the play succumbs to him, but because the so-called Christians refuse to live their professed faith. The devil wins by default.

About this play, Donald Costello concluded, "Jones strains to be shocking; and the play ends up incoherent and adolescent, with scatter-shot fury."[18] One is hard put to find this fury that Costello speaks of; one can find some narrative incoherence; and one can with some reason adjudge the play somewhat adolescent in dramatic approach. But, assuredly, one can hardly miss the play's shock value.

The shock springs mainly from four elements: the overall blasphemous theme, the irreverent characterization, the use of profanity and obscenity, and the anti-Christian humor. Indeed, in this play one sees Jones' use of profanity as both technique and weapon. It seems even more objectionable because it is delivered as rather effortless, routine speech by characters whose speech would be expected to be "pure." For example, when the homosexual calls the minister an "interminable liar, executioner of the ignorant," this religious man's rejoiner is "You are becoming unpleasant Miss Cocksucker and I don't like it." In another episode, when the good church women think that the boy is not the Son of God after all, they cry out, "Ohh. Christ. Fucked for nothing." The shock value is increased when such expressions are juxtaposed with pious religious cliches.

The humor is both irreverently "hip" and broadly gross. Much in the same manner that the profanity is intensified because of its incongruity, quite a bit of the play's humor is predicated upon ludicrous circumstances. For instance, shortly after the minister has pontifically reassured the boy of God's wisdom, charity, and mercy, the minister descends from his pontifical manner to scuffle with the homosexual, accusing, "You've cheated in the collections. Withheld the beautiful money of the poor. Shouted the chorales out of key, and groped the organist in the trustees' room." There are lines that satirize the pseudo-intellectual, as when the homosexual tells the women to "Go home and pin up some Picasso prints or something. . . . Go home to your wretched Electra complexes." There are topical gags, as when the praying women intone, "God bless mommy and daddy, and Rochester, and Uncle Don. . . . And bring me a new doll, and a monopoly set, and an FM radio and a picture of Monk." And as is frequently the case when the devil appears in literature, he (the homosexual) gets some of the best lines.

What LeRoi Jones has done, then, in *The Baptism* is to use the Jonesian humor and clever line as techniques in an attempt to make a philosophical-religious point. Whether or not he succeeds depends upon the individual viewer's or reader's perspective and religion. The outcome may all depend on whether the individual can bear up under the medium long enough to get the message.

Of death and dessert: *Experimental Death Unit #1* and *J-E-L-L-O*

Experimental Death Unit #1 and *J-E-L-L-O* are two of the earliest plays of LeRoi Jones that manifest his theories of drama as expressed in his landmark essay, "The Revolutionary Theatre," written in 1964, his most prolific year in drama. *Death Unit,* to apply phrases from this essay, seeks to "expose," to "Accuse and Attack," to "show victims so that their brothers in the audience will be better able to understand," and to "force change." *J-E-L-L-O* seeks to "teach them [whites] about silence and the truths lodged there," to "take dreams and give them a reality," to present "new kinds of heroes—not the weak Hamlets."

Using sex as a symbol-motif, the short *Death Unit* shows two derelict white males, Duff and Loco, both heterosexual but one also perverted in his sex habits, who chance upon a somewhat bedraggled black woman about forty years of age but "still gallantly seductive." A prostitute, she entices them, weighing their intentions of how they would have her sexually and enjoying observing their desire for her rising to the point where they are willing to fight each other over her. Before the first can consummate a sex act with the woman, the other kills him and then proceeds to take her sexually. They are interrupted, however, by a group of paramilitary black youths who shoot both the white man and the black woman just after she has reassured her customer, "Ohh, honey...it's just a soul-brother...don't worry. I'll cool everything out." Then the soldiers regroup into formation and march off.

The lesson in this play is plain enough for almost any audience to grasp. A black who would literally or symbolically prostitute or, worse still, pervert himself (in this play, herself) to the white world deserves summary execution. The malefactors' judgment has come quickly, for, as poet-critic Lance Jeffers points out, their moral disease is "beyond the hope of redemption"; it is a disease which has descended "into the psychic marrow." Recalling the ending of T. S. Eliot's "The Hollow Men," Jeffers notes that they have died whimpering, "bereft of dignity," their last whimpers signifying "what the Western world has wrought." Continuing, Jeffers says, "But while Eliot turned inward into despair and snobbery, Baraka turns outward to the great breadth of black people, turns outward to the cleansing fire."[19]

To reinforce and to carry the larger symbolism of the play, Jones has operative, in addition to his sex symbolism, several of his symbol-images: windows—as in Duff's line, "Well sufferer, my windows are as icy as the rest of the world"; wet—as in Loco's observation that "Her wet thighs make prints under the skirt"; rooms and hallways—as when the woman tells Loco and Duff, "No rooms...just the hallway. . . . Come on in. Strip down." Although the symbolic action is easy enough to follow, the figurative language which Jones puts into his characters' mouths is at times a bit abstruse, sounding at times like his more difficult poetry. Yet one also finds in *Death Unit* the easy-to-interpret street language that Jones was to employ so much more in his later drama.

J-E-L-L-O, almost pure farce, also has a clear message. A parody of the Jack Benny radio and television show, it presents a "long hair, postuncletom" Rochester who defies the orders of his employer of long years, Jack Benny. To add insult to injury, he force-robs Benny, and when Mary and Dennis, other characters on the show, appear he reinforces their impression that Benny is joking when Benny accuses Rochester of insubordination and robbery. Mary

and Dennis eventually learn the truth, however. Dennis is too timid to do anything about the situation, and faints. Alone now with Mary, Rochester declares,
"Yeh, I know you got somethin' I need...right up between them nasty thighs...
and it's me for takin' it...right now." Resigned, Mary prepares to enjoy what
she thinks is going to be a rape. Instead, Rochester pulls a money bag from
under her skirt, saying, "Never touched you." Disappointed, she responds,
"You fiend. You...you..." and then faints. Finally, yelling goodbye to the pros-
trate figures and to announcer Don, Rochester howls with laughter and leaves.

Subtlety is not a technique in this play. The major point is that in every
"Negro" there is a potential black man — a point which is not missed by most
black audiences. The major weapon for achieving this point is humor — humor
in the actions and humor in the dialogue. *J-E-L-L-O*'s humor is not the intellectual wit that Jones displays in certain other works. Here there is the universally
funny motif of an inferior turning on his superior, the humor that is a part of
slangy street language, the ribald humor of the Rochester-Mary episode, the
gross humor of an excruciatingly effeminate Dennis Day characterization, the
timeless humor of a miser's agony at giving up his treasures, and the openly
symbolic humor of announcer Don Wilson faithfully making a sales pitch for
Jello despite the chaos about him. Such is the type of fun-and-games that does
not often fail to convulse audiences composed of society's common folk or
"underdogs" of any time and place.

Part of this humor is one of the things that kept Bobbs-Merrill from publishing the play. It had been scheduled for publication along with four other of
Jones' plays, but the company feared possible libel suits because of *J-E-L-L-O*'s
characterization of the public figures involved. So *Five Black Revolutionary
Plays* never was printed; instead *Four Black Revolutionary Plays* appeared, with
a note, "Why No J-E-L-L-O?" by Jones, reading in part:

> In an era when Lyndon Johnson is accused in a dumb joke evenings of
> having knocked off the first Kennedy, and Maddox is molested by jewish
> liberals for having had the honesty to be the true devil that they all are, this
> publisher has the nerve to censor and refuse to publish the play, J-E-L-L-O, as
> attacking a public figure's private life.
>
> It sound seems like something shaky in the state of white head. How this is
> figured we can tell right off. This play J-E-L-L-O has been censored, kept off
> the set for all the years since its writing (1965) except that its been seen by
> more Black People than most plays, aside, unfortunately, from the tv sets, be-
> cause this was one of the plays we took out into the streets in harlem and in
> other streets across the country.

He promises that "Jihad is publishing the play as a side order, and this like is no protest, but an advertisement." As things turned out, Jihad did not publish the play; late in 1970 another black press, Third World Press, did.

During a panel-critique of another writer's play, Baraka told his fellow black playwrights that what "we have to do at this point in our lives . . . is to try to say it like a big poster."[20] *Death Unit* and *J-E-L-L-O* both are big posters. The letters on the *J-E-L-L-O* poster just happen to be bolder.

More posters: *A Black Mass, Madheart,* and *Great Goodness Of Life*

Three plays that followed in the year or so after Jones' "big" 1964 year bear mentioning. They are not truly transitional plays, but they do show in several ways the evolution of Jones the playwright.

Called by one critic Jones' "most accomplished play to date,"[21] *A Black Mass* is based upon the original man theory of the Nation of Islam (Black Muslims) as espoused by Elijah Muhammad. In this play an evil thing is created by one of the original "black magicians," Jacoub, the one who could not resist experimenting to create new organisms. In the beginning all is at peace, and fellow magician Tanzil tells Jacoub, "It's a fool's game to invent what does not need to be invented." But Jacoub persists, reasoning, "Let us be fools. For creation is its own end." He succeeds, and when the third magician, Nasafi, looks into the heart of Jacoub's creature he finds "Where the soul's print should be, there is only a cellulose pouch of disgusting habits. . . . THIS THING WILL KILL, JACOUB...WILL TAKE HUMAN LIFE. . . . Jacoub, this creature will take human life...because IT HAS NO REGARD FOR HUMAN LIFE!"

The creature which Jacoub has created is the white man, a wild thing who will not be taught humaneness. Further, Tanzil discovers, "It has merely to touch something to turn it into itself. Or else it sucks out the life juices." It is particularly predatory around women. This white creature is recognized as being incorrigible, so it is banished to the cold places of the earth. The closing words of the play's narrator are:

> And so Brothers and Sisters, these beasts are still loose in the world. Still they spit their hideous cries. There are beasts in our world, Brothers and Sisters. There are beasts in our world. Let us find them and slay them. Let us lock them in their caves. Let us declare the Holy War. The Jihad. Or we cannot deserve to live. Izm-el-Azam. Izm-el-Azam. Izm-el-Azam.

In other words, *A Black Mass* "explains" the existence of the white man (the evil) in the world, and it defines in the closing statement what black people must do to restore the "eternal concentration and wisdom" to the world. It is Jones' strongest dramatic statement of the original-virtue-of-black-people theme.

Madheart presents Mother and her blonde-wig-wearing daughter, named Sister, both infected with whiteness, and a white-masked Devil Lady and their encounter with Black Man and Black Woman ("with soft natural hair"). A lovers' triangle of sorts develops with the young females vying for Black Man. Black Man realizes, however, that "This is the nightmare in all of our hearts. Our mothers and sisters groveling to white women, wanting to be white women, dead and hardly breathing on the floor."

He stabs the Devil Lady, but Sister falls, too, as if the man has stabbed her, for, as Black Woman explains, "You're killed if you are made in the dead thing's image, if the dead thing on the floor has your flesh, and your soul. If you are a cancerous growth. Sad thing." Black Man feels guilty, believing that he has killed one of his own. But Sister is still alive. "She's not even dead," says Black Woman to him. "She just thinks she has to die because that white woman died. She's sick." Black Man then turns upon Black Woman, slapping her, demanding that she "Go down, submit, submit...to love...and to man, now, forever." Black Woman submits. When Sister regains consciousness, she and her mother comfort each other. As the play ends Black Woman asks, "You think there's any chance for them? You really think so?" Black Man answers, "They're my flesh. I'll do what I can—We'll both try. All of us, black people."

The allegorical texture of the play is apparent. Written for the Black Arts Alliance in San Francisco and first performed at San Francisco State College, *Madheart* is a bit more poetic and a bit more intellectual in language than Jones' plays intended for audiences from the black masses. This is not to say that the dialogue as a whole is consistently symbolic or cerebral. There is mass-directed humor. There are many lines heavy with obscenities. Subtitled *A Morality Play,* this work is intended as a message, and the closing lines are clearly indicative of the role that Jones expects young black people to play in dealing with their white-oriented brothers and sisters. The theme preaches a doctrine that Jones espoused in a magazine article—the black woman must inspire, submit to, complement, and praise her black man and in that way contribute to the development of the black nation.[22]

The central character in *Great Goodness of Life* has as his genesis Coyt Jones, LeRoi Jones' father. "Some of it obviously involves situations he was involved in, like, you know, the post office," Jones says. "Still, what I did was take that situation and draw an obvious extreme."[23]

The obvious extreme, Court Royal, is a respectable, middle-aged post office supervisor, who, in a sort of fantasy, finds himself summarily brought before a court and accused of shielding a wanted criminal, a murderer. Alternately perplexed, embarrassed, and mildly indignant, Royal persists in pleading not guilty, upon which he is told that under the circumstances he will not need a lawyer. When he protests that he is a "good man," the Voice replies, "Royal, you're not a man!" Then he is forced to look at a screen upon which are flashed the faces of "Malcolm. Patrice. Rev. King. Garvey. Dead nigger kids killed by the police. Medgar Evers." Royal breaks down and calls them "My sons." Then in a bit of Jonesian irony the Voice declares, "We have decided to spare you. We admire your spirit. . . . You are absolved of your crime, at this moment, because of your infinite understanding of the compassionate God Of The Cross. Whose head was cut off for you, to absolve you of your weakness." But before he can be released, Court Royal must perform a rite, which he does: He shoots to death his own son, then declares, "My soul is as white as snow."

Called by Jones *A Coon Show,* this play, too, is a combination allegory and morality play. The lesson to be learned is that Negroes unintentionally kill the black spirit if they are not aggressively involved in discovering and nurturing their blackness and their children's blackness. Court Royal never realized that he had committed a crime (killing his own blackness), never saw his judge face to face (the determinants of his fate are invisible to him), and he carries out his destiny (the killing of his own son) unquestioningly, feeling this to be an act of expiation.

"Plays of human occasion": The more recent dramas

The plays that LeRoi Jones wrote, produced, or published through 1966 set precedents for or had elements or features that were to become more readily noticeable in his succeeding drama, features that are now looked upon as typically Barakan. The wordless, ritualistic *Resurrection of Life* is in dramatic method not unlike the ritualistic, pantomimic parts of *Slave Ship. Junkies Are Full of (SHHH...)* "teaches" in much the same way as *Experimental Death Unit #1* "teaches," that is, by example. *Great Goodness* uses broad caricature as does the earlier *J-E-L-L-O.* The mixture of fantasy and history in *The Death of Malcolm X* has a precedent in the myth-histories that are a part of *Madheart* and *A Black Mass.* The theme of misunderstanding among people in *Dutchman* is also a theme in *Home on the Range.* As these examples imply, the Barakan features have always been in his drama—the question is just a matter of emphasis and intensity. As he was becoming in his other literary genres, Jones in drama was becoming what he would term "less uselessly 'literary.'"

His more recent plays such as *Home on the Range, Police, The Death of Malcolm X, Resurrection of Life, Junkies Are Full of (SHHH . . .), Columbia the Gem of the Ocean,* and *Bloodrites* are not subtle in terms of action, characterization, or theme. They are, by and large, "common experience theatre in the sense of being able to teach very literally."[24] Jones feels that it is the playwright's job to synthesize the black experience, to present a "collective consciousness," using as materials "the stuff that a lot of people are talking about in *Muhammed Speaks* and the *National Guardian* and on the sidewalks. . . . All the people who are walking around making statements that contribute to our lives have to be dealt with by artists, as in all societies."[25] This "collective consciousness" must be presented with such clarity that *all* black people can understand: "Like they say, you know, in religion, that you can meditate and study spiritualism for a hundred years but there's nothing as valuable as one clearly stated idea. That's the most valuable thing. The most valuable gift there is. One clear idea that rings true and cannot be refuted . . . And that's what I'd like to see."[26]

Two examples of his plays that use "the stuff that a lot of people are talking about" are *The Death of Malcolm X* and *Police.* The first is predicated upon rumors, that have persisted, to the effect that Malcolm X was murdered with the federal government's sanction, either by Central Intelligence Agency type agents or by gunmen encouraged by the government. In montage and kaleidoscopic fashion, Jones depicts such things as a lascivious politician-klansman in Washington planning, between sessions with a frowsy woman, Malcolm's death; a classroom where blacks are being indoctrinated to love whiteness and to hate blackness; a man helplessly afflicted with "the Gandhi syndrome" (clearly Dr. Martin Luther King) leading a group of people in a bland demonstration; another man, obviously Roy Wilkins, receiving an award, "a life sized watermelon made of precious stones and gold"; and "Malcolm dead on floor with weeping hysterical mourners." Then "We hear the tv announcer: 'Today black extremist Malcolm X was killed by his own violence.'" Jones' point is that white America, with the indirect help of certain types of Negroes, is responsible for Malcolm's death.

Police has as its premise the notion held by some blacks that black policemen are traitors and/or reluctant killers of their black brothers and sisters. Black Cop in the play repeats "I don wanna" but nevertheless finally has to change to "I didn' wanna!" One of the characters who leap from the "audience" and participate in the drama speaks the line which directly expresses the play's theme: "Black cop crazy shit in America."

According to Jones, "It is easier to get people into a consciousness of black power, what it is, by emotional example than through dialectical lecture. Black people seeing the recreation of their lives are struck by what is wrong or missing in them."[27] To this end, he is increasingly including elements of ritual and "agit-prop" theatre and hints of street or guerilla theatre in his drama. By no means is his later drama subtle or abstract. Realism and audience involvement are paramount techniques for these kinds of theatre. At times it appears that Jones is moving toward the type of guerilla or street or instant theatre that he called for in a 1967 article:

> In the street, at the spot where such . . . is taking place. Have your actors shoot mayors if necessary, right in the actual mayor's chambers. Let him feel the malice of the just. Let the people see justice work out repeatedly. Examples. Explain evolution.
> Plays for the police department. Jew plays, whether con rolling big ass communications or laying in southorangeavenue always dough producing swamps. Light in every element. Show the chains. Let them see the chains as object and subject, and let them see the chains fall away.[28]

In his review of a performance of *Slave Ship* at Theatre in the Church, Harold Clurman asserted that "The *Slaveship* company is in the purest sense of the word *tribal,* hence unassumingly impressive."[29] It has no plot, in the strict sense of the term. The play[30] is a fusion of words, many in Yoruba, many really only human sounds rather than words:

> WOMAN 3—Moshake, chile, calm, calm be you. Moshake
>   chile. O calm, Orisha, save us!
> WOMAN 2—AAAI-IIEEEEEEEEE

of various sounds:

> Drums (African *bata* drums, and bass and snare
> Rattles and tambourines
> Banjo music for plantation atmos.
>
> Ship noises
> Ship bells
> Rocking and Splashing of Sea
>
> Guns and cartridges
> Whips/whip sounds

of smells:

> Sea smells. In the dark. Keep the people in the dark, and gradually the odors of
> the sea, and the sounds of the sea, and sounds of the ship, creep up. Burn in-
> cense, but make a significant, almost stifling, smell come up. Urine. Excrement.
> Death. Life processes going on anyway. Eating. These smells, and cries, the
> slash and tear of the lash, in a total atmos-feeling, gotten some way.

of music:

> (In background, while preacher is frozen in his "Jeff" position, high hard sound
> of saxophone, backed up by drums. New-sound saxophone tearing up the
> darkness. At height of screaming saxophone, instruments and drums, comes
> voices screaming...)

and of lighting effects:

> (Lights on suddenly, show a shuffling "Negro". Lights off...drums of ancient
> warriors come up...hero-warriors. Lights blink back on, show shuffling black
> man, hat in the hand, scratching his head. Lights off. . . . Lights flash on briefly,
> spot on, off the dance. Then off. Then on, to show The Slave raggedy . . .

All of these elements are fused with the pageantry of action and dialogue, and
Jones handles all of them with consummate artistic skill. That the play has an
electrifying effect upon audiences is generally agreed upon: critic Clurman
called it "a theatrical phenomenon";[31] Newsweek's Jack Kroll reported the
"overwhelming intensity"[32] of the Free Southern Theater production of it; reviewer Edith Oliver declared "The music by Archie Shepp and Gilbert Moses,
and performed by six instrumentalists, sounds absolutely wonderful."[33]

Productions of Slave Ship achieve a realism that approaches street theatre
in method: Kroll reported that ". . . slaves reached out clawing for help from
the New York Times' Clive Barnes, a nausea-racked slave retched realistically
in the lap of Norman Nadel of the Scripps-Howard papers, and during a slave
auction a little black boy was 'sold' to the New Yorker's Edith Oliver."[34] In a
different article from the one just mentioned above, Harold Clurman said that
"The audience is caught in the overall ferment. . . . One realizes the possibility
of a frenzied and overpowering outbreak."[35]

Jones must have intended impromptu theatre, "agit-prop" theatre that edi-
fies and motivates the audience. This being so, is Slave Ship a "get-whitey"

play as Clive Barnes thinks? When LeRoi Jones appeared on a David Frost television program, he was asked about Clive Barnes' assessment of the play. Jones answered:

Well, it's unfortunate that Clive Barnes is the only drama critic that you can make reference to. The play is not written. I think maybe he feels that way because maybe he feels the need to be gotten. But that's not why I wrote it. I wrote it to express a certain people's feeling about what is real in the world. And I think if he has apprehensions about the reality of his own life, you know, and his own guilt, well, that's his problem.

FROST: What did you write the play to get across, in fact?

JONES: Well, to try to explain naturally to sensitive people, black people exactly what the realities of the slave ship were and how they have carried over, how America in a lot of sense is just a reply or a continuation of that same slave ship, that it's not changed. (APPLAUSE)[36]

A concomitant of the trend toward impromptu theatre is the presence of elements of theatre-of-the-absurd. In *The Death of Malcolm X,* Jones has, for example, "The fat klansman with a blonde riding on his shoulders around the room. He has the top of his klansuit down, leaving his chest naked. She is licking his shoulders. She is screaming, 'Giddyap, big pappa...giddyap!' He makes whinnying sounds, like a horse, and bucks stupidly." In *Police* people in the audience become a part of the play, and there are numerous nonsense lines. In *Home on the Range* there are nonwords: "Vataloop bingo. Vashmash. Cratesy. Ming." Indeed, *Police* has been described as a "piece for voices and music,"[37] electronically mixed. *Resurrection of Life* is wordless, its pantomimes suggesting ritual abstractions as well as narrative line.

In addition, his later plays have taken on characteristics of pageantry, appealing to the eye and ear and depending less upon the type of cerebral reaction necessary for an appreciation of, say, *Dutchman. The Death of Malcolm X* moves rapidly from mini-scene to mini-scene, creating almost a blur of visual images. *A Black Mass* relies heavily upon "(Sun-Ra). Music of eternal concentration and wisdom." *Slave Ship* employs pageantry. Much of *Columbia the Gem of the Ocean* depends upon mime for dramatic effect.

Despite his use of nonverbal language, LeRoi Jones, unlike some other current playwrights, has not abandoned language as a primary dramatic technique. His dialogue is not without occasional brilliance whether he is using street idioms or highly original and poetically charged language. In fact, even some of his stage directions are poetic. Neither has he forsaken the Jonesian verbal humor.

As he has attempted new dramatic forms and techniques, he has not neglected the traditional. Richard Schechner noted that "Surprisingly, among the writers who have maintained a steady relationship with the avant-garde is LeRoi Jones. His militancy has not militated against his powerful use of new forms. As he has used them, these forms are also traditional. Tom Dent of the Free Southern Theatre pointed out to me how dear black culture holds participation, song, tragic and triumphant celebration."[38] There is no doubt that Jones draws heavily on the dramatic traditions and conventions of minstrelsy, ritual, allegory, morality, and pageant.

The drama of LeRoi Jones has had wide and deep influence on other black playwrights. The testimony of Ed Bullins is typical of what young black writers are saying:

> I didn't really find myself until I saw *Dutchman.* That was the great influence on my life. LeRoi has greatly influenced many young black artists. I say without reservations that LeRoi Jones is one of the most important, most significant figures in American theater. Now, hardly anybody knows it but we playwrights and artists. We know that the Man (LeRoi) has changed theater in this country by creating or influencing or whatever he has done to black theater, which will have a great effect on the overall theater of this country.[39]

David Littlejohn, not famed for being an admirer of Jones the writer, believes that "no Negro playwright except LeRoi Jones has even begun to take advantage of the dynamic potential of living theatre in the manner initiated by Genet."[40] Finally, the words of Toni Cade demand to be repeated: "The LeRoi Jones plays from 1962 to 1964 were more than a beginning of Black Theater. It [sic] was."[41]

Part III

Chapter 8. Latter day romantic, early black aesthetician
Summary and conclusions

The findings presented in part one of this book lead to the following general-izations. First, the study of LeRoi Jones' life reveals a gifted young person who while living a racially integrated life during the late 1950's and early 1960's became a major literary figure in the intellectual and artistic avant-garde; who then turned from this social, intellectual, and artistic ambience to become the leading theoretical and practicing black cultural nationalist, a community leader, and a political organizer and catalyst. Second, Jones' characteristic ways of perceiving and thinking show the following: he conceives of culture as the total of life's activities and of art as process; he anticipates the atrophy of Western culture and a concomitant rise of a black culture; he gives some evi-dence of being anti-white America, anti-Semitic, and anti-Negro middle-class, or positively stated, he is strongly pro-black (not pro-Negro). He believes in the superiority of separatism and active resistance over assimilation and passive resistance as methods of dealing with America's race problems. He advocates cultural, social, spiritual, economic, and political black populist nationalism. Third, his characteristic modes of expression reveal a versatile writer keenly aware of the power of words as laws—that is, as a means of molding public attitudes and ultimately as a means of attaining and maintaining power; highly inventive in the use of language; dadaistic in matters of mechanics and form; humorous both in a general way and satirically; original, occasionally to the point of being cryptic, in style; and highly original and personal in the use of figurative language, particularly in the use of symbol-images.

These three—his experiences, his characteristic ways of thinking, and his characteristic ways of writing—interact in such a way that it is difficult to say what is cause and what is effect in any given situation. The Jones-to-Baraka movement was an evolutionary process, Barakan characteristics always having been present to some degree and in some form.

The examination of Jones' literary works in part two shows: His nonfiction prose, more than any other genre, is revelatory of his ideologies, philosophies, and theories. It is also indicative of his stylistic versatility. His fiction is the most consistent of all genres in terms of style, being essentially of two types, "as-sociation complexes" and "fast narratives." He has written practically no fiction since *System* and *Tales.* His poetry has changed in content, form, and style from private and lyrical poetry of the avant-garde type to public and exhortative poetry of the black aesthetic persuasion. As his poetry has changed, it has depended less upon compression and symbol-images, more upon prose-like declarations. His drama has changed drastically in structure and technique but not basically in theme since his early success, *Dutchman*. His later drama tends to be impulsive, pageant-like, and ritualistic, and it has become openly a medium for teaching, evangelizing, and motivating.

On the basis of the examination of Jones' works, what identifying and evaluative conclusions can be reached?

It would be well to consider first the conclusions of critics, remembering that critics, too, must be evaluated. In any attempt to assess the literature of any writer, a good critic is careful before looking at the writer's work to make a distinction between personal preferences of types and styles and objective judgments of types and styles. Carrying this a step further, assuming that a critic is objective in his judgment of types and styles of literature, the good critic is then careful to judge the work rather than the writer. For so controversial a man as LeRoi Jones, objectivity is important, for it is easy to like or dislike his work on ethnic, ideological, or political grounds.

About the only generalization that can be made about critics' evaluation of Jones' work is that there is no way to generalize. It is almost a truism that one can tell the ethnic and cultural (and sometimes, political) orientation of a reviewer or critic of a given work by Jones. Too often the non-black, culturally traditional, or artistically conventional critic will find Jones lacking in technique and offensive in content. Too often the black (as different, in current connotation, from Negro), culturally nontraditional, or artistically unconventional critic will find Jones, especially as Baraka, progressive in technique and a well of truth in content. So to various critics, Jones is artist, eyegouger, illuminator, racist, moral conscience, demagogue, or prophet. But no matter what critics term him, LeRoi Jones affects indifference. "Critics," he asserts, "are supposed to be people in a position to tell what is of value and what is not, and hopefully, at the time it first appears. If they are consistently mistaken, what is their value?"[1] To Jones, the white critic grounded in Western artistic values is likely to be mistaken often, for "a society whose only strength lies in its ability to destroy itself and the rest of the world has small claim toward defining intelligence or beauty."[2] Moreover, he says, "They rely on their experience, not realizing that we have a totally different experience. They criticize us if we don't meet their particular references."[3] Where does he turn for critical reactions? "Our critics, he claims, "are the ones on the streets."[4]

Classifying or typing Jones as a writer is not easy, for he is versatile in both genre and style. Within his writing one can find elements of different literary periods, schools, and movements. For example, he is "baroque" in his asymmetrically structured fiction, in his juxtaposition of the unexpected with the expected in poetry, in writing whatever his mind unfolds at the time he is writing. He is "realistic" in his use of actual speech idioms and in, for example, his emotional and physical setting for *The Toilet.* He is "neoclassical" in his use of subway riders as a sort of chorus in *Dutchman.* He is "folk" in his depiction of life in the subculture known as the inner-city and in his use of ethnic language and lore. He is "naturalistic" in his tracing of the social causes of man's experiences, as in his tracing in *Blues People* of the causes of changes in jazz. But more than anything else, categorized according to literary labels he is "romantic."[5]

In a general way, Jones is a romantic in the sense that many literary historians and scholars consider the post-Romantic Period symbolists, imagists, realists, naturalists, dadaists, impressionists, and other modern writers as latter day romantics or as part of a romantic continuum. He is a romantic in more specific ways as well. Like Emerson and certain other romantic writers, in a transcendentalistic way Jones places great faith in intuition, in feelings. As he applies this faith in an ethnocentric way, he would have blacks place faith in what he assumes to be their singular mystical impulses. He is antirational in the way that romantics of Western European literature were opposed to the "cold" rationality of neoclassicism. Moreover, in connection with this reliance upon innate urgings and promptings, Jones inescapably asserts, as Blake and other romantic mystics contended, that man is divine, although, as Baraka, Jones would argue that the white man has perverted his, the white man's, divinity. Also, Jones is, like those romantics who would not conform to neoclassical religious dogma and traditions, romantic in that he is disdainful of the organized and orthodox religion of the majority and in that he has been himself a religous speculator and seeker. Next, Jones is romantic in his concern for the well-being, freedom, and dignity of the economically and politically weak, the dispossessed, the oppressed, and the downtrodden, as were the past century's romantic political and social libertarians and romantic champions of "humble" people. Further, Rousseau-like in his concern for the full development of man's potential, Jones sees his contemporary social, cultural, and political institutions as destructive of (black) man, so he would have man destroy, change, or control these institutions so that they, in his opinion, serve man rather than have man serve them. Further, Jones, like the Shelleys of the Romantic Period, is a visionary who sees creative artists as providers of philosophical and ideological bases for change. Next, in regard to technique, Jones, like many romantics of the past, will have little to do with conventional and prescribed forms and techniques, insists upon using the "language of the people," and constantly strives for new ways of writing, searching for what he calls a "post-American form." And it is obvious that Jones, as have countless romantics, uses his creative imagination to inform and shape his literary work.

Assuming then that according to commonly recognized identifying criteria for literary categories Jones is essentially a romantic, what is his stature according to commonly recognized Western criteria for literature regardless of category or label? On such a scorecard, he would rate very high on originality of expression, and he would be credited for creative use of his materials, individualistic thinking, and aptness of expression (figurative language). By conventional standards, he would be found lacking in control of his materials (form), undisciplined as a craftsman, and lacking in the expression of, for want of a better term, what would be called philosophical (in the sense of being commonly agreed upon) truth. As to those inescapable canons, universality and timelessness, he would be scored minus in one sense and plus in another sense. He would be downgraded on these two in that the very ethnocentrism and topicality of his content and method are antithetical to concepts of unlimited time and space. But he would be upgraded on these two in that the essential problem with which he concerns himself — man's inhumanity to man and what this does to all concerned — has existed everywhere, always. Jones is topical in the sense that the writer of Psalm 137 is topical, ethnocentric or provincial in the sense that Robert Burns is provincial — and Jones is universal and timeless in the sense that these writers are universal and timeless. But in terms of degree, of quality of writing, Jones is not recognized as being of their stature, according to accepted standards.

On balance then, on the basis of established and generally accepted Euro-American criteria for great literature, it cannot be said that LeRoi Jones has produced great literature.

Let us now consider Jones as a black aesthetician. It must be stressed that it is not our purpose here to argue if there is or is not a black aesthetic, nor, assuming that there is a black aesthetic, to argue whether or not a Western aesthetic and a black aesthetic are in the final analysis significantly different or mutually exclusive, nor to argue if a black aesthetic is or is not properly a part of a larger Western aesthetic, nor to argue whether the corpus known as black literature in the final analysis is or is not analogous to literary schools, categories, or movements of different times and places.[6]

But let us assume that Jones, as he says, is not trying to write according to generally recognized principles of a Western aesthetic. Let us assume that there is a black aesthetic and that Jones, as he says, is writing according to principles of this black aesthetic as they apply to literature. At this point we are somewhat blocked, for there now exist no codified and commonly recognized criteria for such literature. This being so, what we can do is look at the elements and characteristics of this literature as pronounced by those who speak or write about the black aesthetic and as exemplified by those who profess to be or seek to be creative black aestheticians. These interrelated elements and characteristics include prominently: utilitarianism; strong ethnocentric content; black nationalistic content; identification with the black masses; collective or communal black, as opposed to an individualistic or private, attitude; cynicism about or rejection of Euro-American culture values; disregard for the type of universality which black aestheticians claim the American literary establishment wrongly equates with Westernism (Euro-Americanism) rather than with worldism; usefulness for social, political, and economic change; ethnic pride and celebration of a hitherto sometimes avoided or disdained black culture (life style and value system); urban and rural black folk elements; "black language"; energetic diction; experimentation in search of new, or black, forms and techniques. Jones' writing exhibits all these elements and characteristics, and in high degree.

Jones, especially as Imamu Amiri Baraka, is not in the business of composing poems, constructing plays, or creating fiction for the sake of poetry or drama or fiction. He is in the business of effecting change that will be to the advantage of black people. He is a political organizer and catalyst and a cultural theorist and leader. To the extent that it will aid him in these areas, his writing is, to him, art. An essay, a poem, a story, or a play that will get across a point, convert an unbeliever, destroy an enemy, promote the Jihad, organize a fragmented group, or raise a black's appreciation of himself is an artistic essay, poem, story, or play. In other words, Jones is attempting to practice an important tenet of black aestheticism, that literature be of practical value to black people.

There remains a primary principle of the black aesthetic, that the literature be written by blacks about blacks for blacks, that is, for the black masses. It is on the last part of this criterion that one may find fault with Jones the avowed black aesthetician. There is no doubt that his intention is to write for black people. But can the masses understand him? Do the masses of black people read his works? Is he communicating with black people on the streets? Is he writing clear "posters?" The answer is, too frequently, no. Baraka has not succeeded in eliminating his early Jonesian inclination to esoteric, academic, metaphysical, and abstruse writing. The majority of his readers still are the white intellectuals, the black college students, and the relatively small "in-group" of black cultural nationalists and other Afro-Americans not identified as being a part of the bulk of the black masses. The average inner-city "dude," the average black man-on-the-street knows little if anything at all about either LeRoi Jones or Imamu Amiri Baraka and his literary works. (This is not to say, however, that Jones' literature does not or will not eventually in some way touch the lives of the black masses.) To Jones' credit as a black aesthetician, though, he is making a conscious attempt to get his writing directly to the black masses in comprehensible form.

By and large, according to the existing principles of black literary aesthetics, LeRoi Jones is considered to be the supreme writer. Moreover, he is recognized to be the leading theorist and spokesman for the current black cultural movement.

Testimonials to Jones' paramountcy in this respect are typically like that of Eugene Perkins, who says that of the newer, young black writers who seek critical acceptance in the black community rather than in the mainstream of the American literary community, "Perhaps the most prominent is the dynamic and gifted poet/playwright/essayist—LeRoi Jones . . ."[7] Or they are like Llorens who says, "Today he is regarded by those closest to black art as the nation's leading black writer, which of course suggests that no other, however talented, has proven—in this time and place—more valuable to black people."[8] There are those who will say that Jones was the first and most important mover and exponent of his age's black aestheticism and its concomitant black cultural nationalism, for instance, "Ameer Baraka . . . LeRoi Jones . . . set in motion the whole new Black Arts movement and . . . as playwright and polemicist, and as poet and practical politician, steers an imaginative course toward community consciousness."[9] In fact, Larry Neal credits Jones with first using "in a positive sense" the term "Black Arts."[10]

Young black writers almost invariably begin writing in the Jonesian style and continue to "use" him in the sense that Jones defines the term "use" (see p. 73, Black Music). The same applies to his ideology. In poetry, he is the standard, the prototype. One need only casually peruse a collection of poetry by young black writers to see poems in the Jonesian style. For example, in the propagandistic "Re-Act For Action," Don Lee uses "yr," "blk," and the diagonal (/); in "Down Wind Against The Highest Peaks," Clarence Major uses "Tonto Sambo Willie" as a symbol-image; in "Time Poem," Quentin Hill speaks of Roy

Wilkins as a ghost "walking along KNEEGRO tarbaby streets." The Jonesian prose style is immediately apparent to one perusing, say, the book reviews in an issue of *Black World* or an article in an issue of *Black Theatre.* The Jonesian theory about jazz as a social and spiritual phenomenon and his way of writing about jazz can be seen in the works of almost any critic in, say, an issue of *The Cricket.* As to drama, we have noted earlier Bullins' and Cade's estimations of Jones' influence. Larry Neal claims that "In drama, LeRoi Jones represents the most advanced aspects of the movement. He is its prime mover and chief designer."[11]

It is significant that in a survey conducted by *Negro Digest* in 1968 among some thirty-eight Afro-American writers, Jones was named the "most promising" black writer, the "most important living black poet," and the "most important black playwright."[12] Significant, too, was the election of Jones, in the fall of 1970, to the Black Academy of Arts and Sciences, in the company of such established literary people as Saunders Redding and Dorothy Louise Porter.

To return to the overall impact and value of LeRoi Jones, it seems to me that in addition to his other accomplishments as a writer he is performing an extremely valuable public service. "He has shown us," writes John Tryford, "the black-white confrontation in the frankest possible terms."[13] Paul Velde writes, "Jones and the whole problem of racism in the country calls upon whites to truly use their imaginations. Jones is performing the minimum Western ritual to bring this about."[14] Henry S. Resnik writes, ". . . a black man in a nation of shattered white dreams, Jones has focused his visions on himself and his life with such intensity and honesty that he has made himself a symbol of America's deepest troubles."[15] Certainly he is, as Maloff says, "a lyricist, a moralist, even a sentimentalist."[16] But, says Lance Jeffers, Jones is above all "a cleansing fire . . . the most cleansing of consciences."[17]

By using his gift with language and his particular sensibilities to explore situations afresh, to challenge existing beliefs, to rage against what he perceives as evil, to provide fresh insights, to propose new directions, in short, to illuminate life and to seek to better the quality of life, our author—Mr. LeRoi Jones, or Imamu Amiri Baraka—is accomplishing a prime function, is fulfilling a prime responsibility of the literary artist.

Notes

Notes to chapter 1

1. Quoted from a transcript of a tape-recorded interview of Jones by Theodore R. Hudson, Newark, New Jersey, July 29, 1970. Hereafter after the first documentation, this and other interviews conducted by Hudson are identified simply by the word "Interview" and the date.
2. Quoted from an interview of Mr. and Mrs. Jones by Theodore R. Hudson, Newark, New Jersey, October 24, 1970. This interview was not tape-recorded; the transcript is from notes taken during the interview.
3. "Suppose Sorrow Was a Time Machine," *Yugen,* issue No. 2 (1958), 10.
4. Ibid.
5. Ibid., p. 11.
6. *Blues People,* p. 96.
7. Ibid., p. 38.
8. Interview, July 29, 1970.
9. *Four Black Revolutionary Plays,* p. 17.
10. *The System of Dante's Hell,* p. 154.
11. Judy Stone, "If It's Anger . . . Maybe That's Good," San Francisco *Chronicle,* August 23, 1964, p. 42.
12. Jones quoted in David Llorens, "Ameer (LeRoi Jones) Baraka," *Ebony,* August, 1969, p. 78.
13. *Tales,* p. 73.
14. *Blues People,* p. 58.
15. New York *Herald Tribune Magazine,* December 13, 1964, as quoted in *Current Biography,* May, 1970, p. 16.
16. Interview, July 29, 1970.
17. Ibid.
18. Stone, p. 42.
19. Interview, October 22, 1970. Like the interview of October 24, 1970, documented in footnote 2, this interview was not tape-recorded, and the transcript is from notes taken during the interview.
20. *The System of Dante's Hell,* p. 41.
21. "Biographical Info" [sic], a photo-reproduced, single sheet distributed by Jones/Baraka, undated but circa 1969 inasmuch as it lists in its bibliography *Four Black Revolutionary Plays,* which was published in 1969.
22. Interview, July 29, 1970.

23. Stone, p. 42.
24. *Home,* p. 102.
25. Stone, p. 42.
26. "Philistinism and the Negro Writer," *Anger, and Beyond,* ed. Herbert Hill, pp. 51–52.
27. *Home,* p. 109. Jones now says that he does not remember exactly who this professor was; he recalls only that she was a young speech teacher (Interview, July 29, 1970).
28. "Philistinism and the Negro Writer," p. 52.
29. Ibid., pp. 51–52.
30. Interview, July 29, 1970.
31. Ibid.
32. "Biographical Info."
33. "Philistinism and the Negro Writer," pp. 52–53.
34. See, for example, James A. Emanuel and Theodore L. Gross, eds., *Dark Symphony,* p. 513.
35. "Biographical Info."
36. *Tales,* pp. 83–84.
37. *Current Biography,* May, 1970, p. 16.
38. Interview, October 24, 1970.
39. Quoted from a transcript of a tape-recorded telephone interview by Theodore R. Hudson, New York, N.Y., October 22, 1970.
40. Interview, July 29, 1970.
41. Quoted from a transcript of a tape-recorded interview of Theodore Wilentz by Theodore R. Hudson, New York, N.Y., October 22, 1970.
42. Interview, October 22, 1970.
43. Ibid.
44. Interview, October 22, 1970.
45. Interview, October 22, 1970.
46. Saul Gottlieb, "They Think You're an Airplane and You're Really a Bird," an interview, *Evergreen Review,* December, 1967, p. 53.
47. Interview, July 29, 1970.
48. Wilentz interview, October 22, 1970.
49. Hettie Jones interview, October 22, 1970.
50. *Catalog Ninety-three: Outside In* (New York: The Phoenix Book Shop, undated but in use by the store in 1970), p. 35.
51. Interview, October 22, 1970.
52. Stone, p. 42.

53. Today a copy of the issue of *The Trembling Lamb,* undated but c. 1960, containing *The System of Dante's Inferno* [sic] has a catalog price of $5.00. See *Modern First Editions,* Catalog Six (Spring, 1969), 30.
54. Interview, July 29, 1970.
55. Ibid.
56. Toni Cade, "Black Theater," *Black Expression: Essays by and about Black Americans in the Creative Arts,* ed. Addison Gayle, Jr., p. 137.
57. Stephen Schneck, "LeRoi Jones or, Poetics & Policemen or, Trying Heart, Bleeding Heart," *Ramparts,* July 13, 1968, p. 14.
58. Quoted in Schneck, p. 14.
59. Llorens, p. 75.
60. Ibid.
61. Schneck, p. 14.
62. *Black Magic Poetry,* p. viii.
63. Interview, July 29, 1970.
64. Stone, p. 42.
65. Ibid.
66. Llorens, p. 77.
67. Interview, July 29, 1970.
68. Ibid.
69. Interview, October 22, 1970.
70. James W. Sullivan, "The Negro 'National Consciousness' of LeRoi Jones," New York *Herald Tribune,* October 31, 1965, p. 34.
71. Interview, October 22, 1970.
72. "Tax Funds for a 'Hate the Whites' Project," *U.S. News and World Report,* December 13, 1964, p. 17.
73. Ibid.
74. Schneck, p. 16.
75. Interview, October 24, 1970.
76. Sullivan, "The Negro 'National Consciousness' of LeRoi Jones," p. 34.
77. James W. Sullivan, "HARYOU and the '5 Percenters,'" New York *Herald Tribune,* October 19, 1965, n.p.
78. Ibid.
79. Cy Egan and Frank Borsky, "Raid 'Pakistani Muslims,'" New York *Journal American,* March 18, 1966, p. 2.
80. Ibid.
81. Interview, July 29, 1970.
82. "Negro Theater Pimps Get Big Off Nationalism," p. 5.
83. Gottlieb, pp. 53–96.

84. Interview, July 29, 1970.
85. Gottlieb, p. 52.
86. Gerald Weales, "The Day LeRoi Jones Spoke on Penn Campus What Were the Blacks Doing in the Balcony?" New York *Times Magazine,* May 4, 1969, p. 38.
87. Letter from Mwanafunzi Katibu to Theodore R. Hudson, undated but postmarked September 11, 1970.
88. Llorens, p. 82.
89. "Black Women," *Black World,* July 1970, p. 9.
90. For Jones' version of events and forces which led up to this outbreak and for his description of incidents during the outbreak, see "Newark: Before Black Men Conquered" and "From: The Book of Life," both in *Raise.*
91. Gottlieb, p. 51.
92. Quoted in Schneck, pp. 16–17.
93. Sentencing proceedings, State of New Jersey v. Everett Le Roi Jones, Charles McCray & Barry Wynn, Essex County Court, Law Division, Criminal Indictment No. 2220–66, January 4, 1968, pp. 19–24, passim.
94. Quoted in "Poetic Justice," *Newsweek,* January 15, 1968, p. 24.
95. Jack Richardson, "Blues for Mr. Jones," *Esquire,* June 1966, p. 108.
96. "New Script for Newark," *Time,* April 26, 1968, p. 17.
97. Speech, Towson State College, Towson, Maryland, October 10, 1970. Quotation is from notes taken by Theodore R. Hudson.
98. Gottlieb, p. 52.
99. Stewart Alsop, "The American Sickness," *Saturday Evening Post,* July 13, 1968, p. 6.
100. "New Script for Newark," *Time,* April 26, 1968, p. 19.
101. Alsop, p. 6.
102. "The Need for a Cultural Base to Civil Rites & Bpower Mooments," *The Black Power Revolt,* ed. Floyd B. Barber, p. 120.
103. "An Interview with Mayor Kenneth Gibson of Newark," transcript of the David Frost Show, televised over WNEW-TV and other stations, Friday, August 28, 1970, p. 12.
104. "Interview with LeRoi Jones," transcript of the David Frost Show, televised over WNEW-TV and other stations, January 5, 1969, p. 3.
105. Murray Kempton, "Newark: Keeping Up with LeRoi Jones," *New York Review of Books,* July 2, 1970, p. 22.
106. Haynes Johnson, "Gibson Is Elected Mayor of Newark," Washington *Post,* June 17, 1970, p. A18.
107. "New Chance for Newark," Washington *Evening Star,* June 18, 1970, p. A8.

108. Interview, July 29, 1970.
109. Emory Lewis, "The Voice of Black Newark," Hackensack, N.J., *Record Call,* August 17, 1969, p. 7A.
110. Marvin X and Faruk, "Islam and Black Art: An Interview with LeRoi Jones," *Negro Digest,* January, 1969, p. 5.
111. Ibid., p. 7.
112. Ibid., p. 80.
113. Interview, July 29, 1970.
114. Hoyt M. Fuller, "A Warning to Black Poets," *Black World,* September 10, 1970, p. 50.
115. *Four Black Revolutionary Plays,* p. 89.
116. Gottlieb, p. 96.
117. Schneck, p. 19.
118. Letter from Chester Himes to James Landis, William Morrow and Company, October 16, 1968.
119. Llorens, p. 82.
120. Lennox Raphael, "Roi," *Negro Digest,* August, 1968, p. 84.
121. Stone, p. 39.
122. Schneck, p. 18.
123. See Ed Bullins, "The King Is Dead," *The Drama Review,* 12, No. 4 (Summer, 1968), 24, for an account of how Jones and his friends reacted to the news of King's death.
124. Lewis, p. 1.

Notes to chapter 2

1. William Butler Yeats, *A Vision* (New York: Macmillan, 1956), p. 270 ("A Reissue with the Author's Final Revisions").
2. Gottlieb, p. 53.
3. In a letter to Theodore R. Hudson, dated July 8, 1970, Jones recommends this essay as revelatory of his thoughts on the artistic process.
4. *Black Music,* p. 109.
5. Ibid., p. 63.
6. *Black Magic,* p. 41.
7. *Home,* pp. 164–65.
8. Ibid., p. 109.
9. *Tales,* p. 68.
10. *Home,* p. 113.

11. Ibid., pp. 114–15.
12. "Philistinism and the Negro Writer," *Anger, and Beyond,* ed. Herbert Hill, p. 56.
13. *Home,* pp. 65–66.
14. Stone, p. 39.
15. *Home,* p. 200.
16. Ibid., p. 137.
17. Ibid., p. 66.
18. Ibid., p. 150.
19. Ibid., p. 73.
20. Ibid., p. 202.
21. Ibid., pp. 152–53.
22. *Tales,* p. 100.
23. "New Script for Newark," *Time,* April 26, 1968, p. 18.
24. *Home,* p. 206.
25. Ibid., p. 207.
26. Ibid., p. 84.
27. Gottlieb, p. 96.
28. *Black Music,* p. 195.
29. "A School of Prayer."
30. *A Black Mass,* p. 24.
31. In *Home,* p. 142, Jones defines the free world as "merely that part of the world in which the white man is free to do as he wants with the rest of the people there."
32. Marvin X, p. 7.
33. Ibid.
34. "Negro Theater Pimps Get Big Off Nationalism," p. 5.
35. Marvin X, p. 7.
36. *Home,* pp. 198–200.
37. *Blues People,* p. 236.
38. *Home,* pp. 61–62.
39. Ibid., p. 96.
40. *A Black Value System,* p. 4.
41. *Home,* pp. 150–51.
42. Llorens, p. 83.
43. "The Black Aesthetic," *Negro Digest,* September, 1969, p. 5.
44. *A Black Value System,* p. 10.
45. *Home,* p. 196.

46. Ibid., p. 86.
47. Gottlieb, p. 96.
48. *Raise Race Rays Raze*, p. 107.
49. Marvin X, pp. 77–78.
50. *Negro Digest*, July, 1968, pp. 20–21.

Notes to chapter 3

1. Granville Hicks, "Literary Horizons: The Poets in Prose," *Saturday Review*, December 11, 1965, p. 32.
2. H. S. Resnik, "Brave New Words," *Saturday Review,* December 9, 1967, p. 28.
3. Faith Berry, "Black Artist, Black Prophet," *New Republic,* May 28, 1966, pp. 24–25.
4. *Current Biography,* May, 1970, p. 16.
5. Stone, p. 42.
6. Resnik, p. 29.
7. *Home,* p. 176.
8. *Black Music,* pp. 71–72.
9. *Home,* p. 168.
10. Owen Dodson, "Playwrights in Dark Glasses," *Negro Digest,* April, 1968, p. 34.
11. "Books: Current & Various," *Time,* November 19, 1965, pp. 140–41.
12. Interview, October 24, 1970.
13. Llorens, p. 80.
14. Interview, July 29, 1970.
15. Hill, pp. 56–57.
16. *Black Music,* p. 107.
17. Ibid., p. 210.
18. Ibid., p. 179.
19. *The Drama Review,* 12, No. 4 (Summer 1968), 53–57.
20. Interview, October 22, 1970.
21. *Tales,* p. 107.
22. *Black Music,* p. 85.
23. *Tales,* p. 107.
24. Ibid., p. 60.
25. *The System of Dante's Hell,* p. 78.

26. My method for establishing meanings of recurring symbols and images was as follows: first, to compile a list of the words and phrases that tended to recur as symbol-images throughout his works in all genres; next, to record on file cards the contextual instances in which each was found; then, when a possible meaning or interpretation for a given symbol-image seemed to be apparent, to test this tentative meaning by substituting it in each of that symbol-image's contexts. Happily, a reasonable meaning or interpretation did occur for a number of these. Later, when I had an opportunity to talk briefly with LeRoi Jones about most of these symbol-images, he corroborated most of the theoretical findings, with some ememdations, of course.
27. *Black Music*, p. 174.
28. *Home*, p. 241.
29. "Three Modes of History and Culture."
30. *Home*, p. 198.
31. *Black Music*, p. 136.
32. *The System of Dante's Hell*, p. 38.
33. Ibid., p. 28.
34. *Black Music*, p. 137.
35. Interview, July 29, 1970.
36. *The System of Dante's Hell*, p. 146.
37. Ibid., p. 42.

Notes to chapter 4

1. Faith Berry, "Black Artist, Black Prophet," *The New Republic*, May 28, 1966, p. 23.
2. Cecil M. Brown, "Black Literature and LeRoi Jones," *Black World*, June, 1970, pp. 30–31.
3. *Choice*, 3 (October, 1966), 622.
4. Oscar Handlin, "Reader's Choice: Style, Form, and Chaos," *Atlantic*, May, 1966, p. 128.
5. "Books: Short Notices," *Time*, May 6, 1966, p. 110.
6. "The Jones Boy," *Newsweek*, May 2, 1966, p. 106.
7. Robert Bone, "Action and Reaction," New York *Times Book Review*, May 8, 1966, p. 3.
8. "This Week," *Christian Century*, May 4, 1966. p. 588.

9. "The Jones Boy," *Newsweek,* May 2, 1966, p. 106.
10. Faith Berry, p. 25.
11. Joe Goldberg, "Music, Metaphor, and Men," *Saturday Review,* January 11, 1964, p. 69.
12. Nat Hentoff, "Critics' Choices for Christmas," *Commonweal,* December 4, 1964, p. 358.
13. Goldberg, p. 69.
14. Edward Margolies, *Native Sons: A Critical Study of Twentieth Century Negro American Authors,* p. 197.
15. Richard Howard, "Some Poets in Their Prose," *Poetry,* 105 (March, 1965), 403–4.
16. "Blues and Roots, Cool, Funky and Soul" London *Times Literary Supplement,* June 18, 1964, p. 524.
17. Howard, p. 397.
18. Goldberg, p. 69.
19. From liner notes for *Four for Trane* (New York: ABC Records, Inc., 1965), quoted in *Black Music,* pp. 160–61.
20. From liner notes for *New Wave in Jazz* (New York: ABC Records, Inc., 1965), quoted in *Black Music,* p. 175.
21. From *A Jazz Great: John Coltrane* (New York: Metronome Corporation, 1963), quoted in *Black Music,* pp. 58–59, 61, passim.
22. *The Dark Lady of the Sonnets* (liner notes, Guide Music, Inc., 1962), quoted in *Black Music,* p. 25.
23. John Wilson, "The New Jazzmen," New York *Times Book Review,* March 17, 1968, p. 46.
24. Mel Watkins, "Talk with LeRoi Jones," New York *Times Book Review,* June 27, 1971, p. 26.
25. "Interview with LeRoi Jones," transcript of the David Frost Show, televised over WNEW-TV and other stations, January 5, 1969, p. 3.
26. Kalamu Ya Salaam, "Books Noted," *Black World,* January, 1972, p. 78.
27. Jan Carew, "About the Black Accused and the White Accusers," New York *Times Book Review,* June 27, 1971, p. 31.

Notes to chapter 5

1. Interview, July 29, 1970.
2. Bernard Bergonzi, "Out Our Way," *The New York Review of Books,* January 20, 1966, p. 22.

3. Emile Capouya, "States of Mind, of Soul," New York *Times Book Review*, November 28, 1965, p. 4.

4. It is interesting to note that Jones accuses Dante of being an imitator: ". . . *Dante's Hell* is an imitation. The Inferno is him copying some Arab, Ibn Arabi, or—who was it that he stole it from. That's Arab theology. The whole thing is an imitation" (Marvin X, p. 79).

5. John Williams, "LeRoi Jones' Novel: Not a Novel," New York *Post*, November 18, 1965, p. 34.

6. Peter Prescott, "Books," *Women's Wear Daily*, November 26, 1965, p. 41.

7. Granville Hicks, "Literary Horizons: The Poets in Prose," *Saturday Review*, December 11, 1964, p. 31.

8. Ibid. It should be mentioned that Hicks seems not to have considered this book on the allegorical or symbolic level; one may easily infer that he understood the book only on the literal level.

9. Capouya, p. 4.

10. Despi Tralis, "Alone in a Dark Wood," *Freedomways*, 6, No. 2 (Second Quarter), Spring 1966, 175.

11. Dudley Randall, "Books Noted," *Negro Digest*, March, 1966, p. 52.

12. Letter from Michael Rumaker to Morrie Goldfischer, undated.

13. "Out of Touch," *Newsweek*, November 22, 1965, p. 115.

14. Adams, p. 122.

15. *Bibliographic Survey: The Negro in Print*, 4, No. 3 (September, 1968), 12.

16. Bergonzi, p. 22.

17. Saul Maloff, "The Crushed Heart," *Newsweek*, December 4, 1967, p. 103B.

18. Robert Bone, "De Profundis," New York *Times Book Review*, February 4, 1968, p. 36.

19. Resnik, p. 28.

Notes to chapter 6

1. *Home*, p. 123.

2. "Poetry: Actual Sweet Black Fury," *Diplomat*, November, 1966, p. 72.

3. Stone, p. 42.

4. Richard Howard, "Two Against Chaos," *The Nation*, March 15, 1965, p. 289.

5. Richard M. Elman, "Moments of Masquerade," New York *Times Book Review*, January 31, 1965, p. 26.

6. Clarence Major, "The Poetry of LeRoi Jones," *Negro Digest,* March, 1965, p. 54.
7. "Poetry: Actual Sweet Black Fury," p. 72.
8. In another place Jones has identified this poem as "Anon. Street Yell/20th Century U.S."
9. Jascha Kessler, "Keys to Ourselves," *Saturday Review,* May 2, 1970, p. 36.
10. Emanuel and Gross, p. 514.
11. Published in *Black Theatre,* issue No. 4 (April, 1970), 32, and in *Black World,* June, 1970, pp. 12–13.
12. Published in *Black Theatre,* issue No. 4 (April, 1970), 35.
13. Weales, p. 52.
14. Margolies, pp. 194–95.
15. Steve Hussein, "The Call Board," *Bay State Banner,* November 20, 1969, p. 14.
16. Darwin T. Turner, ed., *Black American Literature: Poetry,* p. 119.

Notes to chapter 7

1. Interview, July 29, 1970.
2. Published as an introductory essay in *JELLO* (Chicago: Third World Press, 1970), pp. 5–8. (In other places, the title of the play is spelled with hyphens between the letters: *J-E-L-L-O.*)
3. "A Symposium on 'We Righteous Bombers,'" *Black Theater,* Issue No. 4 (April, 1970), 25.
4. Ibid.
5. *Home,* pp. 187–88.
6. "Underground Fury," *Newsweek,* April 13, 1964, p. 60.
7. For discussion of this legend in relation to Jones' play, see Hugh Nelson, "LeRoi Jones' *Dutchman:* A Brief Ride on a Doomed Ship," *Educational Theatre Journal,* March, 1968, pp. 53–59.
8. David Littlejohn, *Black on White: A Critical Survey of Writing by American Negroes,* p. 78.
9. Stone, p. 42.
10. Littlejohn, p. 75.
11. George Dennison, "The Demagogy of LeRoi Jones," *Commentary,* February, 1965, p. 69.
12. Interview, October 22, 1970.

13. Stone, p. 42.

14. Mel Watkins, "Talk with LeRoi Jones," New York *Times Book Review,* June 27, 1971, p. 26.

15. Stone, p. 42.

16. See the discussion of the terms in quotes in the third chapter of this book.

17. Interview, July 29, 1970.

18. Costello, p. 436.

19. Lance Jeffers, "Bullins, Baraka, and Elder: The Dawn of Grandeur in Black Drama," *CLA Journal,* 16 (September, 1972), 47.

20. "A Symposium on 'We Righteous Bombers,'" p. 25.

21. K. William Kgositsile, "Towards Our Theater: A Definitive Act," *Black Expression,* ed. Addison Gayle, Jr., p. 146.

22. See "Black Woman," *Black World,* July, 1970, p. 8.

23. Interview, July 29, 1970.

24. Ibid.

25. "A Symposium on 'We Righteous Bombers,'" p. 20.

26. Ibid., p. 25.

27. "The Need for a Cultural Base to Civil Rites & Bpower Mooments," p. 125.

28. "What the Arts Need Now," *Negro Digest,* April, 1967, pp. 5–6.

29. Harold Clurman, "Theatre," *The Nation,* February 2, 1970, p. 125.

30. *Slave Ship, Negro Digest,* April, 1967.

31. Clurman, p. 125.

32. J. K. [Jack Kroll], "Dark Voyage," *Newsweek,* December 1, 1969, p. 86.

33. Edith Oliver, "The Theatre," *The New Yorker,* December 6, 1969, p. 168.

34. Kroll, p. 86.

35. Harold Clurman, "Theatre: Le Roi Jones," *The Nation,* January 4, 1970, p. 125.

36. Transcript of the David Frost Show for January 5, 1969, pp. 1–2.

37. Velde, p. 440.

38. Richard Schechner, "White on Black," *The Drama Review,* 12, No. 4 (Summer, 1968), 27.

39. Marvin X, "An Interview with Ed Bullins: Black Theatre," *Negro Digest,* April, 1969, p. 16.

40. Littlejohn, p. 70.

41. Cade, p. 137.

Notes to chapter 8

1. *Black Music,* p. 17.
2. *Blues People,* p. 232.
3. Interview, July 29, 1970.
4. Gottlieb, p. 53.
5. Because romantic, like other labels applied to literature, does not submit to absolute, static, and universal definition, it would be digressive at this time to attempt an in-depth definition of the term. It is useful, however, to consider important synthesizing statements on the subject such as Rene Wellek's "The Concept of Romanticism in Literary History," A. O. Lovejoy's "On the Discrimination of Romanticisms," and Henry H. H. Remak's "West European Romanticism: Definition and Scope" and to consult widely used references such as Thrall and Hibbard's *A Handbook to Literature,* Baugh's *A Literary History of England,* and Hornstein's *The Reader's Companion to World Literature* to find common identifying and defining elements and characteristics for romantic and romanticism. Such a process provides generally accepted elements and characteristics by which Jones' work may be reasonably assayed. The same process may be profitably applied for arriving at identifying and defining elements and characteristics for Western aesthetic, black aesthetic, and other terms useful in the assaying of Jones' literary work.
6. Basic philosophical and critical statements about the black aesthetic include pertinent essays by Jones himself (especially those mentioned in the discussion under "Theory of Culture and Art" in chapter two and in the discussion of *Home* and *Raise* in chapter four of this book), Larry Neal's "And Shine Swam On" in *Black Fire,* Julian Mayfield's "Into the Mainstream and Oblivion" in *Cavalcade,* and the illuminating essays in *The Black Aesthetic,* edited by Addison Gayle, Jr. Stephen Henderson's *Understanding the New Black Poetry: Black Speech and Black Music as Poetic References* promises to be a landmark, a reference point, for subsequent longer critical studies on the black aesthetic. Not only does Henderson explore the blackness of the content of black poetry, he also goes into some detail about the blackness of form and technique, and he introduces a concept of what he calls "saturation" inherent in the creation and successful reception of black poetry.
7. Eugene Perkins, "The Changing Status of Black Writers," *Black World,* June, 1970, p. 96.

8. Llorens, p. 75.
9. "Perspectives," *Negro Digest,* April, 1970, p. 49.
10. Larry Neal, "The Black Arts Movement," *The Drama Review,* 12, No. 4 (Summer, 1968), 31.
11. Ibid., p. 33.
12. "A Survey: Black Writers' Views on Literary Lions and Values," *Negro Digest,* January, 1968, pp. 16–18, passim.
13. John Tryford, "Who Is LeRoi Jones? What Is He?" *Trace,* No. 65 (Summer, 1967), 297.
14. Velde, p. 441.
15. Resnik, p. 28.
16. Maloff, p. 104.
17. Jeffers, pp. 45–46.

Bibliography

Works by LeRoi Jones

Books

Arm Yrself or Harm Yrself. Newark: Jihad Productions, 1967.

The Baptism and *The Toilet.* New York: Grove Press, 1966.

Black Arts. Newark: Jihad Productions, 1966.

Introduction to Larry Neal, *Black Boogaloo.* San Francisco: Journal of Black Poetry Press, c. 1969.

Co-editor, with Larry Neal, *Black Fire: An Anthology of Afro-American Writing.* New York: William Morrow and Co., 1968.

Black Magic Poetry. New York: Bobbs-Merrill Company, 1969. This volume includes "Sabotage," "Target Study," and "Black Art."

Black Music. New York: William Morrow and Co., 1967.

* *Bloodrites.* In *Black Drama Anthology,* ed. Woodie King and Ron Milner. New York: New American Library, 1971, pp. 25–31.

* *A Black Value System.* Newark: Jihad Productions, 1970.

"Blues, Jazz, and the Negro." In *The American Negro Reference Book,* ed. John P. Davis. Englewood Cliffs, N.J.: Prentice-Hall, 1966, pp. 759–65.

Blues People: Negro Music in White America. New York: William Morrow and Co., 1963.

Cuba Libre. New York: Fair Play for Cuba Committee, 1966.

The Dead Lecturer. New York: Grove Press, 1964.

The Death of Malcolm X. In *New Plays from the Black Theatre,* ed. Ed Bullins. New York: Bantam Books, 1969, pp. 1–20.

Dutchman and The Slave. New York: William Morrow and Co., 1964.

"Epistrophe (for yodo)." In *The Beat Scene,* ed. Elias Wilentz. New York: Corinth Books, 1960, pp. 56–57.

Four Black Revolutionary Plays. New York: Bobbs-Merrill Company, 1969. This volume includes *Experimental Death Unit #1, A Black Mass, Great Goodness of Life: A Coon Show,* and *Madheart (A Morality Play).*

Editor, *Four Young Lady Poets.* New York: Totem Press, 1961.

Home: Social Essays. New York: William Morrow and Co., 1966.

---

*Published under the name of Amiri Baraka or Imamu Amiri Baraka.

**Published under the name of Ameer Baraka or Imamu Ameer Baraka.

"How You Sound??" In *New American Poetry, 1945–1960,* ed. Donald M. Allen. New York: Grove Press, 1960, pp. 424–25.

*With Fundi (Billy Abernathy), *In Our Terribleness* (*Some Elements and Meaning in Black Style*). New York: Bobbs-Merrill Company, 1970.

* *It's Nation Time.* Chicago: Third World Press, 1970.

* *JELLO.* Chicago: Third World Press, 1970.

* *Junkies Are Full of* (*SHHH...*). In *Black Drama Anthology,* ed. Woodie King and Ron Milner. New York: New American Library, 1971, pp. 11–23.

* *Kawaida Studies: The New Nationalism.* Chicago: Third World Press, 1972.

Editor, *The Moderns: An Anthology of New Writing in America.* New York: Corinth Books, 1963.

"The Need for a Cultural Base to Civil Rites & Bpower Mooments." In *The Black Power Revolt,* ed. Floyd B. Barber. Boston: Porter Sargent Publisher, 1968, pp. 119–26.

* "Negro Theater Pimps Get Big Off Nationalism." In *JELLO.* Chicago: Third World Press, 1970, pp. 5–8.

"Philistinism and the Negro Writer." In *Anger, and Beyond: The Negro Writer in the United States,* ed. Herbert Hill. New York: Harper and Row, 1966, pp. 51–61.

Preface to a Twenty Volume Suicide Note. New York: Totem Press, 1961.

* *Raise Race Rays Raze: Essays since 1965.* New York: Random House, 1971.

Slave Ship: A Historical Pageant. Newark: Jihad Productions, 1969.

"SOS." In *Anthology of Our Black Selves* (originally published as *Afro-American Festival of the Arts Magazine*). Newark: Jihad Productions, 1966. Under title "Anon. Street Yell/20th Century U.S."

Spirit Reach. Newark: Jihad Productions, 1972.

Strategy and Tactics of a Pan-African Political Party. Newark: Jihad Productions, 1971.

The System of Dante's Hell. New York: Grove Press, 1965.

Tales. New York: Grove Press, 1967.

* "Technology and Ethos." In *Amistad 2: Writings on Black History and Culture,* ed. John A. Williams and Charles F. Harris. New York: Random House, 1971, pp. 319–22.

Periodicals

* "The Ban on Black Music." *Black World,* July, 1971, pp. 4–11.

** "The Black Aesthetic." *Negro Digest,* September, 1969, pp. 5–6.

*"Black (Art) Drama Is the Same as Black Life." *Ebony,* February, 1971, pp. 74–82.

A Black Mass. Liberator, 6, No. 6 (June, 1966), 14 ff.

**"Black Power Chant." *Black Theatre,* issue No. 4 (April, 1970), 35.

*"Black 'Revolutionary' Poets Should Also Be Playwrights." *Black World,* April, 1972, pp. 4–6. (Also in *The Black Scholar,* November, 1969.)

*"A Black Value System." *The Black Scholar,* November, 1969, pp. 54–60.

*"Black Woman." *Black World,* July, 1970, pp. 7–11.

"Communications Project." *The Drama Review,* 12, No. 4 (Summer 1968), 53–57.

**"The Coronation of the Black Queen." *The Black Scholar,* June, 1970, pp. 46–48.

*Co-editor, *The Cricket,* 1969–.

"The Evolver." *Negro Digest,* September–October, 1968, pp. 58–59.

Co-editor, with Diane di Prima, *The Floating Bear,* 1961–c. 1962.

*"For Maulana Karenga & Pharoah Saunders." *Black Theatre,* issue No. 4 (April, 1970), 4.

"Harlem Considered: A Symposium." *Negro Digest,* September, 1964, pp. 16–26.

Home on the Range. The Drama Review, 12, No. 4 (Summer 1968), 106–11.

"If It's Anger...Maybe That's Good." An interview by Judy Stone. San Francisco *Chronicle,* August 23, 1964, pp. 39, 42.

"Islam and Black Art: An Interview with LeRoi Jones." An interview by Marvin X and Faruk. *Negro Digest,* January, 1969, pp. 4–10, 77–80.

*"Jim Brown on the Screen." *Black Theatre,* issue No. 4 (April, 1970), 32.

*"Jim Brown on the Screen." *Black World,* June, 1970, pp. 12–13.

"The Negro Middle Class Flight from Heritage." *Negro Digest,* February, 1964, pp. 80–95.

* "New Work by Imamu Amiri Baraka." *Black World,* May, 1973, pp. 40–48. Includes "We Know Directions," "OK Shoot!," "US," "In the Midst of Chaos," "Look Inside," "Habari Gani," and "Afrikan Revolution."

"Poetry: Actual Sweet Black Fury." *Diplomat,* November, 1966, pp. 70–73.

Police. The Drama Review, 12, No. 4 (Summer 1968), 112–15.

Slave Ship: A Historical Pageant. Negro Digest, April, 1967, pp. 62–74.

"Suppose Sorrow Was a Time Machine." *Yugen,* issue No. 2 (1958), 9–11.

*"A Symposium on 'We Righteous Bombers.'" *Black Theatre,* issue No. 4 (April, 1970), 15–25.

"They Think You're an Airplane and You're Really a Bird." An Interview by Saul Gottlieb. *Evergreen Review,* December, 1967, pp. 51–53, 96–97.

"Three Poems of Protest" ("Numbers, Letters," "Ka 'Ba," and "Newshit"). *Diplomat,* June, 1966, p. 61.

*"Toward the Creation of Political Institutions for All African Peoples." *Black World,* October, 1972, pp. 54–78.

"What Does Non-Violence Mean?" *Negro Digest,* November, 1964, pp. 4–19.

*"What Is Black Theater?: An Interview with Imamu Amiri Baraka." An interview by Mike Coleman. *Black World,* April, 1971, pp. 32–36.

"What the Arts Need Now." *Negro Digest,* April, 1967, pp. 5–6.

"Who Will Survive America? / Few Americans / Very Few Negroes / No Crackers at All." *Negro Digest,* July, 1968, pp. 20–21.

Co-editor, with Hettie Cohen (Jones), *Yugen,* 1958–63.

Others

*"Biographical Info." A photo-reproduced sheet distributed by Jones/Baraka. Undated, c. 1969.

Black and Beautiful. A phonograph recording featuring Yusef Iman, the Jihad Singers, and LeRoi Jones. Distributed by Jihad Productions, Newark, N.J.

A Black Mass. A phonograph recording of a live performance of the play featuring an "All Star Cast" and the music of the "Sun-Ra Myth-Science Arkestra." Distributed by Jihad Productions, Newark, N.J.

"Interview with LeRoi Jones." Transcript of the David Frost Show televised over station WNEW-TV, New York, N.Y., on January 5, 1969. New York: Radio and TV Reports, Inc., for Group W Productions, January 5, 1969.

Sonny's Time Now! A phonograph recording featuring Sonny Murray and other musicians and featuring LeRoi Jones reading "Black Art." Distributed by Jihad Productions, Newark, N.J.

Writing About Jones and His Works

Books

Allen, Donald M., ed. *New American Poetry, 1945–1960.* New York: Grove Press, 1960.

Baker, Houston A., ed. *Black Literature in America.* New York: McGraw-Hill Book Co., 1971.

Barber, Floyd B., ed. *The Black Power Revolt.* Boston: Porter Sargent Publisher, 1968.

Bullins, Ed, ed. *New Plays from the Black Theatre.* New York: Bantam Books, 1969.

Cade, Toni. "Black Theater." In *Black Expression: Essays by and about Black Americans in the Creative Arts,* ed. Addison Gayle, Jr. New York: Weybright and Talley, 1969, pp. 134–43.

Clurman, Harold. *The Naked Image: Observations of the Modern Theater.* New York: Macmillan, 1966.

Couch, William, ed. *New Black Playwrights,* New York: Avon Books, 1970.

Dace, Letitia. *LeRoi Jones: A Checklist of Works by and about Him.* London: Nether Press, 1971.

Davis, Arthur P., and Redding, Saunders, eds. *Cavalcade: Negro American Writing from 1760 to the Present.* Boston: Houghton Mifflin Co., 1971.

Davis, John Preston, ed. *The American Negro Reference Book.* Englewood Cliffs, N.J.: Prentice-Hall Publishing Co., 1966.

Emanuel, James A., and Gross, Theodore L., eds. *Dark Symphony: Negro Literature in America.* New York: The Free Press, 1968.

Ford, Nick Aaron. *Black Insights: Significant Literature by Black Americans — 1760 to the Present.* Waltham, Mass.: Ginn and Co., 1971.

Gayle, Addison Jr., ed. *The Black Aesthetic.* New York: Doubleday and Co., 1971.

———, ed. *Black Expression: Essays by and about Black Americans in the Creative Arts.* New York: Weybright and Talley, 1969.

Gibson, Donald B., ed. *Five Black Writers: Essays on Wright, Ellison, Baldwin, Hughes, and LeRoi Jones.* New York: New York University Press, 1970.

Henderson, Stephen. *Understanding the New Black Poetry: Black Speech and Black Music as Poetic References.* New York: William Morrow and Co., 1973.

Hill, Herbert, ed. *Anger, and Beyond: The Negro Writer in the United States.* New York: Harper and Row, 1966.

Jahn, Janheins. *Neo-African Literature: A History of Black Writing,* trans. Oliver Coburn and Ursala Lehrburger. New York: Grove Press, 1968.

Kearns, Francis E., ed. *The Black Experience: An Anthology of American Literature for the 1970s.* New York: Viking Press, 1970.

Kgositsile, K. William. "Towards Our Theater: A Definitive Act." In *Black Expression: Essays by and about Black Americans,* ed. Addison Gayle, Jr. New York: Weybright and Talley, 1969, pp. 146–48.

King, Woodie, and Milner, Ron, eds. *Black Drama Anthology.* New York: New American Library, 1971.

Littlejohn, David. *Black on White: A Critical Survey of Writings by American Negroes.* New York: Viking Press, 1966.

Margolies, Edward. "Prospects: LeRoi Jones." In *Native Sons: A Critical Study of Twentieth-Century Negro American Authors.* Philadelphia: J. B. Lippincott Company, 1968, pp. 190–99.

Mitchell, Lofton. *Black Drama: The Story of the American Negro in the Theatre.* New York: Hawthorne Books, 1967.

Neal, Larry. *Black Boogaloo.* San Francisco: The Journal of Black Poetry Press, c. 1969.

The Negro Handbook. Chicago: Johnson Publishing Co., 1966.

Ossman, David. "LeRoi Jones." *The Sullen Art: Interviews by David Ossman with Modern American Poets.* New York: Corinth Books, 1963, pp. 77–81. (Originally broadcast over radio stations of the Pacifica Foundation.)

Parone, Edward, ed. *New Theatre in America.* New York: Dell Publishing Co., 1970.

Turner, Darwin T., ed. *Black American Literature: Poetry.* Columbus: Charles E. Merrill Publishing Co., 1969.

Wilentz, Elias, ed. *The Beat Scene.* New York: Corinth Books, 1960.

X, Marvin. "Interview with Ed Bullins." In *New Plays from the Black Theatre,* ed. Ed Bullins. New York: Bantam Books, 1969, pp. vii–xv.

Periodicals

Adams, Phoebe. "Potpourri." *Atlantic Monthly,* January, 1966, p. 122.

Alsop, Stewart. "The American Sickness." *Saturday Evening Post,* July 13, 1968, p. 6.

Bergonzi, Bernard. "Out Our Way." *The New York Review of Books,* January 20, 1966, p. 22.

Berry, Faith. "Black Artist, Black Prophet." *The New Republic,* May 28, 1966, pp. 23–25.

Bibliographic Survey: The Negro in Print, 4, No. 3 (September, 1968), 12.

"Blues and Roots, Cool, Funky and Soul." London *Times Literary Supplement,* June 18, 1964, p. 524.

Bone, Robert. "Action and Reaction." New York *Times Book Review,* May 8, 1966, p. 3.

_____. "De Profundis." New York *Times Book Review,* February 4, 1968, p. 36.

"Books: Current & Various." *Time,* November 19, 1965, pp. 140–41.

"Books: Short Notices." *Time,* May 6, 1966, p. 110.

"Books: The Undaunted Pursuit of Fury." *Time,* April 6, 1970, pp. 98–100.

Brecht, Stefan. "LeRoi Jones' *Slave Ship." The Drama Review,* 14, No. 2 (Winter, 1970), 212–19.

Brown, Cecil M. "Black Literature and LeRoi Jones." *Black World,* June, 1970, pp. 30–31.

Buckley, Thomas. "Six Who Heckled Beame and Powell in Harlem Linked to Theatre Group." New York *Times,* October 20, 1965, p. L–37.

Bullins, Ed. "An Interview with Ed Bullins: Black Theater." An interview by Marvin X. *Negro Digest,* April, 1969, pp. 9–11.

_____. "The King Is Dead." *The Drama Review,* 12, No. 4 (Summer 1968), 23–25.

_____. "A Short Statement on Street Theatre." *The Drama Review,* 12, No. 4 (Summer 1968), 93.

Capouya, Emile. "States of Mind, of Soul." New York *Times Book Review,* November 28, 1965, pp. 4, 42.

Carew, Jan. "About the Black Accused and the White Accusers." New York *Times Book Review,* June 27, 1971, pp. 4, 31.

Choice, 3, No. 8 (October, 1966), 622.

Choice, 1, No. 9 (November, 1964), 378.

Choice, 5, No. 1 (March, 1968), 50.

Clurman, Harold. "Theatre." *The Nation,* February 2, 1970, pp. 124–25.

_____. "Theatre: LeRoi Jones." *The Nation,* January 4, 1965, pp. 16–17.

Coleman, Mike. "What Is Black Theater?: An Interview with Imamu Amiri Baraka." *Black World,* April, 1971, pp. 32–36.

Costello, Donald P. "LeRoi Jones: Black Man as Victim." *Commonweal,* June 28, 1968, pp. 436–40.

"Curtains for LeRoi." *Time,* January 12, 1968, p. 14.

Davis, Arthur P. "The New Poetry of Black Hate." *CLA Journal,* 13, No. 4 (June 1970), 382–91.

Dennison, George. "The Demagogy of LeRoi Jones." *Commentary,* February, 1965, pp. 67–70.

Dodson, Owen. "Playwrights in Dark Glasses." *Negro Digest,* April, 1968, pp. 31–37.

Duberman, Martin. "Visionaries with Blind Spots." *Book Week,* April 24, 1966, pp. 3, 8.

Egan, Cy, and Borsky, Frank. "Raid 'Pakistani Muslims.'" New York *Journal-American,* March 18, 1966, pp. 1–2.

Elman, Richard M. "Moments of Masquerade." New York *Times Book Review,* January 13, 1965, p. 26.

Fabio, Sarah Webster. "Who Speaks Negro?" *Negro Digest,* December, 1966, pp. 54–58.

Faruk and X, Marvin. "Islam and Black Art: An Interview with LeRoi Jones." *Negro Digest,* January, 1969, pp. 4–10, 77–80.

Fuller, Hoyt W. "A Warning to Black Poets." *Black World,* September, 1970, p. 50.

Gayle, Addison. "The Critic, the University, and the Negro Writer." *Negro Digest,* January, 1967, pp. 54–59.

Gilman, Richard. "The Devil May Care." Chicago *Sun Times,* December 26, 1965, pp. 10–11.

Goldberg, Joe. "Music, Metaphor, and Men." *Saturday Review,* January 11, 1964, p. 69.

Gottlieb, Saul. "They Think You're an Airplane and You're Really a Bird." *Evergreen Review,* December, 1967, pp. 50–53, 96–97.

Handlin, Oscar. "Reader's Choice: Style, Form, and Chaos." *Atlantic,* May, 1966, pp. 125–31.

Hatch, Robert. "The Baptism." *The Nation,* February 2, 1970, p. 384.

Hay, Samuel A. "Afro-American Drama, 1950–1970." *Negro History Bulletin,* 36, No. 1 (January, 1973), 5–8.

Hentoff, Nat. "Books: Critics' Choices for Christmas." *Commonweal,* December 4, 1964, p. 358.

_____. "Critics' Choices for Christmas." *Commonweal,* December 6, 1968, pp. 358–59.

_____. "The Square Route to Blues Is White." *Book Week,* October 20, 1963, p. 5.

Hicks, Granville. "Literary Horizons: The Poets in Prose." *Saturday Review,* December 11, 1964, pp. 31–32.

Howard, Richard. "Some Poets in Their Prose." *Poetry,* March, 1965, pp. 397–404.

_____. "Two against Chaos." *The Nation,* March 15, 1965, pp. 289–90.

Hughes, Langston. "That Boy LeRoi." Chicago *Defender,* January 11, 1965, p. 38.

Hussein, Steve. "The Call Board." *Bay State Banner,* November 20, 1969, p. 14.

Jackson, Kathryn. "LeRoi Jones and the New Black Writers of the Sixties." *Freedomways,* 9 (Third Quarter, 1969), 232–47.

J. K. (Jack Kroll). "Dark Voyage." *Newsweek,* December 1, 1969, p. 86.

Jeffers, Lance. "Bullins, Baraka, and Elder: The Dawn of Grandeur in Black Drama." *CLA Journal,* 16 (September, 1972), 32–48.

Johnson, Haynes. "Gibson Is Elected Mayor of Newark." Washington *Post,* June 17, 1970, pp. A–1, 18.

"The Jones Boy." *Newsweek,* May 2, 1966, p. 106. Listed in table of contents as "A Harangue by the Jones Boy."

"Jones, (Everett) LeRoi." *Current Biography,* May, 1970, pp. 16–18.

Kempton, Murray. "Newark: Keeping Up with LeRoi Jones." *The New York Review of Books,* July 2, 1970, pp. 21–23.

Kessler, Jascha. "Keys to Ourselves." *Saturday Review,* May 2, 1970, pp. 36, 42.

"The LeRoi Jones Case: Letter about a Wolf-Pack." *American Dialogue,* 5, No. 1 (1968), 17.

"A Lesson for Pedagogues." *Negro Digest,* July, 1968, pp. 78–79.

Levertov, Denise. "Poets of the Given Ground." *The Nation,* October 14, 1961, pp. 251–52.

Lewis, Emory. "The Voice of Black Newark." Hackensack, New Jersey, *Record Call,* August 17, 1969, pp. 1, 7A.

Lindenberg, Daniel. "Un Théâtre Militant." *Les Temps Moderne,* 21 (1966), 1918–20.

Llorens, David. "Ameer (LeRoi Jones) Baraka." *Ebony,* August, 1969, pp. 75–78, 80–83.

Major, Clarence. "The Poetry of LeRoi Jones." *Negro Digest,* March, 1965, pp. 54–56.

Maloff, Saul. "The Crushed Heart." *Newsweek,* December 4, 1967, pp. 103B–4.

"The Maturing of LeRoi Jones as a Politician." The Washington *Sunday Star,* July 11, 1971, p. A–16.

May, John R., S. J. "Images of Apocalypse in the Black Novel." *Renascence: Essays on Values in Literature,* 23 (1970), 31–45.

Meyer, J. "Opinion: On Negro Aims." *Mademoiselle,* April, 1966, pp. 84ff.

Miller, Jeanne-Marie A. "The Plays of LeRoi Jones." *CLA Journal,* 14 (March, 1971), 331–39.

Mootry, Maria K. "Themes and Symbols in Two Plays by LeRoi Jones." *Negro Digest,* April, 1969, pp. 42–47.

Murray, George B. "Books." *The Critic,* 22 (February-March, 1964), 88.

Neal, Larry. "The Black Arts Movement." *The Drama Review,* 12, No. 4 (Summer 1968), 29–39.

"Negro, 38, Beats Addonizio to Become Newark Mayor." Washington *Evening Star,* June 17, 1970, pp. A-1, 6.

Nelson, Hugh. "LeRoi Jones' *Dutchman:* A Brief Ride on a Doomed Ship." *Educational Theatre Journal,* March, 1968, pp. 53–59.

"New Chance for Newark." Washington *Evening Star,* June 18, 1970, p. A-8.

"New Script for Newark." *Time,* April 26, 1968, p. 19.

Oberbeck, S. K. "Black Daydreams, White Man's Nightmares." *Book World,* December 24, 1967, p. 7.

Oliver, Edith. "The Theatre." *The New Yorker,* December 6, 1969, p. 168.

Otten, Charlotte F. "LeRoi Jones: Napalm Poet." *Concerning Poetry,* 3, No. 1 (Spring, 1970), 5–11.

"Out of Touch." *Newsweek,* November 22, 1965, pp. 114–16.

Peavy, Charles D. "Myth, Magic, and Manhood in LeRoi Jones' *Madheart."* *Studies in Black Literature,* 1, No. 2 (Summer, 1970), 12–20.

Perkins, Eugene. "The Changing Status of Black Writers." *Black World,* June, 1970, pp. 18–23, 95–98.

"Perspectives." *Black World,* June, 1970, pp. 49–50.

"Perspectives." *Negro Digest,* April, 1970, p. 49.

"Poetic Justice." *Newsweek,* January 15, 1968, p. 24.

Prescott, Peter. "Books." *Women's Wear Daily,* November 26, 1965, p. 41.

Randall, Dudley. "Books Noted." *Negro Digest,* March, 1966, pp. 52–53.

Randolph, Vance. "The Roots Go Deep." New York *Times Book Review,* November 17, 1963, p. 22.

Raphael, Lennox. "Roi." *Negro Digest,* August, 1968, p. 84.

Reck, Tom S. "Archetypes in LeRoi Jones' Dutchman." *Studies in Black Literature,* 1, No. 1 (Spring, 1970), 66–68.

Reed, Daphne S. "LeRoi Jones: High Priest of the Black Arts Movement." *Educational Theatre Journal,* 22, No. 1 (March, 1970), 53–59.

Resnik, H. S. "Brave New Words." *Saturday Review,* December 9, 1967, pp. 28–29.

Richardson, Jack. "Blues for Mr. Jones." *Esquire,* June, 1966, pp. 106–8, 138.

"Riots: Poetic Justice." *Newsweek,* January 15, 1968, p. 24.

Rodgers, Carolyn M. "Black Expression: Breakforth. In Deed." *Black World,* September, 1970, pp. 13–22.

———. "The Literature of Black." *Black World,* June, 1970, pp. 5–11.

Roth, Phillip. "Channel X: Two Plays on the Race Conflict." *New York Review of Books,* May 28, 1964, pp. 10–13.

Schatt, Stanley. "LeRoi Jones: A Checklist to Primary and Secondary Sources." *Bulletin of Bibliography and Magazine Notes,* 28, No. 2 (April–June, 1971), 55–57.

Schechner, Richard. "White on Black." *The Drama Review,* 12, No. 4 (Summer 1968), 25–27.

Schneck, Stephen. "LeRoi Jones, or, Poetics & Policemen, or, Trying Heart, Bleeding Heart." *Ramparts,* July 13, 1968, pp. 14–19.

Simon, John. "Theatre Chronicle." *Hudson Review,* 17 (Autumn 1964), 424.

Smith, R. H. "Jersey Justice and LeRoi Jones." *Publisher's Weekly,* January 15, 1968, p. 66.

Sontag, Susan. "Going to Theater, etc." *Partisan Review,* 31, No. 3 (Summer 1964), 389–94.

"Spasms of Fury." *Time,* December 25, 1965, pp. 62–63.

Steinlauf, Martin. "LeRoi." *University Review,* March, 1970, p. 7.

Stone, Judy, "If It's Anger...Maybe That's Good." An interview of LeRoi Jones. San Francisco *Chronicle,* August 23, 1964, pp. 39, 42.

Sullivan, James W. "The Negro 'National Consciousness' of LeRoi Jones." New York *Herald Tribune,* October 31, 1965, p. 34 (Also in *Jazz,* 5, No. 1 (January, 1966), 10–11.)

——. "News Perspective: HARYOU and the '5 Percenters.'" New York *Herald Tribune,* October 19, 1965.

"A Survey: Black Writers' Views on Literary Lions and Values." *Negro Digest,* January, 1968, pp. 10–48.

"A Symposium on 'We Righteous Bombers.'" *Black Theatre,* issue No. 4 (April, 1970), 15–25.

"Tax Funds for a 'Hate the Whites' Project." *U.S. News and World Report,* December 13, 1965, pp. 16–17.

"The Theatre." *The New Yorker,* December 6, 1969, p. 168.

"This Week." *Christian Century,* May 4, 1966, p. 588.

Tralis, Despi. "Alone in a Dark Wood." *Freedomways,* 6, No. 2 (Spring, 1966), 174–75.

Tryford, John. "Who Is LeRoi Jones? What Is He?" *Trace,* No. 65 (Summer, 1967), 294–98.

"Underground Fury." *Newsweek,* April 13, 1964, p. 60.

Velde, Paul. "LeRoi Jones: Pursued by the Furies." *Commonweal,* June 28, 1968, pp. 440–41.

Watkins, Mel. "Talk with LeRoi Jones." New York *Times Book Review,* June 27, 1971, pp. 4, 24, 26–27.

Weales, Gerald. "The Day LeRoi Jones Spoke on Penn Campus What Were the Blacks Doing in the Balcony?" New York *Times Magazine,* May 4, 1969, pp. 38–40, 44, 48, 52, 54, 56, 58.

Welburn, Ron. "Book Review." *Liberator,* August, 1970, p. 20.

Williams, John. "LeRoi Jones' 'Novel': Not a Novel." New York *Post,* November 18, 1965, p. 34.

Wilson, John. "The New Jazzmen." New York *Times Book Review,* March 17, 1968, p. 46.

X, Marvin. "An Interview with Ed Bullins: Black Theatre." *Negro Digest,* April, 1969, pp. 9–16.

_____, and Faruk. "Islam and Black Art: An Interview with LeRoi Jones." *Negro Digest,* January, 1969, pp. 4–10, 77–80.

Ya Salaam, Kalamu. "Books Noted." *Black World,* January 1972, pp. 52, 78–84.

Others

Fouch, Deborah Smith. *Everett LeRoi Jones (Imamu Ameer Baraka).* CAAS Bibliography No. 2. Atlanta: Atlanta University Center for African and African-American Studies, c. 1971.

Hudson, Theodore R. "From LeRoi Jones to Amiri Baraka: The Literary Works. Doctoral dissertation, Howard University, 1971.

_____. *A LeRoi Jones (Amiri Baraka) Bibliography: A Keyed Research Guide to Works by LeRoi Jones and to Writing about Him and His Works.* Washington, D.C., 1971.

"Interview with LeRoi Jones." Transcript of the David Frost Show televised over station WNEW-TV, New York, N.Y., on January 5, 1969. New York: Radio and TV Reports, Inc., for Group W Productions, January 5, 1969.

"An Interview with Mayor Kenneth Gibson of Newark." Transcript of the David Frost Show televised over station WNEW-TV, New York, N.Y., on August 28, 1970. New York: Radio TV Reports, Inc., for Westinghouse Broadcasting Corporation, August 27, 1970.

Index